GERMAN CULTURE THROUGH FILM

An Introduction to German Cinema

GERMAN CULTURE THROUGH FILM

An Introduction to German Cinema

Robert C. Reimer
Reinhard Zachau
Margit Sinka

Focus Publishing
R. Pullins Co.
Newburyport, MA

TABLE OF CONTENTS

PREFACE

German Culture through Film: an Introduction to German Cinema grew out of the frustration of the authors with finding a film book adaptable to an introductory undergraduate course in German film, which for reasons of exigency had to include not only students with German language skills but also those with no knowledge of the language. We were at the same time looking for a book that could be used as an introductory text for students in a film studies program, whose knowledge of German history and culture was not always at a level to understand fully the texts of German films.

This set of texts was written with the needs of such courses in mind. It consists of two texts, one of which covers thirty-one German films in English. The other covers twelve of those films in German. Thus, one or both of these texts can be used for courses in German film in English, courses in German film in German, or courses which for various reasons might cater to students taking either track simultaneously in the same course. In such a way the series is designed to appeal to professors who teach courses in general education, liberal arts, cinema, or who wish to conduct a course in German film exclusively in German, or for those on many campuses, such as ours, where students share the same class (and films) for those two different courses.

For this end, the text in English contains background information on German history and culture, as well as analysis of the films. The text in German covers twelve of the films in the English text, and in addition to background information on the films, culture and history, also offers excerpts from the screenplays, and question and exercises.

Users of both books will have access to the authors' homepage, address listed in the introduction.

INTRODUCTION

Purpose of this book

This introduction to German film consists of thirty-one chapters on select German films from the silent era to the present. There is a threefold focus behind the book: First, the essays use films rooted in a particular time and a specific place to introduce students to the history and culture of German speakers. Second, the essays present history and culture to help students recognize the importance these concepts have for understanding and interpreting films. Finally, the essays introduce students to the rudimentary aesthetics needed for understanding films, even those from their own culture. Therefore the chapters are divided into three parts: the story the film tells, the basic background information on history and culture necessary for understanding films from a particular period, and a discussion of the specific film demonstrating how information about culture deepens our understanding of the film.

As a textbook and general reference tool for undergraduate German film and culture courses, the book is written in English. However, there is also a companion book in German which covers twelve of the films included in the English book. This companion book contains transcripts of scenes from the films and a set of study questions, thereby creating an attractive introduction to film courses that have a German component or are taught entirely in German. A Website with information to complement both books is currently under construction at http://www.sewanee.edu/German-Film and http://www.pullins. com. Information is also available at http://www.languages.uncc.edu/rcreimer.

This book is a first introduction to German film for Americans. For a long time there was only one book suitable as an introductory film text for undergraduates, Frederick Ott's *Great German Films*. Since Ott's book is out of print, nothing has been available and most teachers have to rely on Internet resources and reviews for their students. While the internet and reviews are a valuable resource, their information is limited in scope, can be of varying quality, and is not always accessible.

We hope that our book will be interesting to a variety of readers and viewers, especially viewers and students of film in general, who would like to find out more about German film, people interested in learning more about Germany and its convoluted and fascinating history, people who would like to study German and use films as a tool, and teachers and professors of German language courses, who need a convenient introduction to common German films. We attempted to make this an interesting book to read and tried our best to avoid the academic lingo that prevails in most film books.

As a resource book each film chapter contains the following elements:

- Basic information about the movie including credit information.
- A synopsis of the movie, which gives a brief overview of the plot.
- Background information about the history, the movie, its director, the actors, and the movie style. With this part we tried to make German movies attractive to viewers, audiences and teachers outside the immediate film history classes and to reach social studies and German history teachers.
- An analysis, which summarizes the research for this movie and points out areas for class discussion.

- A number of questions to motivate class discussion. The companion volume for German sections contains another set of linguistic and cultural exercises.
- References. Since teachers of German culture face the decision whether a course is going to be taught in German or English, we have included resource information in both languages in the reference section.

The articles were conceived and written by Margit Sinka of Clemson University (MS), Robert C. Reimer of the University of North Carolina at Charlotte (RCR), and Reinhard Zachau of the University of the South in Sewanee, Tennessee (RZ). The contribution of Wim Wenders's *Himmel über Berlin* (*Wings of Desire*) comes from Amy Hill (AH), Adnan Dzumhur (Adz) and Andrew Doak (AD), students at the University of the South.

Teaching a course on German film

For a course on German film history, we recommend dividing the movies into sections and showing only one film per week to facilitate a good discussion. Excerpts from films relevant to the main feature can be introduced in lectures during that week. It is difficult to show more than twelve movies in one semester, and indeed ten might be a more manageable number, especially if students are assigned written and oral presentations on the films. If the program allows, it might be tempting to offer the course as a two-semester-long introduction, and thus be able to show twenty movies or a few more.

German film courses can be organized around different themes inherent in the films themselves, such as Silent Film, Expressionist Films, Nazi Films, East German Films, The New German Cinema, and Contemporary German Cinema. The most obvious organization for a film course covering these themes would be chronological. In addition to the films discussed at length in the book in each of these areas, there is a list of related films at the end of each chapter. Many of these are available on VHS or DVD and thus can be brought into the discussion. Some, however, are available only in the German format PAL for tapes and region 2 for DVDs.

I. Silent Movies

The silent movie period from 1919 to 1925 marked the most creative period in the history of the German cinema, dominated by heavily symbolic expressionist films such as *Das Cabinet des Dr. Caligari* (*The Cabinet of Dr. Caligari*, Robert Wiene 1920) and by works of Friedrich Wilhelm Murnau. Fritz Lang's silent films, although not covered in the English text, are easily available and lend themselves to student work as they are striking for their style, monumental sets, complex lighting and creation of special effects.

II. Weimar Sound Movies

The early 1930s saw the production of classic sound movies, such as *Der blaue Engel* (*The Blue Angel*, Josef von Sternberg *1930)* and *M* (Fritz Lang 1931). Socially committed films like *Kuhle Wampe* (1932) addressed Weimar's economic and political crisis and offer an aesthetic contrast to the next era's films, those of the Third Reich.

III. Film in the Third Reich

1933 saw the rise of Leni Riefenstahl, Hitler's and Goebbels' supreme propaganda filmmaker. Joseph Goebbels, Nazi Minister of Propaganda, generally preferred an indirect approach, with seemingly apolitical entertaining movies, rather than open propaganda films like *Hitlerjunge Quex* (*Hitler Youth Quex*, Hans Steinhoff 1933). The cinemas were flooded with comedies and operettas; sentimental entertainment designed to take people's minds off problems of the time.

IV. The Post-War Film

In 1945, at the end of the war, the German film had to start all over again. This new beginning involved financial risks, but also offered artistic opportunities. Up until 1949, the German film could still be regarded as a unity – but all of that changed with the division of Germany. While East Germany's DEFA studios produced mainly communist propaganda movies, West Germany's post-war film industry turned out largely kitsch or milieu productions. Demanding, sophisticated movies were very much the exception. The most uncompromising anti-war film in the postwar West German cinema was Bernhard Wicki's 1959 film *Die Brücke* (*The Bridge*), which received considerable international recognition.

V. The New German Film

In the early 1960s, the German cinema faced an artistic and commercial crisis. Light entertainment dominated; television had become a competitor. But some people rejoiced at what they called "the collapse of the conventional German film" in 1962. Twenty six young German film makers, cameramen and producers published a manifesto at the international short film festival in Oberhausen, proclaiming the death of "Papa's cinema." At the same time they announced the creation of the "New German Cinema," a term later generally applied to films between 1962 and 1982. Author filmmakers like Alexander Kluge, Edgar Reitz and Rainer Werner Fassbinder entered the scene and were some of the major adherents to the new cinema.

VI. Political Films

German filmmakers reacted in very different ways to the political events of the 1970s, often with semi-documentary films and movies critical of the social system of the Federal Republic. Volker Schlöndorff's *Die Blechtrommel* (*The Tin Drum* 1979), based on a novel by Günter Grass, became the most successful German film since 1945, winning an Oscar and the Golden Palm. In German cinema, the 70s were above all a period of realism and social criticism. Wolfgang Petersen's *Das Boot* (*The Boot* 1980) was the overall winner in this period, a film which showed that Germany could attain the level of Hollywood blockbusters.

VII. Visions and Adventures: Werner Herzog and Wim Wenders

Werner Herzog ranks alongside Rainer Werner Fassbinder and Wim Wenders as one of the leading representatives of the New German Cinema. He makes poetic, sensitive films about dreamers, adventurers and rebels. Over and over he shows a fascination with extreme situations and bizarre outsiders. Even the actual shooting of a film – especially *Aguirre, der Zorn Gottes* (*Aguirre, the*

Wrath of God 1972) and *Fitzcarraldo* (1982) – became a hazardous adventure. Wim Wenders is one of Germany's internationally recognized directors, known for his road movies and films of searching for identity. Both tell laconic stories of people's encounters and separations.

VIII. Movies of unified Germany

The German movie industry reacted with different approaches to the challenges of unification. With a few exceptions, such as *Das Versprechen* (*The Promise*, Margarethe von Trotta 1995) *Sonnenallee* (*Sun Alley*, Leander Haußmann 1999), or *Good Bye, Lenin!* (Wolfgang Becker 2003), most movies explore the human condition, not political issues. But von Trotta, Haußmann and Becker also focus on the political in the aforementioned highly entertaining films. The nineties were a time of comedies and light dramatic films, indicating a renewed popular interest in movies. However, these light movies should not be seen as a continuation of the fifties entertainment films. Since language courses are often interested in showing modern German culture through film, we have included a good number of these recent German movies.

Teaching a film course on German history

A selection of movies from this book can serve as an excellent source for teaching German history. Beginning with *The Cabinet of Dr. Caligari* and *Nosferatu*, the students get an impression of the confused state of mind Germans were in at that time. Speculation of how and why these movies were so grotesque and gruesome will invariably shift to discussion of the end of the First World War and the earlier part of the Weimar Republic with its street fighting and political instability prior to the hyperinflation of 1923. *Kuhle Wampe* is an excellent example to show how filmmakers speculated about Germany's future and is still capable of engaging students.

The two Nazi movies *Triumph des Willens* (*Triumph of the Will*, Leni Riefenstahl 1935) and *Jud Süß* (*Jew Süss*, Veit Harlan 1940), will for most students be a first impression of the Nazis from the inside, most likely fascinating for most viewers. This fascination will lead to a general discussion of propaganda films and why Riefenstahl is admired by some and condemned by others in the U.S., and finally to the morbid mind behind the destruction of the Jews and the making of a movie such as *Jew Süss*.

The post-war movies, especially *Die Mörder sind unter uns* (*The Murderers Are among Us*, Wolfgang Staudte 1946) give a rare glimpse of the destruction after the Second World War. Other movies, such as *The Bridge* and more importantly *The Boat* or *The Tin Drum* let Americans take a closer look at how Germans learned to deal with the Nazi past.

While some might consider the experimental movies of Germany's New Wave too difficult for students to comprehend, no German film course would be complete without at least one movie by R. W. Fassbinder. Fassbinder combines film experimentation with a progressive message that gives insight into the world of the 1970s, the *Aufbruchsstimmung* (anticipation something is going to happen) and the notion that West Germany was heading the wrong way with its fascist and capitalist baggage. One of the most interesting movies for this phase in West German history is Volker Schlöndorff's and Margarethe von Trotta's *Die verlorene Ehre der Katharina Blum* (*The Lost Honor of Katharina Blum* 1975), with its plot focusing on terrorism.

Purely aesthetic and artistic movies may be unattractive for language courses, but Werner Herzog's and Wim Wender's movies belong in a course on German film. Wenders's *Wings of Desire* (1987) and Herzog's *Aguirre, the Wrath of God* changed critics' opinion about German film.

CHAPTER 1

Das Cabinet des Dr. Caligari

(*The Cabinet of Dr. Caligari*, **Robert Wiene 1920**)

After seeing the beautiful Jane (Lil Dagover) asleep, Cesare (Conrad Veidt) falls in love with her and does not kill her, as Caligari had demanded, but abducts her over the rooftops of Holstenwall. The scene presents a paradigm of expressionist film style with its diagonal lines, geometric shapes, drawn-in shadows, slanting rooftops, and exaggerated acting.

CREDITS

Director...Robert Wiene
Screenplay ....Hans Janowitz, Carl Mayer
Director of Photography ....Willi Hameister
Music.. Giuseppe Becce
Producers .... Rudolf Meinert, Erich Pommer
Production Design ....Walter Röhrig
Set Decoration...Hermann Warm
Costume Design .... Walter Reimann.
Length.. varies by version between 50-78 minutes
(USA releases generally 67 minutes); b/w

Principal Cast

Werner Krauß (Dr. Caligari), Conrad Veidt (Cesare), Friedrich Feher (Francis), Lil Dagover (Jane), Hans Heinrich von Twardowski (Alan), Rudolf Lettinger (Dr. Olson), Rudolf Klein-Rogge (A Criminal).

THE STORY

Das Cabinet des Dr. Caligari (*The Cabinet of Dr. Caligari*, 1920), directed by Robert Wiene, is set in the small north German town of Holstenwall where Dr. Caligari is one of the exhibitors at a small fair or carnival. Francis (Friedrich Feher), the narrator, attends the carnival with his friend Alan (Hans Heinrich von Twardowski). When they visit the stand of Dr. Caligari (Werner Krauß) where the somnambulist (sleepwalker) Cesare (Conrad Veidt) is on display, all dressed in black, Cesare predicts that Alan will die tomorrow. Alan is indeed murdered that night. Coincidentally, Francis and Alan are both in love with Jane (Lil Dagover).

Jane's father has disappeared and she decides to visit Caligari's stand, but flees in horror after catching sight of Cesare in his coffin-like box. Later that night, Cesare rises from his coffin and starts stalking Jane with a knife. Upon seeing the beautiful Jane asleep, Cesare falls in love with her and does not kill her, as Caligari had demanded. Cesare dies after dragging Jane off, first over roof tops (perhaps the most recognized shot from the movie) and finally through fields. Jane's abduction by the monster, itself reminiscent of the "damsel in distress" motif from melodrama, influenced abduction scenes in monster films that came later including *Metropolis*, *Dracula*, and *King Kong*.

Francis breaks through all the confusion in the end and finds out the background to Caligari's story: He is the director of an insane asylum who got interested in historical research. In his research he uncovers information about a mountebank named 'Caligari' in 1612 who ran around with a somnambulist whom he trained to commit murder. Wanting to imitate those actions, Dr. Caligari thus begins his own strange sequence of murders. The film captions "Du musst Caligari werden!"("you must become Caligari!") clearly suggest Caligari's madness.

The story related above describes the body of the film as written by Hans Janowitz and Carl Mayer before a framing device was added, in which Francis tells the story to an old man. The ending frame returns to the asylum, showing that Francis, Cesare, who is still alive, and Jane are all inmates there. When Dr. Caligari appears, the attendants grab Francis and throw him into one of the cells. Dr. Caligari looks at him and mumbles: "Now I know what his problem is. He will be cured."

BACKGROUND

The Cabinet of Dr. Caligari opened in 1920, 25 years after the first movies were shown in Paris in 1895, and in a time of political turmoil in Germany. By early November 1918, many cities had been taken over by workers' and soldiers' councils, as had happened in Russia during the Revolution of 1917. Politicians were thus fearful of a communist takeover in Germany, which had agreed to an armistice on November 11, 1918, after which the German Emperor, Kaiser Wilhelm, abdicated on November 28, 1918. Painfully crippling peace terms were imposed upon the German people in 1919 in the Versailles treaty. In the midst of the chaos surrounding the end of the war, a new government, the Weimar Republic, was created to deal with the worsening political situation.

Since many German soldiers did not believe that they had been defeated, and since Germany was in a constant state of economic chaos with food in short supply, the Weimar Republic had great problems gaining acceptance throughout Germany. The harsh conditions dictated by the Treaty of Versailles angered Germans everywhere, and they directed their resentment at the Weimar government who signed the Treaty. From 1919 to 1923, there was a series of attempted revolutions in Germany. Some were staged by Communists, who hoped to take advantage of the situation and follow the example of Russia; others were carried out by right wing nationalists (among them Hitler and the fledging Nazi Party), who wanted to overthrow the government, blaming the harsh conditions of the Treaty of Versailles on Weimar politicians.

In spite of the economic and political turmoil, the arts started to flourish in Weimar Germany's impoverished capital city Berlin, with the Expressionists dominating the scene. They developed a style notable for its harshness, boldness, and visual intensity. They used jagged, distorted lines; crude, rapid brushwork; and jarring colors to depict urban street scenes and other contemporary subjects in crowded, agitated compositions notable for their instability and their emotionally charged atmosphere. Many of their works expressed frustration, anxiety, disgust, discontent, violence, and generally a sort of frenetic intensity of feeling in response to the ugliness, the crude banality, and the possibilities and contradictions that they discerned in modern life. Woodcuts, with their thick, jagged-lined and harsh tonal contrasts, were one of the favorite media of the German Expressionists.

Strongly influenced by Expressionist stagecraft, the earliest Expressionist films set out to convey through decor the subjective mental state of the protagonist. The most famous of these films is *The Cabinet of Dr. Caligari* (1919), in which Francis, an inmate in a mental institution, tells his story to an old man, another of the inmates, as to how he came to be in the asylum. The misshapen streets and buildings of the set are projections of the asylum's crazy universe. The inmates have been abstracted through makeup and dress into visual symbols.

The film's morbid evocation of horror, menace, and anxiety and the dramatic, shadowy lighting and bizarre sets became a stylistic model for Expressionist films by several major German directors. Paul Wegener's second version of *The Golem* (1920), F.W. Murnau's *Nosferatu* (1922), and Fritz Lang's *Metropolis* (1927), among other films, present pessimistic visions of social collapse or explore the ominous duality of human nature and its capacity for monstrous personal evil. Expressionist elements also influence later films such as Joseph von Sternberg's *The Blue Angel* (1930) and and Lang's *M* (1931), as well as the noir films made in Hollywood in the forties.

At the film's opening on February 26,1920 in the Marmorhaus in Berlin a blend of classical music of Beethoven, Schubert, Rossini, Bellini, Donizetti and Paul Lincke was played. Soon after, the composer Giuseppe Becce wrote his own score of modernist music for the movie, which has been lost. Obviously modernist music works better with Caligari's expressionist style than the original classical score. The film composer Lothar Prox and Emil Gerhardt, who had seen a small piece of Becce's original score, recreated it for a 1984 restoration of the movie. Subsequently, many different scores for the movie have been created, as it has always attracted large numbers of composers, making it one of the most popular silent movies for re-scoring.

EVALUATION

The Cabinet of Dr. Caligari is one of the strangest German movies ever written. Although one of the earliest successful German movies to date (filmed in December 1919 and January 1920) it still holds our attention and still fills us with suspense. The film is an artistic tour de force that makes every viewer experience the power of expressionist filmmaking. Consequently it is also open to multiple and equally extreme interpretations as that of Siegfried Kracauer, for example, who saw Dr. Caligari as an early embodiment of Adolf Hitler.

While the story line is somewhat incoherent and bizarre, the film's artistic quality is without equal for the times. The sets, costumes, performance of the actors, coloring of the scenes, and music present an excellent example of "Expressionism in action", of an almost complete expressionist work of art, a *Gesamtkunstwerk* (total synthesis of the arts), as Richard Wagner might have called it. If we accept the various musical scores that accompany the film, depending on distributor, then the only art form missing is audible dialogue, but captions have been entered into the images in a variety of ways, providing a substitute for the film's silence.

The costumes and make-up are skillfully combined with the exaggerated body movements of the actors. Some of these exaggerations originate in the fact that the adequate lighting we are used to now was absent. Moreover, because audible dialogue was missing, every body movement had to be exaggerated to compensate for the low light.

Conrad Veidt as Cesare is excellent in his mysterious animal-like acting, repulsive and attractive at the same time, a personification of sexual and subliminal desire, the ultimate alter ego figure so popular with expressionist drama and movies. One of the precursors to *The Cabinet of Dr. Caligari* is the first version of *The Student of Prague* (1913) with its shadowy figures, the bearers of the protagonist's conscience, popping up to startle viewers.

The sets with their irregular angles, zigzag shapes, and uneven surfaces are pure Expressionism, dominating the actors' movements which are similarly angular. Conrad Veidt and Werner Krauß represent an eerie, stylized underworld, as when Caligari presents Cesare for the first time or when Cesare slinks by the wall towards Jane's house, shadowy and sinister.

The other actors follow with equally unsettling movements. The town clerk in his over-sized chair and his standoffish attitude suggests Kafka, who wrote his texts at about the same time as this movie was produced. We still marvel at these creations in texts and movies as anticipations of the political horrors to come, Stalin's purges and mass killings, the Holocaust, and the other atrocities of the Second World War committed by Hitler and the Nazis.

In his summary of the film, Mike Budd suggests that the more one tries to make all the movie's details fit, the more difficult and problematic the film becomes, which prompts a critical rereading of the film. The scriptwriter Hans Janowitz had argued that these problems stemmed from Robert Wiene's rewriting of the original script, which he regarded as a story with too conventional a frame. According to the original script, Francis and Jane were supposed to have told Caligari's story at a dinner party, the story of how they met and how the strange Caligari changed their lives.

This opening frame was supposed to be closed again with the mad Caligari's death and Francis and Jane commemorating his death. As Janowitz argued, by

Dr. Caligari (Werner Krauß) displays the somnambulist Cesare (Conrad Veidt) at the fair, all dressed in black. Veidt's Cesare influenced later depictions of monsters, including Boris Karloff's monster in James Whale's Frankenstein.

changing the frame and revealing Francis rather than Caligari as the madman, the entire message became twisted. A film critical of authority was altered into a more conformist one. The edge was removed and what was left was utter confusion, which a benevolent viewer might interpret as modern art.

As Siegfried Kracauer argued in his book *From Caligari to Hitler*, "A revolutionary film was thus turned into a conformist one ... by putting the original into a box, this version faithfully mirrored the general retreat into a shell." Kracauer further writes that since both scriptwriters were pacifists, the original script with Francis and Jane's story contained an anti-authoritarian message where Caligari represents deranged and dangerous authority. For Kracauer, who was attempting to use films to psychoanalyze the German people in order to understand how a man like Hitler could have risen to power, the story becomes prescient: it is the tale of a man leading a double life, first as the respected head psychiatrist of a mental institution, and then as the insane side-show keeper who uses his exhibit, a somnambulist, to commit ghastly murders. In Kraucauer's psychoanalysis Caligari becomes Hitler, who uses innocent people (Cesare the somnambulist representing the German people) to commit horrible atrocities to satisfy the lust for power. Thus Kracauer, looking back on history, contends the movie was able to foreshadow the German political direction leading toward the rise of totalitarianism:

"The character of Caligari ... stands for an unlimited authority that idolizes power as such, and, to satisfy its lust for domination, ruthlessly violates human rights and values. Functioning as a mere instrument, Cesare is not so much a guilty murderer as Caligari's innocent victim ... Whether intentional or not Caligari supposes the soul wavering between tyranny and chaos and facing the desperate situation: any escape from tyranny seems to throw it into a state of utter confusion. Quite logically, the film spreads an all-pervading atmosphere of horror. Like the Nazi world, Caligari's world overflows with sinister portents, acts of terror and outbursts of panic."

Thus Kracauer's entire thesis of equating film with society originates in his reading of Caligari as a mirror of Hitler and of this movie's power to anticipate the horrors of the Third Reich. Kracauer's book was written after the Nazi empire had ended and in a time when everybody was hungry for an explanation of the horrors. In addition, he, Kracauer, a German Jewish émigré, was a likely knowledgeable interpreter to the world of what might have happened to Germany.

It is also a clever way of tying art and society together and of using film as perhaps the most thorough investigation and explanation of the unthinkable horrors to come. However, while Kracauer wants to work in an enlightened rational framework, this method may also suggest the opposite, by giving the movie's obscure and contradictory elements a rational political interpretation. As Expressionism is usually seen as a continuation of irrational romanticism, so can Kracauer's method be regarded as irrational, since he promises an explanation of the mysterious and obscure elements in the movie.

Later interpretations, such as Mike Budd's introduced earlier, center more on textual differences in the movie, such as the contradiction between the surreal settings and the real characters; but Budd does not provide a more convincing interpretation either.

Who then is the real madman in the movie, Francis or Caligari? As we have seen, Janowitz and Mayer intended Caligari to be the evil madman, whereas Wiene's altered frame had turned Francis into the lunatic. A clue for deciphering the movie may be found in the latest restoration of the original tints for the DVD version. Here, the color brown is used for all daylight scenes (inside or out), blue for all scenes at night and for all titles, pink for three scenes in Jane's bedroom, and two-tone colors with blue on brown for two scenes where Frances narrates his story, the opening scene and the scene where he tells of Alan's murder. These two scenes at last may add meaning to the puzzle of what really happened, since they add another layer of interpretation. The two-tone colors separate Francis's story from the rest of the story and point to the fact that the events are indeed told from his perspective. With this information the possibility is introduced that Francis's rivalry with Alan could have caused harm to his friend—whether he murdered his friend or not remains open.

However, a political interpretation along Kracauer's lines cannot be excluded either. Thus, the movie serves as a catalyst for discussing political events in Germany during the Weimar Republic, although it will probably never be deciphered completely. (RZ)

QUESTIONS

1. Locate examples of Expressionism in *The Cabinet of Dr. Caligari*.

2. Describe the acting style in *The Cabinet of Dr. Caligari*. In what ways do the exaggerated movements help the story?

3. How does the musical score contribute to the atmosphere of the movie? If you were to score the movie, what kind of music would you use?

4. Make a list of important scenes and the tints used.

5. Describe the political situation in Germany immediately after the First World War and relate it to the film's themes of insanity and authority.

6. Why would Siegfried Kracauer describe Dr. Caligari as a precursor to Hitler?

7. What is your own interpretation of the movie and its inconsistencies?

RELATED FILMS

Der Golem (*The Golem*, Henrik Galeen and Paul Wegener 1915) This film, based on a Jewish legend of a clay statue that was brought to life, is one of the earliest Gothic tales of horror produced in Germany. In this version the statue goes on a killing rampage after it is discovered in the twentieth century, brought to life, and spurned in love.

Der Golem, wie er in die Welt kam (*The Golem: How He Came into the World*, Carl Boese and Paul Wegener 1920). In this second version of the legend, the clay statue is brought to life in the sixteenth century to help the residents of the Jewish quarter resist the despot Rudolf II.

Nosferatu, eine Synphonie des Grauens (*Nosferatu, a Symphony of Horror*, W. Murnau 1922). An early version of the Dracula legend. See discussion elsewhere in this book.

Der Student von Prag (*The Student of Prague*, Hanns Heinz Evers and Stellan Rye 1913). This film, based on a story by the German Romanticist E. T. A. Hoffmann, tells of a student who sells his mirror image to the devil in return for fame and fortune. The film offers an early example of German film's interest in horror movies.

Der Student von Prag (*The Student of Prague*, Henrik Galeen 1926). This remake of the E.T.A. Hoffmann story, when contrasted with the first version, demonstrates the advance made in film production values in the thirteen years since the original was released. It also serves as an excellent example of cinematic Expressionism.

INFORMATION

The Cabinet of Dr. Caligari (1920) DVD, silent with musical score, b/w, approx. 74 minutes, English intertitles, Gotham Distribution, released 2002.

Das Cabinet des Dr. Caligari (1920) VHS/ PAL, silent with musical score, b/w (tinted), approx. 74 minutes, German intertitles, BMG Video, released 1996.

Das Cabinet des Dr. Caligari. Drehbuch von Carl Mayer und Hans Janowitz zu Robert Wienes Film von 1919/20. Munich: Edition Text und Kritik, 1995.

Barlow, John D. *German Expressionist Film*. Boston: Twayne Publishers, 1982.

Heß, Klaus-Peter. *Das Cabinet des Dr. Caligari: Materialien zu einem Film von Robert Wiene*. Klaus Peter Hess. Duisburg: Atlas-Film u. Av, 1988.

Wiene, Robert. *The Cabinet of Dr. Caligari: a film by Robert Wiene; Carl Mayer; Hans Janowitz*. Engl. transl. and description of action by R. V. Adkinson. New York: Lorrimer Publishing, 1972.

Das Kabinett des Dr. Caligari: Presse-Informationen. Frankfurt a. M.: Zentral-Pressestelle des. Centfox-Film, 1962.

The Cabinet of Dr. Caligari: texts, contexts, histories. Edited by Mike Budd. New Brunswick NJ: Rutgers UP, 1990.

Eisner, Lotte H. *The Haunted Screen*. Berkeley: U of California P, 1973. First published in France as *L'Ecran Démoniaque*, 1952. Translated from the French by Roger Greaves, 1969.

Kracauer, Siegfried. *From Caligari to Hitler: A Psychological History of German Film*. Princeton NJ: Princeton UP, 1947.

CHAPTER 2

Nosferatu, eine Sinfonie des Grauens

(*Nosferatu, a Symphony of Terror*, **F. W. Murnau 1922**)

Nosferatu (Max Schreck) has come out of hiding from the hold of the ship bringing him to Wisborg. Here he stands on the upper deck of the ship, the camera angle and verticals of the ship's rigging emphasizing his height and menacing nature. Notice how the ropes on the right reinforce the monster's claw-like fingers.

CREDITS

Director .... F.W. Murnau
Screenplay .... Henrik Galeen
Director of Photography .... Günther Krampf and Fritz Arno Wagner
Music.. Hans Erdmann
Producers ....Enrico Dieckmann, Albin Grau, Wayne Keeley
Production Companies........... Jofa-Atelier Berlin-Johannisthal, Phana-Film GmbH
Length...varies depending on version, average is
ca. 80 minutes. Silent, b/w and tinted

Principal Cast

Max Schreck (Graf Orlock), Alexander Granach (Knock), Gustav von Wangenheim (Thomas Hutter), Greta Schröder (Ellen), Georg H. Schnell (Harding), Ruth Landshoff (Harding's sister), John Gottowt (Professor Bulwer), Gustav Botz (Dr. Sievers), Max Nemetz (Captain of the *Demeter*), Wolfgang Heinz, (First Mate).

THE STORY

Nosferatu, eine Sinfonie des Grauens (*Nosferatu, a Symphony of Terror*, F. W. Murnau 1922) tells a variation of the vampire story that has fascinated the public since Bram Stoker first published his novel *Dracula* in 1897. Thomas Hutter (sometimes referred to as Jonathan) travels to Transylvania at the request of his boss to interest Count Orlock in an old house in Wisborg (in some VHS titles and reviews referred to as Bremen). Although the trip will be long and dangerous, Hutter undertakes the commission for the financial gain and adventure that the trip promises. Once in Transylvania, in spite of warnings from the local populace, Hutter visits the Count, who agrees to purchase the house but attacks the agent during the night. Hutter escapes the Vampire's attack only because Ellen (sometimes referred to as Nina), his wife, hundreds of miles away, calls out his name in her sleep, just as the count is ready to bite him. The Count travels to Wisborg by sea, killing all the crew on the ship that transports him. Hutter returns home via land after a bout with fever. An outbreak of plague in Wisborg coincides with Count Orlock's arrival, but the town is saved further suffering when Ellen, having read that a woman pure of heart could kill the Vampire, sacrifices herself by keeping Nosferatu at her bedside until the break of dawn.

BACKGROUND

Germany fought England, France and Russia in the First World War from 1914-1918, during which millions of Germans died on the battlefield. Returning home after the war, military men, many made physically and mentally infirm by the fighting, returned to a country beset by unemployment and inflation. At the same time, fighting between leftist revolutionaries, who were intent on establishing Soviet styled governments as had occurred in Russia, and rightwing militias caused more death and suffering. Finally, a devastating outbreak of influenza that eventually killed twenty million people worldwide also attacked Germany, killing thousands already weakened by war and deprivation.

German films of the 1910s and early 1920s reflected the pessimism caused by so much suffering, often turning to themes of darkness and evil. Finding inspiration in nineteenth century romanticism, especially the gothic tales of English authors and of E.T.A. Hoffmann, filmmakers emphasized the duality of man's nature, in which good and evil struggle to possess the soul of the same individual. The German director Robert Wiene, for example, creates a sleepwalking monster that kills at the bidding of his psychiatrist master in *The Cabinet of Dr. Caligari* (1920). Henrik Galeen in *The Golem* (1915) and Paul Wegener in a second version of the legend, *The Golem, How He Came into the World* (1920) tell of a clay statue that has come to life, murdering and destroying as he seeks revenge for perceived wrongs. In addition to reflecting the unease of society during bleak times, these films and others also capitalize on the public's new-found interest in the subconscious, tracing back to Sigmund Freud's studies of psychoanalysis and in particular to his work on the *Interpretation of Dreams* (1900). Furthermore the films reflect a darker side of Expressionism, the prevalent style of the decade, whose obsession with expressing the inner nature of people and objects through distortions and shadows influenced the film industry as well. Finally, scenes of death and destruction, monsters of doom, and overall evil replay the fears prevalent at the time and occasioned by the First World War and its aftermath.

Particularly popular in the nineteenth century was the legend of Dracula, whose original persona of avenging angel had been turned into that of a bloodthirsty monster. Bram Stoker, capitalizing on the legend's darker side and also on the Victorian era's repressed nature in matters of sexuality, created a novel of a monster who was at once a threat to women wanting sexual adventure and men who were insecure about their own sexuality. F. W. Murnau, the director of *Nosferatu*, adapts this theme and as a consequence his film reflects the frightening tone of German expressionist lyric and painting, and resembles the horror stories being told by other German directors. Even though the film little resembles Bram Stoker's Victorian novel on which the film is based, the author's widow, Florence Stoker, filed and eventually won a lawsuit against copyright infringement of *Dracula*. Murnau changed the names of his characters and location of the action, but Mrs. Stoker pursued her case and in 1925 a German court ordered all copies destroyed. Some prints did survive, however, and the film had a New York premier in 1929 and by 1943 was recognized as one of Murnau's masterpieces. (BBC film reviews http://www.bbc.co.uk/films/2000/11/09/nosferatu_1922_article.shtml). Yet, as mentioned, in spite of Mrs. Stoker's suit and the court's ruling, Murnau's film resembles Stoker's novel very little. Even had he not changed the names and location, the movie's story departs sufficiently from Bram Stoker's novel as to suggest a radically different reworking of the Dracula legend, which predates Stoker's story by centuries and was a particularly popular subject in the nineteenth century.

Nosferatu is a silent film but the term is somewhat of a misnomer, as films were never silent, or at least they were seldom experienced in a silent mode. Even if the visual track could run without sound of any sort, it was general practice in the early days of cinema to have music in the background. Major films often had a score composed especially for them and played by a full orchestra at the premier and in first run metropolitan film houses. In less affluent settings, organ or piano music replaced the orchestra. Often the organists or pianists chose their own music to accompany the visuals, choosing from source books that made suggestions as to what kind of music was appropriate for what kind of scenes. Silent movies often had a narrator as well.

The situation today with the music on various VHS and DVD releases often follows the haphazard choice of scores from the early years. Videocassette distributors choose their own music, adding tracks that are more or less suitable or unsuitable to the visual text. None of the available releases of *Nosferatu*, for example, has the original music by Hans Erdmann. Instead, the visual text is available with scores that range from jazz to electronic to nineteenth century classical. Perhaps the strangest accompaniment is by O-Negative, an alternative rock band.

Just as films from the silent era were not silent, they were also generally not in black and white as we often assume. Instead directors used tinted filters to indicate mood, location, and time of day. Blue generally meant nighttime, for example. Owing to most of the tinted prints having been confiscated after Murnau lost the copyright infringement lawsuit, until recently *Nosferatu* has been known only in a black and white format. Indeed, even though restored in 1995, some DVD and VHS versions still have only the black and white print, which renders scenes as taking place in the daytime, a problem for a movie about a vampire who is injured by daylight.

EVALUATION

Murnau's film tells a story quite different from that traditionally associated with vampire movies. Perhaps as the first of the vampire films it had less to be influenced by, although as mentioned Bram Stoker's novel served as a model, even if extensively altered. Stoker's novel and the vampire films that followed equate vampirism and unrestrained sexuality. Their imagery suggests seduction as well as violation, excitement as well as fear. And even the first Hollywood version with Bela Lugosi suggests irony in the paradox of the Count's immortality. To understand how important sexuality is to the Dracula legend, we should imagine the punch that a modern film like *Interview with a Vampire* would lose were it not for the overt texts of homosexuality and promiscuous sex that make up the story, and the subtext of AIDs that bubbles beneath the surface of this vampire-cum-zombie tale.

In contrast to most other vampire films, Murnau's *Nosferatu* minimizes the subtext of sexuality, although some readings of the film emphasize this theme; indeed some point to an obvious subtext of homosexuality (Fred Thom, http://www.plume-noire.com/movies/cult/nosferatu.html). In place of overt sexuality Murnau focuses on themes of interest to German Expressionism in general and horror films of the time in particular: good vs. evil, sacrifice, and death. *Nosferatu* is a film infused by its time, reflecting the pessimism of postwar Germany, echoing themes of horror found in other films of Weimar cinema, and committed to the idea of movies as art. Yet the film also reaches beyond its era, exploring the issues of identity and alterity or otherness, themes of universal interest, which explains *Nosferatu*'s reputation as a classic and its position on "top" movie lists.

Nosferatu equates evil with rats, disease, and wild animals. Count Orlock embodies what man fears most, a premature death. Evil, as embodied by the vampire, is unrelenting and undiscriminating, infecting all who cross his path, young and old, shipmates and ship captain, women and men, and poor and rich. Indeed not even the virtuous Ellen can escape Nosferatu's power over life, even if she can end that power. For it is only through her death that the vampire's killing can be stopped. Unlike his model/counterpart in Bram Stoker's novel, *Dracula*, Nosferatu possesses no social graces, no handsome physiognomy, and no seductive allure. He is a total and complete outsider; both because of his physical appearance and, of course, his unnatural being. Yet, in spite of his representation of evil, we develop a sympathy for him, if only briefly, as he stands behind a closed window looking at and longing for the woman in the window of the house opposite his. Indeed it is in the polarity evident in scenes such as this, which reveals Count Orlock's loneliness even as it captures the hideousness that produces his evil, that the film gains its power. The same effect occurs early in the film when the count reaches out for human contact after first seeing Ellen's portrait in a locket. The contrast of ugliness and beauty transmutes in the next scenes to a contrast of evil and goodness.

Nosferatu explores other themes in addition to good and evil. Among them are the power of love, the exclusion of those who are different, and the loneliness of the outsider. Love, exclusion, and loneliness all come together in the denouement of the film, Ellen's willingness to seduce the vampire to end his evil reign. Ellen Hutter is sensitive, good, and totally in love with her husband. We recognize the essential decency of her character in the reaction of sadness she has when receiving flowers from her husband and realizing that the flowers will now wilt and die. Furthermore in her husband's absence she develops difficulty sleeping, wandering in her sleep and walking morosely when awake along a coastline strewn with crosses memorializing men who have died at sea. Finally we see goodness in Ellen's reaction as she reads a page from a book on vampires that advises that only a woman of pure virtue can save mankind from the threat of the monster. Upon reading this page she shows a defiant nature, as her husband has forbidden her to read the book, but she also reveals her readiness to sacrifice herself to save her husband and the town.

When contrasted with Ellen's beauty and goodness, it is, of course, not difficult to see why the vampire would be excluded from human discourse. Nor is it difficult to recognize this very exclusion, even if he himself seems to choose this path, as a motivating factor in his killing of the townspeople. Moreover his very nature of possessing a cursed form of immortality that sets him apart from humanity condemns him to a fate of eternal aloneness. His victims die. Unlike Dracula's victims who become his brides and share his vampire existence, Nosferatu is and always will be alone.

Nosferatu is one of the first films not merely to make extensive use of location shooting but also to allow location shooting to reflect the themes of the film. The exterior scenes of the town and harbor of Wisborg were shot in Germany's northern seaports of Rostock and Wismar. Count Orlock's Wisborg dwelling was an old warehouse in Lübeck, still standing as a department store. The Upper Tatras and Orasky Castle in Slowakia substituted for the Carpathian Mountains and the Count's home in Transylvania.

Murnau's decision to shoot on location lends an atmosphere of mystery and decay to *Nosferatu*. At the same time location shots add a sense of realism to this otherwise expressionist and formalist film. In the Transylvania scenes especially, the film builds tension by counterbalancing expressionist form with realistic content. Murnau uses shadows, deliberate pacing, oblique angles, exaggerated speed, and scenes reproduced in negative on the screen to capture the natural settings of a village inn, horses running in a meadow, a coach racing through the heath, a ruined castle on a mountain top, and local villagers. The director thus reverses the usual convention of early horror films as in *The Cabinet of Dr. Caligari* or *The Student of Prague*, which used the artificiality of studio sets to enhance horrific effects. Murnau instead sets his tale of fantasy and horror in the natural world, adding realism to an artificial tale, creating an uneasy feeling of dread in viewers.

The film itself, though, is not scary in the conventional sense. There are no monsters that jump out at the characters and startle viewers, nor bats that fly in through windows foreshadowing danger, as occur in conventional vampire movies. Instead, there are arches that lead from an actual courtyard into the void of total darkness; tower rooms whose windows look out and onto a real but unreachable landscape; and furnishings that transmute into objects of danger. In one of the more effective scenes of the film, Hutter lies in bed when his door slowly opens and the vampire appears in the distance down the corridor. As he slowly advances and reaches the room, he goes up a step or two until his body is framed by the doorway which is shaped like a gothic arch, the monster's head almost reaching the peak of the arch. The doorway emphasizes and even extends the monster's size, generating a deeper fear in Hutter, and vicariously in the viewer, than would have been achieved had Nosferatu appeared suddenly out of nowhere.

Murnau created a likewise ominous atmosphere for the scenes in Wisborg by shooting in once fine but now rather dilapidated patrician houses. Here also he creates fear and dread through blending of natural settings, expressionist techniques, and horrific content. Ellen, for example, stands at her window looking down onto the street watching as a town crier's proclamation signals the spread of the plague. The next time we see Ellen at the window she is watching Nosferatu looking out the window opposite hers, from the run-down building he has leased. Later in a stairwell, we see not Nosferatu but his shadow, as it slinks along the walls of the hallway before the monster appears in Ellen's room. Again there are no surprises, no sudden appearance of objects of danger, but rather a deliberate sequence of movement that builds suspense and leads to Ellen's sacrifice, submitting to the desires of the vampire, which in turn leads to the monster's death.

Reflecting the themes and the tone prevalent in the expressionist plays and films of the era, the movie creates a mood of mystery surrounding themes of sacrifice, love, and death. As the film opens, for example, Knock, a gnomish-sized broker, pores over real estate documents whose strange cabalistic-like symbols suggest hidden meaning. His subsequent commission to Hutter, one of his agents, is likewise suggestively ambiguous, mixing promises of rewards with warnings of danger. Finally, this sequence comes to a close as Hutter offers his wife a bouquet of flowers as a way of breaking the news to her about his trip, which she accepts, at the same time mournfully expressing her sorrow that the flowers are now going to die.

Thomas Hutter, in his own way, also contrasts to the vampire. He is a naïve fellow, totally in love with his wife and full of ambition. With few subtitles to guide us, we sense his pleasure in his wife through his smiles, his gift of flowers, and his willingness to undertake the arduous trip to Transylvania. Once in Transylvania, his love letter home and his reckless attempts to get back to Wisborg to warn Ellen further characterize his noble nature. We can also see in him the beginning of a filmic cliché, the husband/finance who temporarily leaves his partner, thus endangering her life.

Throughout the movie, Murnau's visual text continues to juxtapose the irrational and rational, adventure/sacrifice and danger, and love and death found in the opening sequence. Murnau makes ample allusion throughout the film to polarities such as good and evil, beauty and ugliness, and life and death that in general are especially strong during war years and immediately thereafter, and that in particular reflect the condition found in Weimar Germany. Ellen's perfect features are thus contrasted with Nosferatu's distorted body even when she is absent. At table in Transylvania, Nosferatu remarks about Ellen's beauty (specifically her beautiful neck) as he holds her photo in his exaggeratedly elongated hands. Later in the night, scenes of the vampire beginning to attack Hutter are intercut with scenes of Ellen calling out his name. Finally, in Wisborg, as the monster stares out a window opposite Ellen's bedroom, she stares out her window at him. Evil, ugliness, and death are present in all these scenes. Yet they seem ably dispelled by good, beauty, and love.

Yet much of the film stresses death and illness, as was prevalent in Germany and much of Europe immediately after the war. Nosferatu, for example, brings plague with him as he arrives in Wisborg. At a time not long after the so-called

Nosferatu stands at a window staring out to Ellen's bedroom. Unlike in traditional Dracula films, where windows represent a means of entry for the vampire into society's parlors and bedrooms, here the window remains shut on the hideous-looking monster.

"Spanish influenza" had killed millions worldwide, Murnau associates his vampire with disease-carrying rats. Three scenes develop his motif of death: The first occurs on the boat that brought Nosferatu to Wisborg. Subsequent to showing how the sailors break open Nosferatu's earth-filled coffins, thereby releasing scores of rats, the crew buries the first to die in a shipboard ceremony. In the second, Ellen walks along a deserted coastal shore dotted with dozens of crosses as she looks out to sea, awaiting Hutter's return, but also strengthening her tie to the vampire as he is also at sea at this time. Finally in the third scene, shot from a bird's eye view as Ellen looks out her window, coffin after coffin is carried down an otherwise deserted street.

The vampire's association with disease and death does more than reflect conditions in postwar Germany. By making Nosferatu a hideous, diseased pariah, the film also positions him as a perfect example of the other, the misfit who stands outside society never able to join in. Whereas Count Dracula as conceived by Bram Stoker is a monster to be sure, his guise of a sophisticated Eastern European gains him entry into society's theater boxes and parlors. Even as he remains an outsider he enters easily into social discourse and is virtually welcomed into parlors and even bedrooms through doors and windows conveniently left opened. Murnau's monster in contrast is shut out of social interaction with the other characters both because of his physical appearance but also, as mentioned above, by his own choosing. Murnau never shows him even attempting to socialize, but rather shows him sneaking through the town at night, preferring to enter his new home through an outside wall rather than a door. Murnau also positions the monster both within his own world, looking out of his window, and shut out from society, looking over and into Ellen's window. Indeed this shot, as pointed out earlier, at least to modern sensibilities, elicits a degree of sympathy for the monster, totally alone because of his physical hideousness as well as his metaphysical condition, being unable to die. (RCR)

QUESTIONS

1. Describe the way Murnau uses the following elements of cinema to enhance the evil power of the vampire: (1) camera (movement and placement, looking especially at distance from camera); (2) lighting, including shadows; (3) mise-en-scène (the way people and objects are positioned within the frame); and (4) editing (the way scenes are put together or ordered).

2. *Nosferatu* was released in 1922, less than four years after the end of World War I. At the time Germans were still suffering from effects the war had on their physical and emotional well being. Identify individual scenes that would remind contemporary viewers (those seeing the film in 1922) of the war that had just ended and the misery in which they now found themselves.

3. Some critics have noted an anti-Semitic subtext (secondary meaning buried within an artwork's story and structure) in the film. What evidence is there to support their argument? Others have suggested a homosexual subtext. Can you find evidence to support this claim?

4. How does Murnau use the visual text to prepare us for Ellen's sacrifice?

5. How does the film differ from other film versions of the vampire legend with which you may be familiar? Some other famous versions are *Dracula* (Tod Browning 1931) starring Bela Lugosi, *Dracula* (Terence Fisher 1958) starring Christopher Lee, *Dracula* (John Badham 1979) starring Frank Langella, *Bram Stoker's Dracula* (Francis Ford Coppola 1992) starring Gary Oldman, *Interview with a Vampire* (Neil Jordan 1994), starring Tom Cruise and Brad Pitt, *Blade* (Stephen Norrington 1998), starring Wesley Snipes, *Buffy the Vampire Slayer* (Fran Rubel Kuzui 1992), *Nosferatu* (Werner Herzog 1979) starring Klaus Kinski, and *Shadow of the Vampire* (E. Elias Merhige 2000) starring John Malkovich and Willem Dafoe..

RELATED FILMS

Cabinet of Dr. Caligari (Robert Wiene 1920). This excellent example of expressionist film relates the tale of an inmate of a mental institution and his confrontation with the head psychiatrist, Dr. Caligari, a man he accuses of murder. One of Germany's earliest horror films. See discussion elsewhere in this book.

Der Golem (*The Golem*, Henrik Galeen and Paul Wegener 1915) and *Der Golem, wie er in die Welt kam* (*The Golem: How He Came into the World*, Carl Boese and Paul Wegener 1920). These two films, based on a Jewish legend of a clay statue that was brought to life, tell the tale of horror from a different perspective. The 1915 film locates the legend to the twentieth century. The later film leaves the story in the sixteenth century.

Der Student von Prag (*The Student of Prague*, Hanns Heinz Evers and Stellan Rye 1913) and *Der Student von Prag* (*The Student of Prague*, Henrik Galeen 1926). The original and its remake, based on a story by the German Romanticist

E. T. A. Hoffmann, tell of a student who sells his mirror image to the devil in return for fame and fortune. The films offer an excellent example of the advances in production values made between 1913, when narrative film was still in its infancy, and 1926, the heyday of German silent cinema.

Nosferatu: Phantom der Nacht (*Nosferatu the Vampyre*, Werner Herzog 1979). Herzog remade Murnau's film as a loving homage to the original movie. Klaus Kinski, who worked with Herzog in a number of his movies, creates a monster at once frightening and pitiful, as a man condemned to live forever.

INFORMATION

Nosferatu (1922), DVD, silent with choice of musical score, b/w (tinted), English intertitles, Arrow Video, released 2001.

Barlow, John D. *German Expressionist Film*. Boston: Twayne Publishers, 1982.

Bergstrom, Janet. "Sexuality at a Loss: The Films of F. W. Murnau." *Poetics Today* 6, nos. 1-2 (1985): 185-203.

Eisner, Lotte H. *The Haunted Screen*. Berkeley: U of California P, 1973. First published in France as *L'Ecran Démoniaque*, 1952. Translated from the French by Roger Greaves, 1969.

Kracauer, Siegfried. *From Caligari to Hitler: A Psychological History of German Film*. Princeton NJ: Princeton UP, 1947.

Mayne, Judith. "Dracula in the Twilight: Murnau's *Nosferatu* (1922)." In *German Film and Literature: Adaptations and Transformations*, edited by Eric Rentschler, 25-39. New York and London: Methuen, 1986.

McCormick, Richard W. *Gender and Sexuality in Weimar Modernity: Film, Literature, and "New Objectivity."* New York: Palgrave, 2001.

CHAPTER 3

Berlin: die Sinfonie der Großstadt

(*Berlin: Symphony of a Great City*, **Walther Ruttmann 1927**)

Ruttmann produces a collage of images in his film Berlin: Symphony of a Great City *to present the city as vibrant, energetic, progressive, and playful.*

CREDITS

Director..Walther Ruttmann
Screenplay ....Walther Ruttmann (based on an idea by Karl Mayer)
Director of Photography .....Raimar Kuntze, Robert Baberske, and Laszlo Schäffer
Music... Edmund Meisel (the original compositions are lost),
Timothy Brock (1993 score)
Production Companies................... Deutsche Vereins-Film AG, Berlin; Fox Europa
Length..62 minutes; b/w

THE STORY

The film is a visual symphony that Ruttmann divides into five parts, labeling each part an "Act." A prelude contrapuntally focusing on unblemished nature and on technology precedes the five-part drama consisting of 24 hours in the life of Berlin. Ruttmann segments the day as follows:

Act I—5:00 A.M. to shortly before 8:00 A.M. At the beginning of Act I, most of Berlin is still dormant—its inhabitants, its animals, its vehicles, its traffic, its stores, its factory machinery. No signs of life stir from the buildings. The streets, in spite of occasional late-night revelers or early bird risers, are largely empty. Soon, however, the city starts to awaken. More and more blue-collar workers slowly populate its streets. Coming from all imaginable directions after using different modes of transportation—these ranging from trains to the simple use of their feet—many head toward work in factories. There they put machines into motion, ensuring that the machines produce mass quantities of milk, bread, or steel—the old staples manufactured differently coexisting with the new.

Act II—Immediately before 8:00 A.M. through mid-morning. The beginning of this act continues to focus on workers' tasks, but this time mainly on those of various servants, cleaning women, housewives, garbage collectors, mailmen, sales personnel in small stores, and car washers. By this time, children have also awakened and are shown en route to schools and as they arrive in them around 8:00 A.M. After the film highlights the 8:00 A.M. time, it concentrates on white-collar workers on their way to large office buildings and disappearing into them. Abundant amounts of activity occur in the offices too, as drawers and notebooks open, as papers are sorted, and as typing, printing, and telephoning start and accelerate.

Act III—From mid-morning until noon. Work continues as construction workers repair streetcar rails, people sell clothes, policemen help children cross the streets, and railroad and hotel personnel help new arrivals in Berlin load and unload suitcases. But this act mainly centers on the increasing activity in the streets: the many means of transportation (busses, streetcars, taxis, and trains with signs connecting Berlin to other European cities) and the hectically circulating traffic. The advertising world is conspicuously present in a multitude of signs and display windows, the latter filled with nodding or rotating mechanical dolls energetically emulating the accelerated movement on the city streets. In the midst of the considerable chaos there is room not only for the purposeful workers of society but for a varied assortment of other Berliners. There is, for instance, a woman who goes into a church, a flirting couple and one that gets married, a woman who searches for something in forlorn fashion, and a prostitute who entices a man as they look at each other through the display windows of a store situated at the right angle of two streets. There are quarreling men flanked by onlookers, beggars, political demonstrators along with a political rabble-rouser, newspaper vendors, and marchers in a military parade (this scene leads to a quick glimpse of Paul von Hindenburg). All are representative of the traffic collages incessantly recreated in the film.

Act IV—Noon to dusk/early evening. This act includes perhaps the largest variation of activities and moods. At its outset, a welcome calm prevails as workers put down their tools and the wheels of factory machines come to a halt. A large cross section of Berliners—both humans and animals—eats, drinks, and rests contentedly. Children play in the parks and on the streets, musicians practice in Berlin courtyards, people take leisurely walks or conduct leisurely conversations in garden cafes. After the noon rest period—idyllic except for the inexplicable torturing to which some children suddenly subject animals and a poverty stricken mother's surprisingly harsh rejection of the children approaching her with warmth—Berliners resume activities in the world of work.

But the irrational harshness introduced at noon time increases in the course of the act: the newspapers seem to highlight crises with words such as "murder" accentuated to the accompaniment of ominous rhythms; stormy showers catch Berliners unprepared and cause them to panic; a roller coaster plasters rigid fear on the faces of its riders; suddenly a woman commits suicide by jumping from a bridge; the animals in the zoo become menacingly restless; and two dogs ferociously attack each other. Toward the end of the act, however, the weather no longer poses any danger, and the working day comes to a halt in the offices and factories, allowing Berliners to engage in their various favorite daytime leisure activities. These range from pursuing all sorts of sports to attending a fashion show or simply sitting in the park.

Act V—From dusk to the early morning hours. As night falls, lights appear in residential buildings, advertisements light up the streets, and—much as a light bulb draws moths to it—lit up display windows lure Berliners from the dark. Movie theaters, concerts, theater productions, variety shows, ice hockey and boxing events, jazz evenings, dancing establishments, bicycle races—all imaginable forms of spectacle and entertainment attract large crowds. People— so to speak—drink, dance, and are merry. The ceaselessly circulating traffic of vehicles and pedestrians, the dancing city lights, and the gleaming advertisements seem to merge into a chaotic whole with indistinguishable parts. This entity bursts into a fireworks display spreading all over the sky but ultimately giving way to the light circling from the solitary radio tower of Berlin—the only immediately recognizable Berlin landmark the film features.

BACKGROUND

Berlin: Die Sinfonie der Großstadt (*Berlin: Symphony of a Great City* 1927) is unquestionably a landmark film in the history of German cinema. For the first time, none of the filming occurred in an artificial studio, and barely any props were produced for the film (one of the few exceptions is an advertising column set up so that a cameraman could hide in its interior and film street scenes through a slit in the column). For several tracking shots, a canvas with a slit for the camera was spread over the back of a truck. During approximately one year, Walter Ruttmann (the "h" was dropped from the first name in 1929) and his camera crew immersed themselves with hidden cameras in the life of Berlin, largely unnoticed by the people they were filming. Of the many thousand segments filmed on the life of Berlin, Ruttmann's film includes only two that depended on professional actors: an actor initiated the aggressive street argument between two men that was terminated by a policeman, and clearly the suicide episode was also a staged event.

On the whole, though, Ruttmann was right to pride himself on having produced the first German film departing from Germany's theater tradition. His was also the first German film to feature a city as the main character and the first to dispense with intertitles (there was no need for them, since spectators easily recognized the actual Berlin locations appearing in the film and were not called upon to understand a traditional plot). Diverging from prevalent subjective, expressionistic filmic modes, Ruttmann initiated the realistic tradition in German cinema. Thus his film is generally classified as an example of the New Objectivity (*Neue Sachlichkeit*), the artistic movement of the middle and later 1920s that followed Expressionism.

Perhaps one of the most important innovations connected with *Berlin: Symphonie of a Great City* is the highly sensitive film stock that its producer Karl Freund, a photography expert, developed. It is this new film stock that enabled filming at night and filming inside any city building. Up to Ruttmann's groundbreaking movie, filming had been done almost exclusively in studios, since the expensive, special studio lighting was needed for simulating not only scenes taking place in the dark, whether inside or outside, but also for inside environments in general. Freund's sensitive film stock was thus nothing short of revolutionary. It vastly expanded the areas where filming could occur and it immensely increased the potential of cinema to shape perception—the act of viewing as much as the act of filming.

Despite its reliance on the real people of Berlin rather than on actors, on the real environment rather than on props, and on actual incidents rather than on simulated ones, Ruttmann's film cannot be considered a pure documentary. Reflecting Ruttmann's personal signature, its editing and montage techniques are largely responsible for introducing the concept of urbanism or modernity into German film. In fact, the film needs to be situated in the context of the many hotly argued aesthetic debates of the Weimar era.

Musically talented, Ruttman had nonetheless pursued a career as a painter after abandoning his study of architecture. Yet he eventually became dissatisfied with the static nature of paintings and moved more and more to the forefront of the theoretical positioning pertaining to film. Even before the start of the twenties, he had fervently opposed the use of cinema to film literary works, whether novels or dramas, insisting that film was a new art vastly different from any other. Convinced, moreover, that art needed to capture the quintessential nature of contemporary times—in the case of Berlin's Weimar era the rapidity of change or the intensely accelerated pace of all movement—he no longer felt that his occupation as a painter made any sense. To reflect the times, still life must be put into motion, he decreed. But, how to turn motion—the essence of film—into art, he wondered, much as he puzzled over maximizing the visual potential inherent in film. In these ponderings he was not alone, for others, too, concerned themselves with the question of how to create what was then envisioned as pure film or "the absolute film."

Ruttmann's first attempt at addressing his aesthetic concerns was *Opus I* (1921), a short of about ten minutes that turned into the first German abstract film shown to a wide public. Believing that color and shapes were the most important features of painting, he focused on these rather than on people or on recognizable everyday objects. In *Opus I* and later in the three other *Opus*-shorts that followed (1921-1925), he therefore set colors and shapes into motion—shapes such as circles, spheres, rectangles, triangles, cones, slices of the moon or of the sun, and straight or wavy lines. In concert with the music composed for each *Opus*-work, he put the hundreds of variously colored shapes, each painted by hand, into motion in countless ways (e.g., they jumped, fell, soared, melted, merged, separated, burned, rested, expanded, contracted, and danced). Mostly enthusiastic (except for those who complained about the absence of human beings), critics heralded the advent of "the new art," calling it "painting in motion," "audible light," or "visible music."

When his filmic experimentations with abstract shapes, color, and music seemed to reach a dead end, Ruttmann turned to the concrete objects of the everyday world after all, but without abandoning the aesthetic tenets dearest to him: form and content must be fused, the one signifying the other; cinema alone represents "painting with time"—that is, the visual in motion. In the film he planned on Weimar Berlin, images of the real, unmodified Berlin were to represent the "painting" element; the "motion" to express Berlin's tempo would, in turn, result not merely from the music but also from montage techniques lending rhythm to the Berlin shots. While the optical and the auditory elements were meant to complement each other equally, in reality the music took precedence, necessitating the removal of several Berlin images that were in Ruttmann's view among the best of those filmed.

Although the musical composition created by the composer Edmund Meisel seems to have been irretrievably lost, Arthur Kleiner reconstructed the score on the basis of orchestral fragments and piano scores. Still, Ruttmann is on record for having wished another musical score. It is thus at least possible that the current musical score—the music composed and directed by Timothy Brock in 1993—might have been more to Ruttmann's liking.

EVALUATION

Declared the capital of the Germany founded in 1871, Berlin at that time had a mere 800,000 inhabitants. By 1910, the number had risen to two million—this figure, in turn, swelled to four million by the middle of the 1920s, partly because Berlin had incorporated eight outlying cities and dozens of rural areas in 1920. This substantially enlarged Berlin became the biggest industrial city on the European continent, annually drawing thousands of people looking for work. Understandably, as the youngest industrialized metropolis in Europe, Berlin represented mobility and unlimited possibilities.

Ruttmann's film accentuates Berlin's changes and its dizzying potential by depicting the arrival of more and more people, the abundance of new consumer goods in well-lit display windows, and the flashing electric advertisements on facades of buildings that both fascinate and confuse the senses. Above all, though, the film focuses on the ceaselessly accelerated tempo that had become Weimar Berlin's most prominent attribute. The establishing shots of the film leap from the primordial nature represented by a placid sea of water to the technology-driven modernity characterized by an imposing passenger train completely oblivious to nature as it relentlessly charges, roars toward urban Berlin.

Though spectators do not encounter this same train again after it arrives in Berlin, the more than twenty train episodes in the first four acts of the film do help them to recall it, both in its material reality and in its symbolic functions. Because of the first powerful train, the later ones also connote technological change and its forceful imposition on life, as well as the anonymity of city dwellers (though the many compartment windows of the first train clearly mark it as a passenger train, the high velocity of the train precludes spectators from seeing any of the passengers through its windows—something that does become possible later in the film through the windows of slowly moving streetcars). Only the last act contains no train at all and not even the large quantities of steam that either terminate or suggest the arrival of a train (at one point in Act IV, the steam from a train occupies the entire frame). Entirely dedicated to leisure, the last act has no use for the steam that signifies toil.

The first train acts, moreover, as the harbinger of the increasingly complex city traffic that conditions modernity and thus the changing rhythms and swift tempo of the film as well. The urban traffic depicted in the film consists of all manner of vehicles—from horse and buggy (holdovers from a more bucolic era) to Lufthansa airplanes. Urban circulation is complicated not only by the large number of differing vehicles moving horizontally, vertically, and in circles but also by a vast array of pedestrian legs navigating the cityscapes in myriad ways (up and down; strolling, running, gliding, jumping, dancing). Just how important the legs and feet—like the horse and buggy arguably also holdovers from a more bucolic era—remain in the urban traffic jungle becomes apparent as they infiltrate even leisure moments. Ruttmann's film, for example, captures one moment of a Charlie Chaplin movie shown in the fifth act: The large movie screen shows only a large image of Charlie Chaplin's unmistakable feet. In marked contrast to their customary restlessness, spectators seem glued to this image—an image, one might say, that encapsulates the essence of their era, mobility in their lives.

Since aesthetic concerns, including the conviction that cinema needs to express the times in its filmic form as much as in its content, led Ruttmann to the subject of Berlin and thus to his choice of tempo as the main organizing principle of his film, faulting Ruttmann, as several critics have, either for excluding certain factual information on Berlin (e.g., the stock market and the dehumanizing aspects of technology) or not dealing with the inner life of Berliners—with their so-called soul—seems somewhat misplaced, at least from today's vantage point. To be sure, the contrasts in the film do occur at too rapid a pace to be interpreted. Viewers see many montages—for example, the feet of cattle being herded to slaughter and then the feet of marching soldiers (perhaps they too on the way to slaughter) or an image of fighting dogs juxtaposed with one of a woman indignantly slamming her office phone down after an angry phone conversation. Or, a woman's vertigo as she jumps from a bridge, committing suicide, interrupts a vertiginous roller coaster ride. The petrified gazes of the roller coaster riders hardly differ from the paralyzed fear in the gazes of those witnessing the suicide. Yet, in none of these instances or in any others do viewers have sufficient time to draw connections or to interpret any of the montages at all. Viewers simply have to accept that moments potentially begging for explication are swiftly followed by unrelated, irrelevant episodes—the suicide scene, for instance, by a fashion show. Clearly viewers are meant to experience the whole rather than its parts. That the film consists of abundant movement but contains no goal seems, however, less important to today's audiences, who continue to be intoxicated by the energy Ruttmann released in his film, just as Ruttmann had hoped his Berliners would be.

For some critics *Berlin: Symphony of a Great City* did not seem to portray specifically Berlin but rather any and all urban centers, particularly in its juxtapositions of rich and poor, young and old, work and leisure. For Ruttmann, however, Berlin was not interchangeable with other cities. In his opinion, only Berlin could function as the epitome of modernity—of its restlessness, dislocations, technological rhythms, hectic pace, surface pleasures, easy distractions, chameleonic nature—and thus of the times.

Admired by many in Ruttmann's day too, *Berlin: Symphony of a Great City* became a widely imitated film, causing the British film critic John Grierson to label it in the 1950s as one of the most influential films of all times. Still, Grierson complains of the proliferation, especially among film students, of "one day in the life of the city"-movies, all clad in symphonies, regardless of the city highlighted.

And in all of them, Grierson adds, the urban day draws to a close without anything essential having been imparted. (MS)

QUESTIONS

1. Does Ruttmann make viewers want to visit the city or not? Give examples of positive and negative attributes of Berlin.

2. Why do you think Ruttmann chose to include a suicide in his film? How does he integrate this fictional element with the documentary style?

3. Identify as many scenes as you can that show public transportation and discuss how these are edited. Be sure to include how the editing produces various feelings in viewers.

RELATED MOVIES

Berlin – Sinfonie einer Großtadt (*Berlin Symphony*, Thomas Schadt 2002). A recent documentary of Berlin.

Kino-Eye (Dziga Vertov, Russian 1924). Like Ruttmann, Vertov thought film should do something besides film dramas and novel-like stories, so he took to the streets to film his documentaries.

Metropolis (Fritz Lang 1927). Although the metropolis of the film is never named and indeed is probably meant to be New York, the film nonetheless pays homage to any large city.

INFORMATION

Berlin: Symphony of a Great City (1927), DVD, silent with German and English intertitles, b/w, 62 minutes, Image Entertainment, released 1999.

Berlin: die Sinfonie der Großtadt (1927), VHS PAL, score reconstructed by Arthur Kleiner. Available from ZDF (Zweites Deutsches Fernsehen).

Brodnax, Mary M., "Man's Machine: The Shift from Soul to Identity in Lang's *Metropolis* and Ruttmann's *Berlin.*" In *Peripheral Visions. The Hidden Stages of Weimar Cinema*, edited by Kenneth Calhoon. Detroit: Wayne State UP, 2001.

Goergen, Jeanpaul. *Walter Ruttmann. Eine Dokumentation*. Berlin: Freunde der deutschen Kinemathek, 1989).

Kracauer, Siegfried. From *Caligari to Hitler: A Psychological History of the German Film*. Princeton NJ: Princeton UP, 1947.

Kaes, Anton, "Leaving Home. Film, Migration, and the Urban Experience," *New German Critique* 74 (Spring-Summer 1998), 179-192.

Ott, Frederick W. *The Great German Films*. Secaucus NJ: Citadel Press, 1986.

Vogt, Guntram. "Berlin, Die Sinfonie der Grossstadt (1927). " In *Die Stadt im Kino. Deutsche Spielfilme 1900-2000*. Marburg: Schüren, 2001.

CHAPTER 4

Der blaue Engel

(*The Blue Angel*, **Josef von Sternberg 1930**)

Lola Lola (Marlene Dietrich) performing what became Dietrich's signature song, "Falling in Love Again" at the Blue Angel nightclub. Note how Sternberg crowds the mise-en-scène, placing people and objects on various planes to give the scene more atmosphere and substance, but also because he believed that by filling the space in front of the camera, he could eliminate the hollow sound of many early sound films.

CREDITS

Director ....Josef von Sternberg;
Screenplay .... Heinrich Mann, Carl Zuckmeyer
Director of Photography .... Günther Rittau
Music.. Frederick Holländer
Producer .... Erich Pommer; Production Company: Universum Film A.G. (Ufa)
Length ....99 minutes; b/w

Principal Cast

Emil Jannings (Professor Imannuel Rath), Marlene Dietrich (Lola Lola), Kurt Gerron (Kiepert, the Magician), Rosa Valetti (Gusta, Kiepert's wife), Hans Albers (Mazeppa, the Strongman), Reinhold Bernt (the Clown), Rolf Müller (Pupil Angst), Karl Huszar-Puffy (Innkeeper), Wilhelm Diegelmann (Captain)

THE STORY

One day the fastidious and despotic Professor Rath, instructor of English at a German *Gymnasium* (a secondary school) in an unspecified North German port city, discovers that some of his students are spending their evenings at the Blue Angel, a rough beer hall close to the harbor, and that they have a crush on Lola Lola, the singer currently performing there. Professor Rath visits the Blue Angel, determined to command Lola to desist from turning his pupils' heads. But the pompous professor melts in her presence.

The next night the professor is back at the Blue Angel to pick up the hat he had left behind the previous night. To hide from their professor, his students rush to a cellar beneath Lola's dressing room. Watching through its trap door, they gleefully observe him as he fully succumbs to Lola Lola's charms. Then, to escape the police intending to raid the beer hall, it becomes the professor's turn to hide. He ends up in the cellar with his students, who no longer even pretend to respect him. After he chases them away, Lola comforts the angry and exhausted professor. He remembers his professorial duties only the next morning, when the clock of the town hall chimes as he is having a pleasant breakfast with her. Completely distraught at his tardiness for school, the professor rushes to his class. There, on two blackboards, he confronts caricatures of himself labeled "Unrat" ("garbage" or "filth"), as well as an unruly class of students ridiculing him.

Soon thereafter, defending his behavior and Lola Lola's honor, Professor Rath tells the school director, who has entered the classroom to restore order, that he will be marrying Lola. After the director dismisses Rath from his position, the professor visits Lola and proposes marriage, an offer which amuses her but which she accepts. At the wedding, in a state of uninhibited happiness, the professor merrily responds to Lola's antics: she cackles like a hen; he crows like a rooster

After four years of traveling around with Lola's troupe, living in cheap lodgings, selling postcards of Lola, and later even performing on stage as a clown, the professor is ordered to crow like a rooster during the troupe's impending guest appearance in the town where he had taught. Plenty of advertising preceded this commercially promising event. Consequently the entire town, including the professor's former students, appears for the performance. Forced to go on stage, despite resisting the humiliation to the bitter end, the professor suddenly sees Lola in the arms of Mazeppa, her new lover. Wildly bellowing the rooster's "Kikeriki" ("Kikeriki" is the way German expresses a rooster's crowing), the professor rushes from the stage and attempts to strangle Lola. He is at first restrained but is freed after he calms down. As if in a trance, he stumbles through the town until he reaches his old school. In his former classroom, he sits down at his desk and dies, as the clock chimes strike twelve.

BACKGROUND

Der blaue Engel (*The Blue Angel* 1930) is firmly anchored in German film history. It was Germany's first notable sound film, achieving both critical and commercial success in Germany and abroad. In addition the film created instant fame for Marlene Dietrich, whose interpretation of Lola Lola, the female protagonist, became the star's signature performance. Immediately after the film's release, Dietrich emigrated to Hollywood, beginning a successful career with the director of *The Blue Angel*, Josef von Sternberg. Efforts by Josef Goebbels, Propaganda Minister in Nazi Germany, to lure her back to Germany failed. She instead became active for the Allies, entertaining troops and contributing to the morale efforts of the United States military by promoting U. S. war bonds. These three factors — her role in *The Blue Angel*, the persona that was created in subsequent movies directed by von Sternberg, and her renunciation of Nazi Germany with subsequent willingness to support the Allies — transformed Dietrich into a recognizable star who to this day remains Germany's most internationally acclaimed filmic icon. In 1984 German actor and director Maximilian Schell interviewed Dietrich for a feature length documentary on the actress.

The *Blue Angel* illustrates the international character of the film industry. Even though a German film, financed by a German studio and cast with German actors, *The Blue Angel* has a non-German or only semi-German director, von Sternberg being an Austrian who had emigrated to the United States at the age of 17, made films during the First World War for the Army Signal Corps and was classified as an American. Moreover, his success as a director was in the Hollywood system, for which he had been directing movies since 1924. The international character of the film industry is further illustrated by the fact that an English language version of the film was made concurrently with the German language version, using the same actors, sets, and screenplay, indicating that the intended market was wider than German-speaking countries.

The Blue Angel is based on Heinrich Mann's novel *Professor Unrath* (1905) which takes place early in the twentieth century and is a critique of middle-class society. The film's screenplay rewrites the ending of the novel, in which the professor gets his revenge on the townspeople, substituting a tragic end for the professor. Though he also changed the time frame of the story to 1925-29, the heyday of the Weimar Republic, Sternberg did not include any material specific to the period. While *The Blue Angel* does feature two separate worlds in opposition to each other, none of the particular upheavals of the period, as they appear in Fritz Lang's *Metropolis* (1927) or Georg Wilhelm Pabst's *Die Freudlose Gasse* (*Joyless Street* 1925) enter into the film. References to the stock market crash of October 1929 are also absent, but as the screenplay and some production would have taken place before this historical event, its absence is understandable. Indeed an emphasis on the political economic situation might have detracted from the professor's personal tragedy, for as von Sternberg has structured the story, the socio-economic situation improves as the personal economic and psychological situation of the professor worsens. Weimar reality is thus reflected not through historical allusions but through the ever increasing sophistication of the surroundings in which the cabaret troupe performs, indirectly mirroring the improving economic situation between 1925 and 1929.

EVALUATION

Ufa (Universum-Film A.G.), the studio that produced *The Blue Angel*, brought Hollywood director Josef von Sternberg to Germany to create a prestige sound film worthy of the Ufa name. Ufa films, at least with critics (at the time and still today), were noted for their artistry, which was displayed in the technical, narrative, and stylistic quality of the studio's silent films. *Das Cabinet von Dr. Caligari* (*The Cabinet of Dr. Caligari*, Robert Wiene 1919) adapted the expressionism of theater and art to create an outer world that reflected the psychological terror of the movie's story and physical angst of a defeated Germany. *Der letzte Mann* (*The Last Laugh*, F. W. Murnau 1925) introduced fluidity of storytelling that could narrate without intertitles. *Metropolis* (Fritz Lang 1926) dazzled with special effects, monumental sets, and choreographed crowds. In *The Blue Angel* von Sternberg continues the Ufa tradition of making entertaining and artistic films. He introduces sound to serve the film's story rather than have the story conform to the needs of sound, the case with many early sound films. He continues Ufa's tradition of telling a story through multi-layered, symbolic visuals, and he presents characters that are archetypal at the same time they are individuated.

The opening few scenes introduce all of the above mentioned elements: multi-layered visuals, naturalistic sounds, expressionist symbols, and individuated archetypes. In the series of short establishing shots, viewers see a group of houses with gabled rooftops packed together and filmed at an angle, several threateningly extending into others. It is not easy to tell where one house ends and another begins. Some houses slant in one direction, their roofs in another. Others extend far upward, leaving only small patches of the spacious sky visible. The shot creates uncertainty, claustrophobia, and tension. Viewers suspect they are in the world of German expressionism and its attendant, often unspecified terrors.

The following shot belies the first impression. A morning delivery of live geese is taking place, probably at a town market. As they are individually unloaded, the geese fill the air with their healthy, uninhibited cackling. Now viewers might wonder if the film is taking place in an idyllic small town still filled with natural sounds. Following the geese come scenes of a poster of the seductive Lola, scantily dressed, and a doorplate on which the name Professor Rath appears.

Though the first two shots show areas outdoors, the film contains very few segments taking place outside. The only three times the professor is filmed in the open, these outside environments also represent his inner state and prescribe for the viewers moods of uncertainty, tension, and foreboding, much as the initial establishing shot does. The first two times, the professor is on the way to the Blue Angel, a very unfamiliar territory for him. The film alternates scenes of Lola in the cabaret with shots of the professor on his way there. As Lola sings a song including lines about jabbing a man in his sides and stepping on his feet, words clearly signaling that she may be a harmful lover, the film crosscuts to the professor, mainly his back in view, firmly walking forward on a perilous, foggy night. In classic expressionist filmic style, low, threateningly slanting houses with jagged edges and protrusions flank the street. The beer drinking song "Es war einmal ein treu' Huszar" (There was once a loyal soldier), a tune whose words express a cavalry soldier's undying love for a woman, accompanies the professor part of the way toward Lola Lola's territory. The song is one of several melodies heard in the background during the film. These melodies foreground the new technology as they sound from nearby taverns, intone through open windows, or blare through

Joseph von Sternberg was known for a mise-en scène composed of multiple planes placed in front of the camera. Here Lola Lola (Marlene Dietrich) and Professor Rath (Emil Jannings) sit at a table, the space between them and the camera filled by Lola's makeup mirrors and other clutter. The light above them provides yet another plane and behind them are a dressing screen, curtains, and an open door, providing yet more filled space in the scene.

opened doors. At the same time they further comment on the narrative. Here the melody serves to induce viewer premonition that a fate similar to the soldier's is to befall the professor. The visual scene emphasizes that the woman the professor passes is a prostitute, which disorients the professor, causing him to confusedly turn around in a circle before proceeding on his way. After a crosscut to the Blue Angel, the professor is seen continuing his walk. The closer he comes to Lola, the more dangerous the walk appears. The fog becomes worse, the street lights cast more shadows, the houses seem to slant more, and the professor seems to stagger and lunge toward his goal as a fog horn sounds in the distance, reinforcing viewer awareness of the perils that await the professor. The professor repeats the trip to the Blue Angel on the following night, walking this time with more confidence.

Professor Rath's walk is reprised at the end of the film, when he walks the route in reverse from the Blue Angel to the school. Utterly degraded, he leaves the Blue Angel – both the establishment and the woman – to embark on the return path, the path to his old school. This time viewers see a frontal view of the professor instead of the back view that dominated when he had gone toward the Blue Angel. As the professor tumbles from one street post to another, from one house facade to the next, he casts threatening shadows on the buildings. The foghorn, one of the few clear signs that the film takes place in a port city, punctures the outdoor silence as it had on the professor's first two walks, but now more loudly and more threateningly. Not present before, the patches of ice and snow on the streets also spell greater dangers. When expressionistic visuals (e.g., darkness, searchlight, shadows) dominate in the school building as well, viewers are prepared for the tragic death that occurs in the classroom.

The stark differences between the professor's world and Lola's are accentuated visually throughout the film, as well as by the frequent cross cutting between the two worlds. Expressionist shadow techniques, for example, occur only in scenes with the professor and the domains associated with him. Thus the professor's walks up or down a staircase produce fearsome shadows on the walls. His students also cast terrifying shadows, particularly in the segment when viewers see the grotesquely distorted, magnified shadows of two students on the wall behind the bed of Angst, the professor's favorite student, before they see the students themselves. It is a shot reminiscent of the shadows cast by the monsters in two of the German silent era's best known films, The *Cabinet of Dr. Caligari* and *Nosferatu*, suggesting danger. The fear of danger is justified, for the students do attack Angst, just as the fearful shadows connected with the professor also correctly predict a negative outcome.

The mise en scène of the professor's world and that of Lola contrast sharply. The professor's housekeeper makes his bed flawlessly and immediately notices everything that is out of place in his apartment. The professor's classroom is austere. There is nothing on the walls and very little even in his desk drawers. Barrenness characterizes his world. When the professor is shown either in his apartment or in the classroom, he seems to fill most of the frame. There is very little to distract viewers from looking at him. The opposite holds true for Lola's environment. Barely any space remains unused in her dressing room: clothes of the greatest imaginable variety hang everywhere on the walls; all sorts of make-up paraphernalia are on her large table; there is a large, three-partitioned mirror and a partition behind which Lola can change clothes or students can hide; there are several small mirrors on Lola's table, hats all over the room, glasses and bottles, fishermen's nets, curtains of many sorts, plants, vases, posters—including one of Lola. The prominent circular staircase in the middle of the dressing room takes up valuable space, but it is merely a larger object in the midst of all the others. Despite the disorder, Lola always immediately finds what she is looking for. She seems to reign over the multitude of things; she is certainly not swallowed by them. Above all, when she is in the room, she still commands all the attention.

In contrast to the professor's solid, yet rigid bourgeois world of orderliness, loyalty, and duty, Lola represents a variety of worlds. Engaged in entertainment, in show business, Lola masterfully fabricates a world of make believe from the abundant costumes and the multitude of disparate objects cluttering up her dressing room. During most of her appearances in her dressing room, she is either putting on new makeup or changing attire, not in the least concealing the artificiality of her constructions. Others are welcome to observe her in the processes of self-invention that add to her glamour rather than unmask it.

Lola does not hide her wigs. Occasionally, stiff, cardboard-type materials simulate her skirts. At other times she adorns herself almost exclusively with frills and feathers. Her curious skirts are cut off in the front or in the back, apparently custom-made to expose her thighs. She is an expert at inventing an abundance of sexually provoking poses. In a sense, due to her inventive self-creations, Lola deserves the artist title that Professor Rath accords her at their first encounter. She, more so than the establishment, embodies the idealized color blue of the German Romanticists—that is, *she* is the Blue Angel.

On the one hand, Lola's constant self-reinventions indicate artificiality, on the other they suggest creative participation in the flux of life. The bird happily chirping in her bedroom also implies that her world is brimming with life. Yet, despite her varied, magical outward appearances, Lola has retained her down-to-earth self. After one of her songs, she sits down on stage, flanked by several fat women who make her seem thinner, to take a chug of beer from a beer mug.

Her no-nonsense Berlin humor readily deflates any pomposity uttered in her presence. When one of the students says "I luv you" to her (surely not the kind of English he learned from Professor Rath), Lola tells him to quit producing such silly English sentences. She quickly reformulates the professor's stiff, stylized marriage proposal—that he wants to ask for her hand—into the equivalent of the English "you wanna marry *me*?"

Lola, the femme fatale who remarks that eventually all men return to her and who likens her power over men with the light that entices and then destroys moths, also has a nurturing, motherly side. In the breakfast scene, for instance, she turns into a warm and kind variant of the professor's housekeeper. In contrast to the housekeeper, Lola does not merely place sugar on the table but puts sugar cubes into the professor's mouth, very solicitous about how many he wants.

She helps him into his coat as the housekeeper had done but insists that he stop wiggling so that she can put a flower in his lapel, a flower to help him think of her. Like the housekeeper, Lola remains on top of the stairwell as the professor departs. Again motherly, Lola tells him to watch out for traffic on his way to school.

Lola is alternately kind and heartless toward the professor once he becomes a member of her troupe. Though she certainly could have severed their relationship when his money ran out, Lola does not abandon the professor, not even when he stops shaving and looks more and more unkempt. While Lola chastises the professor when he denounces their audience as a bunch of uneducated people, reminding him that they after all owe their livelihood to these people, she also defends the professor, telling the director to stop molesting him with excessive demands. Still, knowing that he is totally subjugated to her, she fully exerts her control over him once the troupe returns to the Blue Angel. Filmed at low angle in a medium frontal shot on her circular staircase, her hands on her hips, she haughtily looks down at the professor standing at the foot of the stairs, demanding that he go on stage.

Besides showcasing sound through Lola's singing, Sternberg uses sounds masterfully in this first notable German sound film. He contrasts the professor's stilted language with Lola's down-to-earth language, much as he contrasts the professor's stilted behavior with Lola's uninhibited movements. He relegates the professor to many stretches of silence, but Lola is rarely at a loss for words. Often utter quiet commensurate with the barrenness of his life envelops the professor, whereas lively noise surrounds Lola. The one time the professor opens a window (when he asks the students to write a composition in the classroom), the well known song "Ännchen von Tharau" (aka "Der Palmbaum") is heard in the background, an indication of the professor's subconscious longing for the everlasting love expressed by the song. While songs and sayings associated with the professor have been well known to several generations of Germans, Lola's songs were specifically crafted for her and thus truly appropriated as her own. To the public, she embodies the messages of her songs. When a door in Lola's dressing room opens, a frequent occurrence, music almost always enters the room, usually unpredictable, covering a wide range from German beer hall songs to Mideastern bazaar tunes.

As the movie ends, juxtaposition of the film's two major musical motifs reveals the gulf between the professor's world and Lola's. On the stage, Lola, dressed in slacks, straddles a chair in a dominant masculine position as she sings what became Dietrich's signature song, "Von Kopf bis Fuß auf Liebe eingestellt" ("Programmed for love from head to toe"). The song whose English title and opening lyrics, "Falling in Love Again," soften the erotic message, represents love in all its forms, romantic, illusionary, idealistic, inclusive, unavoidable, destructive. Both versions of the song stress Lola's amoral nature in matters of love. Whether we see her infidelity as the realist's "programmed for love from head to toe" or the romantic's "falling in love again, what else can I do," Lola herself has no choice. Her view of love, though, clashes with that of the Professor, whose attitude in such matters is represented by the simple melody of a German folk song whose words are:

Üb immer Treu und Redlichkeit	Be ever faithful, ever honest
Bis an dein kühles Grab,	Until you reach your cold grave,
Und weiche keinen Finger breit	And do not stray a hair's breadth
Von Gottes Wegen ab.	From God's paths.

The melody of the folk song also supplies the first notes of Papageno's aria from Mozart's *The Magic Flute*: "Ein Mädchen oder Weibchen wünscht Papageno sich" ("Papageno longs for a maid or wife"). The closing moments of the film juxtapose the amoral sentiment of a femme fatale that can't help it if men are drawn to her like moths to a flame and the longing of a lonely man who believes in romantic virtues looking for love. (MS)

QUESTIONS

1. It is clearly von Sternberg's intent to foreground the new sound technology in his film. Yet he also wants it to serve his narrative rather than have sound merely for its own sake. Locate those instances in the film when sound is most obvious (besides dialogue) and explain how it serves to point to itself (the use of the new technology) and how it serves the story.

2. Identify as many songs as you can in the film and explain how they advance or comment on the narrative.

3. The only "angel" anywhere in the film is a cupid on the stage of the cabaret. Yet the title has more significance than this angel from which the cabaret gets its name. Discuss the meaning of the title. Be sure to refer to the many instances of winged figures in the film.

4. Professor Rath, Lola, and the Magician are archetypal figures from melodramatic films: lonely man, femme fatale, and catalyst for tragedy. Yet each also has highly individuate characteristics. Discuss the characters as archetypes and as individuals.

5. Discuss the role of the clown as *doppelgänger* in the narrative. Locate and describe the scenes in which he appears.

RELATED FILMS

The Blue Angel (Edward Dmytryk, 1959). This is a fairly faithful remake of the Dietrich/Jannings classic.

Lola (Rainer Werner Fassbinder 1981). Fassbinder's remake changes the professor into a bureaucrat (head of the office for building permits) and the singer into a prostitute in a topless bar. The film is set in the fifties, the time of Germany's *Wirtschaftswunder* (economic miracle).

Marlene (Maximilian Schell 1984). The film offers an extended interview with Dietrich who is filmed so that we cannot see her face.

Emil Jannings was a major star at the time of *The Blue Angel*, known for his roles as a tragic everyman. It was thought no one suffered as well on screen as Jannings. The following films are some of his best known:

Der letzte Mann (*The Last Laugh*, Friedrich Wilhelm Murnau 1924). The original ending was considered too downbeat for audiences, especially American viewers, and so a coda was added changing a tragedy into a comedy.

Varieté (Ewald André Dupont 1925). Jannings plays a suffering lover. The film's story was changed slightly for American audiences, considered too prudish to accept a story about infidelity.

The Last Command (Joseph von Sternberg 1928). Jannings received the first Best Actor Academy Award for his role.

American films with Marlene Dietrich directed by Joseph von Sternberg. Any of the following films will give an idea of how Sternberg and Dietrich capitalized on the persona they established for her in *The Blue Angel*.

> *Morroco* (1930)
> *Dishonored* (1931)
> *Shanghai Express* (1932)
> *Blonde Venus* (1932)
> *The Scarlet Empress* (1934)
> *The Devil is a Woman* (1935)

INFORMATION

The Blue Angel (1930), DVD, in German w/subtitles plus the English language version, b/w, 99 minutes, Kino Video, released 2001.

Bandmann, Christa and Joe Hembus. *Klassiker des deutschen Tonfilms*. Munich: Goldmann, 1980.

Kracauer, Siegfried. *From Caligari to Hitler: A Psychological History of the German Film*. Princeton, NJ: Princeton UP, 1947.

McCormick, Richard W. *Gender and Sexuality in Weimar Modernity: Film, Literature, and "New Objectivity."* New York: Palgrave, 2001.

Ott, Frederick W. *The Great German Films*. Secaucus, NJ: Citadel Press, 1986.

Prawer, S. S. *The Blue Angel (Der Blaue Engel)*. London: British Film Institute, 2002.

Riess, Curt. *Das gab's nur einmal: Die große Zeit des deutschen Films*. Vol. 2. Frankfurt am/M: Ullstein Sachbuch, 1977.

Vogt, Guntram. *Die Stadt im Kino. Deutsche Spielfilme 1900-2000*. Marburg: Schüren, 2001.

CHAPTER 5

M

(Fritz Lang 1931)

Elsie Beckmann (Inge Landgut) encounters the child killer Hans Beckert(Peter Lorre) in front of his wanted poster. The viewer sees only Beckert's shadow, but hears his raspy voice "Du hast aber einen schönen Ball!" (My, but you have a nice ball!).

CREDITS

Director ....Fritz Lang
Screenplay ....Thea von Harbou
Director of Photography ....Fritz Arno Wagner
Music.. From *Peer Gynt* by Edvard Grieg
Producer ....Seymour Nebenzahl
Production Company ....Nero-Film
Length.. varies from 99 to 117 minutes; b/w

Principal Cast

Mrs. Beckmann (Ellen Widmann), Elsie Beckmann (Inge Landgut), Hans Beckert (Peter Lorre), The blind beggar (Georg John), Inspector Lohmann (Otto Wernicke), Schränker (Gustaf Gründgens), Chief of Police (Ernst Stahl-Nachbaur).

THE STORY

M (1931) is divided into three distinct sections. In the first, Lang shows the killer, the victim, and the urban landscape in which the crimes occur. As the movie opens children gather. The first shot introduces the theme with children gathering in a circle to sing the song of the notorious 1920s Hanover mass murderer Haarmann: "Warte, warte nur ein Weilchen, bald kommt auch zu dir, Haarmann mit dem Hackebeilchen, und macht Hackefleisch aus dir" ("Wait, wait only a little while, then he will come for you too, Haarmann with his little hatchet, and he will make mincemeat out of you"). What the children find amusing and playful is scorned by the laundry woman who walks away from the children into the apartment building (the camera follows and moves upward with her) where she delivers laundry to Frau Beckmann. In a quick succession of shots the Beckmann apartment is established, the poverty and cleanliness, and Frau Beckmann's preparation for lunch with her daughter. The movie then cuts to children leaving a school, among them a little girl who walks towards a wanted poster with the camera following, while a figure enters from the right in front of the poster — the killer, casting his shadow onto the poster. We then hear his voice, "Du hast aber einen schönen Ball" ("You have a very nice ball"), followed by a question about the girl's name, which she answers with a cheerful "Elsie Beckmann", Frau Beckmann's daughter. This shot establishes the first of several memorable images in the movie, many still in the expressionist tradition of fusing shadow and light.

This disturbing scene is followed by a series of shots where the murderer establishes his relationship with the girl. He buys her a balloon and she thanks him by curtsying. The murderer whistles a tune, which has been identified as a melody from Edward Grieg's *Peer Gynt*, a tune he will later use over and over, a leitmotif that will become instrumental in his capture.

Back in the apartment building, Mrs. Beckmann is realizing that her daughter Elsie is late. The connection between Mrs. Beckmann and her daughter is established first with a shot of Mrs. Beckmann checking the cuckoo clock, followed by a shot which shows the children leaving school. Mrs. Beckmann's nervousness is expressed in a rapid succession of still shots, the cuckoo clock, the stairs, the empty lunch plate, the empty attic room with Mrs. Beckmann's voice shouting out Elsie's name with increasing anxiety. The sequence of shots finishes with a ball, Elsie's ball, rolling out from the underbrush, and finally, the awkward manlike balloon figure the murderer had bought for Elsie now dangling from telegraph wires. This rapid sequence of opening shots in M is one of the most memorable beginnings of a film since it shows Lang at the height of his craft. The viewer realizes that the movie relies heavily on symbolism, which will engage on a visual and on an intellectual level.

The director's discreet rendering of the murder of Elsie Beckmann engages the viewer to imagine what is not shown—as Lang wrote, "forcing each individual member of the audience to create the gruesome details of the murder according to his personal imagination." This first sequence of the movie ends with a gradual fadeout.

The second sequence continues with the murderer, Beckert, at a desk writing a note to a newspaper in which he incriminates himself, a confession that changes the rapid pace of a police drama to a cat and mouse game with the viewer as a knowing observer. Most of the action of this second sequence of the movie is made up of the activities of the two groups whose interests are most threatened by Beckert's activities: the police, who must satisfy an hysterical populace, and the criminal underground, whose economic interests are jeopardized by increased police scrutiny because of the killings. The hysteria plays in a tavern, around the *Stammtisch* (the regulars' table), where the patrons accuse each other of being the murderer. This macabre scene is reminiscent of a satirical drawing of the Weimar artist George Grosz.

The police activities are shown almost in documentary style with a voice-over narration by the police inspector explaining the various police search activities to his superior, which include raids on underground bars and clubs such as the Crocodile Club. These bar scenes give Lang the opportunity to use expressionist shots of dark arches and shadowy figures. The underworld activities are dominated by Schränker (Gustav Gründgens) who meticulously plans the shadowing and capture of Becker with the help of all organized criminals in Berlin. These scenes are similar to Brecht's *Die Dreigroschenoper* (*The Three Penny Opera*), a musical about petty criminals, which had just been released in Germany as a movie directed by G. W. Pabst. As Brecht and Pabst do in the play and film, Lang underscores the similarities between the police and the underworld.

As in his other crime films, Lang presents the police and the criminals as indistinguishable, intercutting between parallel scenes of each, strategizing on how to "kill the monster." Some of the police station footage has a documentary feel, as then-new technologies like fingerprint analysis are methodically examined. In spite of the superior technology of the police, it is the criminals who capture Beckert.

In the third and final segment of the film, the criminals capture Beckert and try him in a mock or kangaroo court. Here Peter Lorre as Beckert creates a cinematic psychopath that he made famous in many subsequent films, with his pudgy frame, his bulging eyes, and his panicked grimaces. His breakdown speech before the mob demanding his death gives a powerful look into the mind of a madman: "Kann ich denn anders? Dieses verfluchte Ding in mir, das Feuer, der Strom, die Qual. Immer muss ich, ich höre es doch, als ob ich selber hinter mir her liefe. Ich muss rennen, ich will weg, die Gespenster rennen, sind immer da, nur nicht wenn ich es tue. Dann weiß ich nichts mehr. Ich will nicht, ich muss!" ("I can't help myself! Always ... always! I haven't any control over this evil thing that's inside me—the fire, the voices, the torment! It's there all the time driving me out to wander through the streets. Following me. Silently, but I can feel it there...").

The movie ends with the police arriving just in time to remove Beckert to a regular trial.

BACKGROUND

The story of *M* is based on that of the infamous serial killer Peter Kürten, the vampire of Düsseldorf, who drank the blood of some of his victims. Kürten brutally attacked 41 people, nine of whom died; he was finally arrested on May 24, 1930. Before his final arrest over 12,000 leads were followed, over 200 people surrendered themselves claiming to be the killer, and 300 psychics and occultists offered their help. The two letters Kürten sent to local newspapers sparked a flood of copy-cats and the public was in the state of mass-psychosis. Kürten was the perfect example of a serial killer with the exterior of an average citizen. Surviving victims and witnesses described him as well dressed, friendly, trustworthy and respectable. Kürten was executed July 2, 1931 in Cologne.

M turned out to be Fritz Lang's first and most powerful sound film. Born in 1890 in Vienna, Lang was one of Germany's greatest film directors. He celebrated his first successes during the Weimar Republic, leaving Germany in 1933 and immigrating via France to the United States in 1934, where he continued to tie political aspects into his work. His best known films from his work in Germany include *Die Nibelungen* (1924), *Metropolis* (1927), and *Das Testament des Dr. Mabuse* (*The Testament of Dr. Mabuse* 1933).

M is considered one of the first movies with elements of "film noir" whose roots go back to German Expressionism. Many components of noir are present: a dark cityscape and an unstable environment in which children play in the street, singing chants about bogeymen and murderers. Other elements of noir present are the paranoid pathology of the twisted Beckert, who courts and kills his young victims for reasons he can't express, and a frenzied mob that brings its own brand of justice against him. Many of the following classic noirs films of the 1940s and later follow *M*'s attention to the details of the manhunt. Most important, though, is the sense of doom that colors the film, a fatalism Lang renders through lighting effects and high-angle shots that suggest a malevolent spiritual presence hovering above the city and guiding its denizens to their doom.

M made Peter Lorre famous: The Austrian theater actor, with bulging eyes, round face, and nasal voice with a thick Austro-German accent, became familiar to millions of moviegoers. The Nazis used Lorre's portrayal of Beckert as a Jewish prototype in their propaganda film *Der ewige Jude* (*The Eternal Jew*, Fritz Hippler 1940). For Americans Lorre became the classical bad guy in a film career that spanned 33 years and ranged from classics like the two great American film noir works, *The Maltese Falcon* (1941) and *Casablanca* (1942), or Disney's *20,000 Leagues Under the Sea* (1954) to the respectable if bizarre *Mr. Moto* series (1937-1939), in which Lorre played a Japanese detective modeled after the Chinese film detective Charlie Chan. Lorre returned to Germany after the Second World War to direct and act in his last film, *Der Verlorene* (*The Lost One* 1951), in which he once more plays a serial killer.

EVALUATION

Film historians accord *M* a high place in German film history calling it many things: "frightfully good," "the predecessor to all serial killer thrillers like *Psycho* and *The Silence of the Lambs*," and "one of the defining movies of European pre-WWII cinema." Remastered releases of the film indicate that its powerful and original images still startle and frighten and that the film has aged well, still seeming fresh. *M* demonstrates not only an excellent command of camera, lighting and editing, but also examines human sexuality, sin and redemption. As a film historian writes: "It is the chain-linking of images that gives such force to the masterful scenes."

This film has been called Fritz Lang's ultimate vision of urban space where the film structure portrays space through allegorical images. Lang shows that the city of the 1920s had become a space of danger and warfare. In early twentieth century metropolises the police were losing their grip on the city where the

Hans Beckert sees the M placed on his back by a blind man helping the underworld capture the child murderer. Duality plays an important role in the imagery and themes of the movie.

underworld was slowly taking over, not just in Weimar Germany, but in other crime-ridden urban areas as well: Chicago, New York, London. Lang's parallel cutting juxtaposes the two competing worlds, the emerging social group of imaginative criminals with the modern police department.

As the film shows, Fritz Lang's art is the art of arranging objects, similar to the literary style developed during the Weimar Republic, *Neue Sachlichkeit* (New Objectivity). Objects in these texts show more than the surface reality they represent. Objects in these texts are merely signs, or to use the linguistic term, signifiers, that represent reality.

This symbolism can be demonstrated through the film's central images, Beckert's reflection in shopping windows. They are external images of Beckert's tormented soul with the shopping window as mirror to his confused madness. The image of Beckert in a reflection of knives laid out in a diamond shape inside the store is a good image of this externalization. The reflection of the chalk marking of "M" in another scene represents the central image of Beckert's realization of being a murderer. In this shot, Beckert stares straight into the camera for the first time and he tries to run away as he seems to realize that his anonymity has been revealed. Once marked with the "M," Beckert has lost his magical invisibility that he possessed in the first part of the movie.

This *doppelgänger* motif with a split personality plays a central role during the chase with underground figures appearing everywhere to surprise Beckert. After the chase, Beckert is caught almost simultaneously by the police (they discovered his room where he wrote the incriminating letter to the newspaper) and by the underworld organization, who found his last hideout in an office building and captured him just before the police arrived. This race between police and underworld to find Beckert first creates the film's tension, which continues into the final sequence of the movie.

M, Lang's first sound film, weaves together powerful visual and auditory elements. One of the most striking uses of sound in the film is the repeated, obsessive whistling of "the Hall of the Mountain King," from the Peer Gynt suite by Edvard

Grieg (1843-1907). This orchestral suite was an orchestral adaptation of the poetic drama of the same name by the Norwegian Henrik Ibsen. Lang used Grieg's well-known tune as a "leitmotif," or a musical sign that identifies a character or theme. This spooky melody is used to increase the suspense, because viewers know the murderer is near when they hear his whistling. Lang deliberately used a blind beggar to identify Beckert as the murderer – perhaps a play on Tiresias, the seer priest in Greek mythology –in order to demonstrate the power of sound. *M* is really a movie that lives through its sound and its absence of sound. In that sense the beggar is an essential icon of this movie. "I am a musical moron who can't carry a tune but I decided to dub the whistling myself," Lang said in an interview. "It was off key and turned out to be just right since the murderer himself is off balance mentally."

After Beckert's discovery the movie is concerned only with the explorations of Beckert's inner motives for killing, which culminates with Lorre's chilling monologue at the end. With its open end, *M* becomes both a critique on, and an example of Lang's fascination with crime, as in *Das Cabinet des Dr. Caligari* (*The Cabinet of Dr. Caligari*, Robert Wiene 1920) and other famous German films of the time. Siegfried Kracauer presented his thesis in his book *From Caligari to Hitler: A Psychological History of the German Film* that *M* is a reflection of the time in which it was made, and that the film is an expression of the inevitable development of fascism in German society, a reading that would limit a valid interpretation to just the late Weimar context in which it was produced. The universal appeal the movie has to this day indicates that Kracauer's theory is too limiting.

M, as a cinematic text of New Objectivity, is a superb representation of the tormented social and political landscape of Germany at the end of the Weimar Republic. But its universal appeal lies in the fact that the viewer wonders what is going on inside a killer. Through Lang's symbols, images and reflections we have been privy to his inner world—we have become his psychiatrist and we ponder the question, as does the movie, of what justice should be spoken. (RZ)

QUESTIONS

1. Considering that this is Lang's first non-silent film, discuss the use of sound in *M* and its importance.

2. Name some movies or books that may have been influenced by *M*.

3. Explain how Lang sets the tone of the film in the opening scene involving the disappearance of Elsie Beckmann.

4. The conclusion of *M* is open-ended. Why do you think Lang chose to end the film this way? What is your interpretation of the ending?

5. How does the film *M* reflect the political situation in Germany during this time?

RELATED FILMS

Der Verlorene (*The Lost One* 1951). Lorre plays a serial killer in Nazi Germany in this film which he directed.

Testament des Dr. Mabuse (*Testament of Dr. Mabuse* 1933). Many of Lang's films deal with the criminal mind. In this one, he focuses on a killer in a mental hospital.

M (Joseph Losey 1951) This remake of Lang's 1931 film did not do well with critics. At times it is a scene for scene remake, at other times Losey adds details to distinguish it from the original.

INFORMATION

M (1931), DVD, in German w/subtitles, b/w, 117 minutes, Criterion Collection, released 1998.

Aurich, Rolf, Wolfgang Jacobsen and Cornelius Schnauber, eds. *Fritz Lang: His Life and Work, Photographs and Documents*. Berlin: Jovis, 2001. (Text is in German, French and English)

Bandmann, Christa and Joe Hembus. *Klassiker des deutschen Tonfilms*. Munich: Goldmann, 1980.

Gemünden, Gerd. "From 'Mr. M' to 'Mr. Murder': Peter Lorre and the Actor in Exile." In *Light Motives: German Popular Cinema in Perspective*, edited by Randall Halle and Margaret McCarthy, 85-107. Detroit: Wayne State UP, 2003.

Kracauer, Siegfried. *From Caligari to Hitler: A Psychological History of the German Film*. Princeton, NJ: Princeton UP, 1947.

McGilligan, Patrick. *Fritz Lang: The Nature of the Beast*. New York: St. Martin's Press, 1997.

Muth, Jon J.: *M*. Forestville, CA: Eclipse Books, 1991. (Comic based on the story of the film).

Ott, Frederick W. *The Great German Films*. Secaucus, NJ: Citadel Press, 1986.

Riess, Curt. *Das gab's nur einmal: Die große Zeit des deutschen Films*. Vol. 2. Frankfurt am/M: Ullstein Sachbuch, 1977.

CHAPTER 6

Kuhle Wampe oder wem gehört die Welt

(*Kuhle Wampe or Who Owns the World?*, **Slatan Dudow 1932**)

Crowds of students and workers attend a festival of sports organized by a communist youth organization. The platform in the middle will serve as a stage for an agitprop play by the performers on the left. The play's text summarizes the film's basic theme, that the workers must learn to assert themselves.

CREDITS

Director ....Slatan Dudow
Screenplay ....Bertolt Brecht, Ernst Ottwald
Director of Photography .... Günther Krampf
Music.. Hanns Eisler
Production Companies......................................Praesens-Film AG, Prometheus Film
Length...71 minutes (original release 85 minutes); b/w

Principal Cast

Hertha Thiele (Anni Bönike), Ernst Busch (Ballad Singer, voice), Helene Weigel (Ballad Singer, voice), Max Sablotzki (Vater Bönike), Lili Schönborn (Mutter Bönike), Martha Wolter (Gerda, a friend), Adolf Fischer (Kurt, Anni's friend), Gerhard Bienert (man with beard on street car), das rote Sprachrohr (agitprop troupe playing itself).

THE STORY

Kuhle Wampe oder wem gehört die Welt? (*Kuhle Wampe or Who Owns the World?*, 1932 [alternate American title, *Whither Germany?*]) tells three interrelated stories, with each being introduced by the following captions: One Unemployed Less; The Best Years of a Young Person's Life; and To Whom Does the World Belong? The first episode follows Franz, a young man, who rides through the city on his bicycle in search of work. Unsuccessful in his quest, he returns home only to have his parents berate him as lazy. Even though his sister defends him, Franz falls victim to depression and commits suicide. The second story focuses on Anni, the young man's sister, after she and her parents are evicted from their small flat for nonpayment of rent. Following the sister through the city from one bureaucratic office to the other in search of financial or legal help, the camera captures the futility of getting official Germany to listen to the problems of the workers. Eventually the family moves in with the young woman's boyfriend, who lives in Kuhle Wampe, a tent city on the outskirts of Berlin established by and for the working classes. Anni becomes pregnant but rejects her boyfriend's offer of marriage because she believes that Fritz, the boyfriend, has only consented to marry her because of pressure from his friend and Anni's father. She subsequently moves out of the family's tent home to be with other friends. The third episode shows Anni and Fritz reunited, but the third part of the film is less their story than a celebration of young people, using their participation in a sporting event as a metaphor for the vitality of the new generation that will change the world.

BACKGROUND

Kuhle Wampe documents from a working class perspective the misery and economic crisis that led eventually to Hindenburg's dissolution of the Weimar Republic and the takeover of Germany by the National Socialists. The Weimar Republic, established in 1919, has been interpreted as Germany's first experiment with democracy after the 1848/49 Frankfurt Paulskirche parliament. Weimar also continued parliamentary traditions of the second empire, but now, as a republic, the president had taken over the power of the emperor. From its inception, the Weimar government was plagued by political factions on the right and left fighting for control of the people's allegiance. Indeed, part of the impetus behind establishment of the Republic was to counter the private armies on the right and the Soviet style governments being proclaimed by the left. Founders of the Republic such as its first president Friedrich Ebert hoped that a stable, rational form of government could bring order to chaos.

From the beginning, the moderates or centrists took control of most institutions. Leaders such as Ebert (1871-1925), who served as the country's President from 1919-1925, and later Gustav Stresemann (1878-1929), who served briefly as Chancellor in 1923 and as Foreign Minister from 1924-1929, constructed a careful balance between right and left in order to keep the peace. But the division between the two leftist parties, the Communists and the Socialists, grew as the Socialists, now the Social Democrats, opposed the more radical ideas of the Communists and instead joined the Centrist parties. The Socialists' willingness to work with the Centrists helped make the Republic a reality, thus enabling its continued existence. The gulf between Socialists and Communists, which had manifested itself earlier in the Second Empire under Kaiser William II, continued throughout the Republic's brief history. After 1929 when the world economic crisis of that year turned into the deep recession of the early 1930s, the concessions that were needed to hold the government together favored or yielded to the conservatives. As such compromises were often carried out by coalitions involving the Social Democrats, they exacerbated the division that existed between the Communists and the Socialists. Thus the two leading parties on the left continued to compete for control of the working and lower middle classes rather than join forces to defeat the rightist parties, in particular the Nazis, their natural enemies.

Kuhle Wampe cannot be fully understood without an understanding of the political tensions outlined above. The film reflects the real animosity the Communists or KPD had toward the Social Democrats or SPD. In the early days of the Weimar government, the KPD focused on winning adherents from the Socialists, a party they thought was too eager to compromise to gain and hold power. That position won them supporters as long as Germany's postwar crisis continued, which culminated in the hyperinflation of 1923. Once Germany's economic prospects brightened, however, beginning about 1926, the KPD lost adherents to parties that fully supported democratic institutions. Then in 1929 and the years that followed, as the country sank deeper and deeper into economic ruin, the Communists, rather than ally themselves with the SPD, instead saw them as Germany's true enemy. Even though the National Socialists or NSPD were gaining in power and were soon to surpass the voting strength of the Communists, the KPD continued to rail against the policies of the SPD, which they saw as too closely allied with capitalism. Ironically, the Communists, whose non-democratic position reflected the non-democratic character of the NSPD, contributed to the Nazis' eventual takeover of the government. Both parties, Nazis and Communists, wanted to abolish the Weimar constitution, the "system," or "Systemzeit," as it was called by its foes.

Both Slaton Dudow, the director, and Bertolt Brecht, the screen writer, were dedicated Communists. Their combined efforts produced a work that still stands as one of the best examples of Communist propaganda. Dudow brought to the film his sensitivities as the son of a working class father. In one of his first films, *Wie der Berliner Arbeiter wohnt* (How the working class in Berlin lives), using hidden cameras, he filmed a Berlin family being evicted from their apartment for nonpayment of rent. He incorporated the idea as the focus of the three stories of *Kuhle Wampe*. Brecht contributed his experience as a director of plays that combined entertainment with leftist politics. In particular he adapted his style of agitprop theater, in which a central character experiences a series of learning situations that are meant to teach an economic or political lesson from a Communist perspective.

EVALUATION

Kuhle Wampe: To Whom Does the World Belong? functions as a cinematic agitprop play. These leftist plays of agitation and propaganda (agitprop) were especially popular during the Weimar Republic. Performed by lay and professional actors at workers' gatherings, their intent was to raise the political consciousness of the working class. To this end, *Kuhle Wampe* exposes what the Communists saw as the capitalist control of their own lives. It also offers a perspective on how workers can get control of their lives. Following the structure of agitprop skits (one of which is included in the film), the movie is divided into parts or acts. Act one introduces the thesis of social injustice among the classes, showing how political unawareness produces inappropriate responses from the working class to the problems of inequality and exploitation. Act two reveals that political awareness itself will not lead to a satisfactory resolution of the basic problem, that entrenched institutions work against and not for the people. In the final act, the film proposes that the strength of working class solidarity will change the world. By the end of the film viewers will have experienced the despair of helplessness (characterized by the many workers we see unsuccessfully chasing too few or no jobs in 1932 Germany), the inadequacy of working within the system (presented as families unsuccessfully turning to the social welfare systems of Weimar Germany), and the euphoria of awakened class-consciousness (visualized by youth marching side by side to a triumphant tune whose lyrics proclaim worker solidarity). Dudow and Brecht achieve their effect of awakened consciousness through a dialectical method of point and counterpoint in their film style: Music underscores and contradicts images, but musical styles also clash; visuals support and also contradict their content through lighting, angles, and motion. Characters argue, agree, contradict, and support each other.

Slaton Dudow emulates the style of the Russian film masters Sergei Eisenstein and Vsevolod Pudovkin, whose editing techniques defined Soviet filmmaking in the twenties. As Eisenstein and Pudovkin, Dudow employs montage sequences to create a masterpiece of Communist propaganda: a tale of working class misery that exposes the cruel injustices of capitalism. In a lengthy opening sequence, a series of newspaper headlines highlight Germany's increasing unemployment. The final headline reports on the number of unemployed in Berlin. The headlines are followed by a sequence showing bike riders arriving in a newspaper delivery area, job lists being distributed, and bike riders leaving and racing to the possibility of work. Dudow presents this sequence in a frenetic series of cuts of the group, of individuals, bikes, bike wheels, and of their rejection at factory gates. Viewers see the frustration in the bike riders' faces.

A montage sequence of children and babies in the second half of the film highlights the social and economic problems of women and their children in a capitalist society. Anni, who has just discovered that she is pregnant, walks with her boyfriend Fritz. They pass children, which leads Anni to hallucinate, and the ensuing scene presents her vision as a waking nightmare. Anni imagines the faces in closeup, as they appear to her at an ever more rapid pace until finally they are appearing so quickly that each dissolves into the next. The shots of children are followed by shots of babies which are intercut with birth certificates, small caskets, a hearse, and dolls before ending the sequence with a return to Anni and Fritz walking. In this brief sequence Dudow not only presents Anni's personal dilemma of having an unplanned child but also exposes the political reality of children born into the working class. The short sequence anticipates arguments formulated thirty years later in the feminist discourse of the sixties that the personal is political.

Anni is the only character in the movie developed beyond stereotype. The other characters of *Kuhle Wampe* are for the most part stock figures from two related traditions in socialist entertainment. On the one hand, as suits the melodramatic nature of their predicament, they are from socialist oriented films. The strength of Anni, the daughter in *Kuhle Wampe*, is reminiscent of the daughter Erna's strength in Piel Jutzi's *Mother Krausen's Trip to Happiness*, a Weimar Republic film in which other characters, also as in *Kuhle Wampe*, seem lost in self-pity. The nagging mother and drunken and bullying father of Dudow's film also have their origins in the tenement films of the twenties, in which generational conflicts infuse the melodramatic plots. On the other hand, as already mentioned, the characters originate in the agitprop tradition of the period and as such are stereotypes. They represent workers who over the course of a play are meant to learn a Marxist economic lesson, that those in power exploit them. They are meant to draw conclusions from the economic lessons the play gives them, and they are created to show the audience, presumably composed of workers living in similar conditions, how to change matters.

Anni is the catalyst who will teach the workers. The first episode reveals her as sensitive and politically more astute than her parents. She understands why her brother cannot find work, why he is morose. The second episode broadens her character, showing her as a dutiful daughter, trying to prevent the eviction of herself and her parents from their flat. The second episode also shows she is in need of male companionship and love, and naïve to the consequences of her affair. Her pregnancy allows Anni to show her independent spirit, as she refuses to marry just because of the pregnancy.

Anni's development satisfies the criteria of agitprop. Unlike her brother and parents, whose awareness of politics and economics is completely lacking, Anni reveals the potential for understanding the class struggle from the beginning. She is the character who develops awareness, representing the agitprop figure who learns the economic, moral lesson posed in the title of the film, "To whom does the World belong?" Although the question is answered by her friend Gerda, a stereotypically dedicated Communist, it is clear that Anni understands the answer: the world belongs to the young, but only if they are politically aware.

Seldom has music played as important a political role in film as it does in *Kuhle Wampe*. The background score, composed by Hanns Eisler, augments the dialectical interplay of the visuals, the characters, and themes. Eisler, who often collaborated with Brecht and like Brecht and Dudow was a Marxist, composed music for German, French, and American films. His discordant, jazz-influenced scores, based on Schönberg's twelve-tone music, avoid the harmonious, romantic clichés of music that often accompany stories about the social injustices endured by the working classes and the unemployed. In place of heart-rending strings or low register laments, he offers a sprightly and energized jazz score, consisting of brass, piano, and percussion. The result is a score that invites interest and understanding for the characters in the film without eliciting false sympathy. At the same time it imbues the characters with political energy and lends their situations dynamic tension. Eisler's score thus dovetails perfectly with Brecht's theories of alienation and Dudow's visualization of them. Dudow's direction and Eisler's music realize Brecht's desire to create a film which empowers the working class, and as a text of propaganda hopes to empower its viewers. The textual message of *Kuhle Wampe* is that in spite of their troubles and their position at the bottom of the economic ladder, the working class characters are in control of their destiny, or more accurately, the workers will be in control once they learn they are in control of their destiny. Even the young man who commits suicide at the end of the first part of the film has enough resolve to remove his watch and leave it behind for his family, as his fall from a fifth story window would surely have destroyed the timepiece and reduced its economic value to his family.

Eisler's discordant jazz score begins over the credits, preparing viewers for a narrative that is never visually comfortable or familiar, just as the music we hear is not comfortable or familiar. As riders bike through the city looking for work, the hectic, chaotic nature of the music reflects their haste as it suggests the futility of their ever finding rest from their search. At the end of the day, the camera follows a young man returning home, as the music first stops and then changes into a more upbeat piano and theremin-like electronic melody. The musical background in the second part of the film comments in similar fashion on the futility of a search for housing assistance at the same time that it makes the audience aware of the search. A quiet, slightly discordant phrase, which moves down the register, corresponds to the futility of Anni's quest, contrasting with the increasing tempo of the phrase, suggesting the intolerability of the outcome of the quest.

At times Eisler's music accompanies Bertolt Brecht's lyrics, creating a counterpoint of speech, lyrics, and music and offering ironic comment on the visual text. Thus in the second third of the film, Anni and her boyfriend Fritz walk into the woods as the visuals show swaying tree tops, flowing water, moving clouds, and waving stalks of grass. The lyrics over the visuals tell of spring's awakening, when people in love act on their feelings. The music, though, is as discordant and chaotic as at the beginning. Moreover, the voice, true to the style of Brechtian dramas, is rough and unsettling. The demystifying power of Eisler and Brecht's collaboration strips young love of its sentimentality and false romanticism, lending it instead a mode of sensuality. Voice, lyrics, and music prepare viewers for Anni's preganacy and her eventual breakup with her boyfriend.

The music changes in the third act of the film. Here a martial hymn to youthful solidarity plays throughout, increasing in intensity as the film draws to a close and leaving viewers with a feeling of optimism. As the film closes, Dudow presents a montage sequence that contrasts the stale political outlook of the older generation, whether apolitical, social democrat, liberal, or conservative with the vibrancy and political awareness of youth. A group of young people who have enjoyed the day at a Communist-sponsored sports festival board a tram and interact with a number of the older passengers. Through a series of cuts, Dudow introduces the major criticism of capitalism and the way it privileges markets and profits over people and common sense. As older passengers argue about the reasons Brazil coffee dealers raise the price of coffee, the camera intercuts close-ups of the smug and arrogant faces of the supporters of the political system of the Weimar Republic. Eventually the cuts focus on older women, where the economic conversation has devolved to the proper way to make coffee. After another few edits that further the discussion, someone asks, who will change the world? The next edits cut to older faces as Fritz remarks that neither of the older people will. Eventually the film cuts to Anni whose answer "those who don't like the way things are" underscores the film's intent, that the world will be changed by the young. Finally, the hymn and visuals of the young marching forward answers the question proposed in the title: "To whom does the world belong?" The film suggests that it clearly belongs to those who march together and don't abandon working class ethos. Given that the Naizs came to power shortly after release of the film and banned the Communists from government, the film seems appropriately prophetic. (RCR)

Questions

1. Note the music and lyrics of the song that accompanies the lovers' walk in the woods and relate them to the visuals. How do they comment on what we see and do not see?

2. How does the film characterize Anni and Kurt's parents?

3. Describe the Mata Hari sequence in detail, paying particular attention to Mr. Bönike's reading of the newspaper article, and Mrs. Bönike's activities. How many shots are there in this sequence?

4. What does the Mata Hari scene suggest or imply in terms of the montage theories of Sergei Eisenstein? Stated simply, Eisenstein's theory of montage held that if you put shot A together with shot B you can produce an abstract idea in the mind of the viewer, a sort of unseen shot C. Applying this to the Mata Hari sequence, how does Dudow's juxtaposition of shots support a Communist interpretation of the family's problems?

5. Discuss the sports rally as a metaphor of the Communist youth movement.

6. What are the political-economic arguments being advanced on the streetcar in the discussion of coffee?

Related Films

Battleship Potemkin (Sergei Eisenstein, Russian 1925) Eisenstein's film about a marine mutiny set the standard for political propaganda for directors on both the left and right.

Westfront 1918 (G.W. Pabst 1930). A pacifist film banned as soon as the Nazis came to power in 1933.

Kameradschaft (*Comradeship*, G.W. Pabst 1931). Set on the border between France and Germany immediately after the First World War, the film makes a plea for friendship between the two former enemies.

Dreigroschenoper (*Three Penny Opera*, G.W.Pabst 1931). Pabst's controversial version of Bertolt Brecht's popular stage musical. Brecht unsuccessfully sued Pabst for changes the director made that the playwright felt altered the meaning of his text.

Hitlerjunge Quex (*Hitler Youth Quex*, Hans Steinhoff 1933). This movie of propaganda on the right was inspired by a German marching song and the death of a young Nazi. In spite of its heavy propagandistic message in support of the Nazis, Joseph Goebbels, the Nazi Minister of Propaganda, criticized the film for its lack of subtlety.

Information

Kuhle Wampe (1932), VHS (PAL format, requires converter), in German w/ subtitles, b/w, 71 minutes, released 1999.

Film und Realität in der Weimarer Republik : mit Analysen d. Filme "Kuhle Wampe" u. "Mutter Krausens Fahrt ins Glück." Edited by Helmut Korte. Frankfurt am Main: Fischer-Taschenbuch-Verlag, 1980.

Kracauer, Siegfried. *From Caligari to Hitler: A Psychological History of German Film*. Princeton NJ: Princeton UP, 1947.

Kuhle Wampe oder wem gehört die Welt? : Filmprotokoll u. Materialien / Edited by Wolfgang Gersch and Werner Hecht. Leipzig: Reclam, 1971

Murray, Bruce: *Film and the German Left in the Weimar Republic: From Caligari to Kuhle Wampe*. Austin: U of Texas P, 1990.

Taylor, Richard. *Film Propaganda: Soviet Russia and Nazi Germany*. New York: I. B. Tauris, 1998.

CHAPTER 7

Triumph des Willens

(*Triumph of the Will*, **Leni Riefenstahl 1935**)

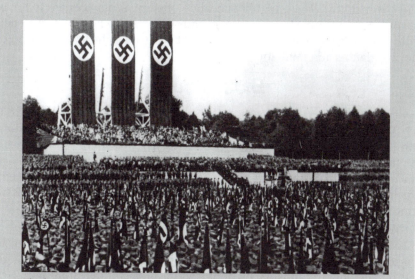

The banners that dominate many of the mass rally scenes in Triumph of the Will *have been effectively parodied in later movies, most notably at the end of* Star Wars *and near the end of* Jewel of the Nile.

CREDITS

Director .... Leni Riefenstahl
Screenplay ....Leni Riefenstahl, Walter Ruttmann
Directors of Photography............. Sepp Allgeier, Karl Attenberger, Werner Bohne, Walter Frentz; Willy Zielke
Editor .... Leni Riefenstahl
Music... Herbert Windt
Producer .... Leni Riefenstahl
Production Companies.......... Leni Riefenstahl-Produktion, NSDAP-Reichsleitung
Length...114 minutes; b/w

Appearing in the documentary are: Adolf Hitler, Joseph Goebbels, Rudolf Hess, Hermann Göring, Alfred Rosenberg, and other dignitaries of the Nazi Party.

THE STORY

Triumph des Willens (*Triumph of the Will* 1935) documents the party rally of the National Socialists (Nazis) held in Nuremberg in 1934. The film opens with a preamble of titles mourning Germany's defeat in 1918 and following through to Hitler's rise to power in 1933. The titles promise vindication for what the Nazis saw as Germany's humiliation in the First World War at the hands of the Allies and, in the eyes of the Nazis, also as a result of pacifist actions by socialists and Jews. The opening credits are followed by Hitler's arrival in Nuremberg, shown from his plane as it flies through scattered clouds before landing to a tumultuous welcome. Hitler's arrival is followed by a lengthy segment on participants in the rally, showing them washing up, having breakfast, and engaging in physical games of various sorts. The levity gives way to a choral introduction to the German workers' corps that climaxes with an emotional ode to the soldiers who fell in the First World War. These highly evocative opening sequences are followed by scenes of marching, mustering of troops, and speeches. In the center of all activity is Hitler as orator, commander, and leader. At other times he is the focused object of adoring glances and laudatory words.

BACKGROUND

Triumph of the Will has its roots in a film Riefenstahl made a year earlier on the 1933 Party Congress, *Der Sieg des Glaubens* (*The Victory of Faith*, 1933). Running 61 minutes, that film is an hour shorter than *Triumph of the Will* and possesses none of the later film's powerful editing and evocative imagery. Indeed Riefenstahl distances herself from the final result by suggesting the film was rushed into production at the last minute and that she had only three cameramen to assist her, limiting the amount of footage from which to edit the film.

According to Riefenstahl, Adolf Hitler asked her to direct *Triumph of the Will* as a way to make amends for the obstacles Joseph Goebbels, Minister of Propaganda, threw in her way during production of *Victory of Faith*. Although she at first refused, hoping to work on another film project, the feature film *Tiefland*, she finally consented to make the film after Hitler met her conditions, foremost of which was to have complete control of the project. There is little to no evidence that Riefenstahl's version of the genesis of her film is accurate, but she uses the story as evidence that the film was not made under the supervision of the Nazi Party and is therefore not propaganda for Germany. She claims she would have made the same movie, only with different characters, if Stalin and the Communist Party had commissioned the film for the Soviet Union.

Controversy has accompanied Leni Riefenstahl since the release of *Triumph of the Will*. Considered by many film historians to be one of the best propaganda films ever made, the documentary nonetheless prevented Riefenstahl from having a film career after the end of the Third Reich. Many have argued that the film documents a rally staged for the aggrandizement of Hitler and the Nazi party and hence is itself not a true documentary, but a construction of an ideology. The facts are, however, that the rally took place and would have taken place whether Riefenstahl had made her movie or not. But it is also true that by focusing on certain aspects of the rally and by inserting staged speeches by Nazi leaders, the film goes beyond documenting the event and instead helps to structure, if not create, the event.

Even during the Third Reich, before the Second World War had started, Riefenstahl found her reputation in the United States tarnished. On a tour to promote her film of the 1936 Olympics, critics in the press referred to her as Hitler's girlfriend. After the war, while other German directors were resurrecting their careers in spite of having made films for the Nazis, Riefenstahl was defending herself against charges of being an unreconstructed Nazi. Although critics also sometimes cited her film of the 1936 Olympics as proof of her Nazi ideology, for the most part, the evidence of her Nazi sympathies came from her participation on *Triumph of the Will*. Amidst all the criticism, Riefenstahl refused to acknowledge the moral issues inherent in having made a film for the Nazis. In spite of the film's obvious and aggressive championing of the Nazi cause, she never wavered on her insistence that she was not a Nazi and that the film was not made to promote Nazi ideology. Riefenstahl died on September 9, 2003 at the age of 101.

Riefenstahl maintained that her primary intent in making *Triumph of the Will* was to show Germany as a land of peace and employment under Hitler and the National Socialists. To this end she devotes a number of visually striking sequences to Germany's labor corps, its youth, and its cheering populace. Furthermore, she includes numerous speeches with abundant references to Germany's desire for peace. Finally, she edits the scenes in a fashion that produces a feeling of forward movement, of a land progressing under the leadership of its Führer, Adolf Hitler. Thus quiet scenes are followed by busy scenes, night scenes by day scenes. Shots that might otherwise be static are given movement through editing. The processions of peasants, soldiers, and motor vehicles seem endless.

Riefenstahl's critics maintain that she intended the film as a propaganda piece for Hitler and the Nazis. That is, the film's main purpose was to sell Hitler and the Nazis to the German people and also to the rest of the world. Moreover, the film was meant to show the people and the world Germany's military presence. Thus, they point out, she alternates scenes of speeches about peace with scenes of marching troops; scenes of workers reciting in chorus to a memorial for the soldiers who fell in the First World War. She also includes a scene of the laying of a wreath at the tomb of an unknown soldier, a military presentation of tanks and other war machinery, and a workers' corps as disciplined as any army.

The nature and degree of propaganda that Riefenstahl included in her film becomes clear when the film is placed in its historical political context. Hitler became Chancellor of Germany in January 1933 with the Nazis in control of only one third of the Reichstag (parliament). Moreover, in spite of harassment of the Communists and other political opponents, the Nazis won only 43.9% of the vote in the March 1933 elections. To achieve the power he wanted, Hitler introduced an enabling bill that would in effect make him dictator. But after silencing much of the opposition, in order to get the three fourths majority needed for passage, Hitler still had to offer the Catholic Centre Party a quid pro quo, protection for the CCP in exchange for its support. Even the burning of the Reichstag on February 27, 1933, which although shrouded in mystery was most likely set by a Communist sympathizer, did not give the Nazi Party the total allegiance it sought. Despite these facts, Riefenstahl's goal in *Triumph of the Will* was to present Hitler and the Nazi Party to the world, but particularly to Germans, as the legitimate heirs to Germany's past and the beneficent leaders necessary for a peaceful and prosperous future. At the same time the film was also to show Nazi leaders, in particularly Hitler, as all powerful.

EVALUATION

Triumph of the Will is more than a film introducing Hitler and the Nazis to the Germans and the international community, and extolling that Nazi leadership will lead to peace and prosperity. If we study the film's visual and aural text, it becomes clear that the film lends Hitler and the Nazi Party legitimacy, it connects Germany present to Germany past, and it offers the Nazis a place in world history. First, given that the Nazis came to power with a plurality rather than majority of voter support, the leadership's task was to continue the momentum after the takeover of the government and persuade the German public that the National Socialists were the country's legitimate leaders. Second, after the Nazis came to power, the left and right wings of the party struggled to control the political agenda. Members on the right, among them Hermann Goering and Heinrich Himmler, worried that the growth of the Sturmabteilung or SA, the private Army of the National Socialists under Ernst Röhm's leadership, posed a threat to their leadership. With Hitler's sanction, Röhm and hundreds of his men in the SA were arrested and eventually executed on fabricated charges of treason. In one of his speeches in the film Hitler obliquely acknowledges the political infighting in general and this event in particular, known as the "night of the long knives." Finally, the arrest and placement in camps of the Communist opposition made clear that the Nazis were not yet in complete control of the people's minds. Riefenstahl's film speaks to these concerns for the Nazis by putting a positive spin, to use the cynical language of today's politics, on the Party's problems.

The film opens with a written prologue that establishes Nazi Germany as the rightful heir to the Germany of the Second Empire under Kaiser Wilhelm. In Gothic script, the prologue places the time of the film twenty years after the start of the First World War and sixteen years after the beginning of Germany's suffering, a reference to the end of the war and the founding of the Weimar Republic. Nazis attributed the Allies' victory over Germany to the country's betrayal at the hands of the socialists, Communists, and Jews. The idea that the country was humiliated by the terms of the Versailles Treaty, and that Germans suffered because of it, became a refrain in Nazi speeches and writings. Hitler had advanced the so-called "stab in the back" (*Dolchstoß*) theory in his autobiography *Mein Kampf* (*My Struggle*), written while he was in prison for treason for his involvement in the unsuccessful Beer Hall Putsch of 1923. For Hitler and his adherents, the Weimar government, which in their eyes was controlled by Jewish leftists, was a constant reminder of the "stab in the back." The credits close with a reference that Hitler is opening the congress nineteen months after Germany's "rebirth," which here is equated with the coming to power of the National Socialists. The opening conflates prewar Germany and post-1933 Germany, as it marginalizes Weimar Germany and discredits the democratically elected government. Riefenstahl appeals to Nazi sentiment that Germans are victims of the Communists. The prologue's religious tone resembles that of a passion play, identifying Germans as Christian martyrs. The theme of martyrdom is reinforced a few scenes later in which a workers' chorus invokes the memory of fallen comrades. Even the format of the text, Gothic script designed to resemble woodcuts, relates the Third Reich to Germany's rich history, as the woodcut letters pay homage to Nuremberg, the site of the meeting and the home of Albrecht Dürer, a sixteenth century artist famous for his woodcuts. The prologue was actually written by Walter Ruttmann, the intended director of the film who, after he had backed out, was replaced by Riefenstahl at Hitler's insistence.

Two sequences stand out above all others in the film that valorize the film's underlying text of celebrating Hitler and the Nazis as the legitimate heirs to Germany's historical past, perhaps even to the role of the Third Reich as the reincarnation of the Holy Roman Empire of German Nations. After the prologue, the film cuts to the inside of an airplane showing its descent from the perspective of its chief occupant, Adolf Hitler. We watch as the plane descends through clouds, seeing even the shadow of the plane on the ground as it glides to its landing. Noted film historian Siegfried Kracauer interpreted the sequence as showing Hitler as Germany's savior coming to free the people (Kracauer, 291). One need not resort to religious exaggeration, though, to read the importance of historical allusion for the scene. For the scene that directly follows the plane's landing shows Hitler disembarking to a throng of cheering crowds, as if he were a Roman emperor returning after battle.

The second sequence shows a chorus of workers, in military-like formation, as they introduce their regions, their duties, and also recite an ode to Germany's fallen heroes. The workers' chorus proclaims that comrades who fell in the First World War are not forgotten but live on in Germany. The swastikas on the flags have been hidden to this point. Their appearance as the word "Germany" is shouted relates Germany to the Nazis and Hitler.

What makes the scene remarkable is the Eisenstein-like juxtaposition of two images to create an ideological image in the viewer's mind. The manner in which the film has been edited – Riefenstahl alternates contrasting images and scenes – makes the whole greater than its parts. The scenes alternate group shots with close-up shots of individual faces with shots of feet and shovels. Spliced into these are shots of Hitler or the Nazi flag whenever the text mentions Germany. In this way individual workers become one mass force, their Heimat or region becomes one united Germany, and Germany becomes the Nazi flag, but also and most importantly, Germany becomes Hitler.

Similar to the visual text, Herbert Windt's musical score for *Triumph of the Will* establishes Nazi Germany's ties to the past, particularly the Germany of nineteenth century romanticism. In the opening sequence, for example, Windt alludes to Germany's past greatness with lush orchestration reminiscent of Richard Wagner. The Wagnerian melodies give way to the Nazi anthem, "Die Fahne hoch." In a subsequent scene, as the visuals show Nuremberg's cathedrals at dawn, the orchestra plays a melody from Wagner's *Meistersinger von Nürnberg*. Windt continues to intemix the grandeur of Wagner with other musical forms, including martial music for the many parade scenes, the German national anthem for extremely patriotic moments, and the military song "Ich hatt' einen Kamaraden" ("I had a good friend") for more sentimental moments. Except for the Nazi anthem, the music, whether it is Wagner-like, actual Wagner, folk music, or martial music, references pre-1918 Germany — romantic Germany.

In spite of the controversy surrounding the director and her film, and perhaps because of the controversy, *Triumph of the Will* has a major place in German film history. Its influence can be seen even in Hollywood film productions. Among the more obvious references to the film are the final scene of George Lucas's *Star Wars* (1977), the scene of the Arab leader's speech in Lewis Teague's *Jewel of the Nile* (1985), and the visual aesthetics of Paul Verhoeven's *Starship Troopers* (1997). Perhaps the most outrageous reference comes near the end of Jim Sharman's *The Rocky Horror Picture Show* (1975), in which the character Magenta tells Frankenfurter that Rocky, his creation who is a blond, blue-eyed Aryan, is a "triumph of your will." (RCR)

QUESTIONS

1. Give a shot-by-shot breakdown of the sequence in which the members of the workers' chorus first introduce themselves to the point where they lower and then raise flags in honor of Germany's war dead. Be sure to describe both what the shots show and also how they are filmed. Include the audio track in your analysis.

2. Locate the scenes with Hitler. How does Riefenstahl present him?

3. Many people find this film tedious. Why do you think this is the case, and do you agree?

RELATED FILMS

Der Sieg des Glaubens (*Victory of Faith*, Riefenstahl 1933). The film is Riefenstahl's documentary of an earlier Nuremberg rally.

Olympia (Riefenstahl 1938). The documentation of the 1936 Olympic Games held in Berlin. The film is considered by some to be Riefenstahl's best film and also the best film ever made of a sporting event.

Jud Süß (Veit Harlan 1940). Discussed elsewhere in the book, *Jud Süß* comprises one half of a pair of anti-Semitic films made in 1940, the other being the pseudo-documentary *The Eternal Jew*.

Der ewige Jude (*The Eternal Jew*, Fritz Hippler 1940). Soldiers and students were required to attend showings of *The Eternal Jew*, one of the most vicious anti-Semitic films ever made.

Deutschland erwache (*Germany Awake*, Erwin Leiser 1968). Using film clips, Leiser introduces viewers to the major themes of Nazi cinema.

Die Macht der Bilder: Leni Riefenstahl (*The Wonderful, Horrible Life of Leni Riefenstahl*, Ray Müeller 2000). The director interviews Riefenstahl at length and allows her to comment on her films and editing techniques.

INFORMATION

Triumph of the Will (1935) DVD (special edition with commentary), b/w, in German with English subtitles, Synapse Video, released 2001.

Berg-Pan Renata. *Leni Riefenstahl*. Boston: Twayne Publishers, 1980.

Hinton, David B. *The Films of Leni Riefenstahl*. Metuchen, NJ: Scarecrow Press, 1978.

Hull, David Stewart. *Film in the Third Reich: A study of the German Cinema 1933-1945*. Berkeley and Los Angeles: U of California P, 1969.

Infield, Glenn B. *Leni Riefenstahl: The Fallen Film Goddess*. New York: Thomas Y. Crowell, 1976.

Knopp, Daniel: *NS-Filmpropaganda: Wunschbild und Feindbild in Leni Riefenstahls "Triumph des Willens" und Veit Harlans "Jud Süss"*.—Marburg : Tectum-Verlag, 2004.

Kracauer, Siegfried. *From Caligari to Hitler: A Psychological Study of the German Film*. Princeton, NJ: Princeton UP, 1947.

"Leni Riefenstahl – Regisseurin, Schauspielerin" in *CineGraph: Lexikon zum deutschsprachigen Film*, edited by Hans-Michael Bock, Munich.

Loiperdinger, Martin: *Triumph des Willens: Einstellungsprotokoll*. Frankfurt/M.: Institut. für Historische-Sozialwissenschaftliche Analysen e.V. (IHSA), 1980.

Mueller, Ray (director). *Die Macht der Bilder Leni Riefenstahls*. New York: Kino Video, 1993.

Sontag, Susan. "Fascinating Fascism." *The New York Times Review of Books*, 6 February 1975, 23-25.

Schwartzman, Roy J. "Racial Theory and Propaganda in *Triumph of the Will*." In *Authority and Transgression in Literature and Film*, edited by Bonnie Braendlin and Hans Braendlin, 136-51, Gainesville, FL: UP of Florida, 1996.

CHAPTER 8

Jud Süß

(*Jew Süss*, Veit Harlan 1940)

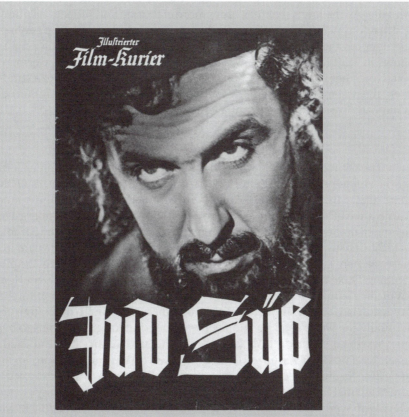

The poster for the infamous film starring Ferdinand Marian as Jud Süß. Marian was a matinee idol, which arguably contributed to the popularity of the film.

CREDITS

Director .... Veit Harlan
Screenplay .... Veit Harlan, Eberhard Wolfgang Möller, Ludwig Metzger
Director of Photography .... Bruno Mondi
Music .... Wolfgang Zeller
Production Company .... Terra Filmkunst
Length .... 98 minutes; b/w

Principal Cast

Ferdinand Marian (Jud Süß), Heinrich George (Duke Karl Alexander), Hilde von Stolz (Duchess), Werner Krauß (Rabbi Loew, Levy), Eugen Klöpfer (Sturm), Kristina Söderbaum (Dorothea Sturm), Malte Jäger (Faber), Albert Florath (Obrist Röder), Theodor Loos (von Remchingen), Walter Werner (Fiebelkorn), Charlotte Schulz (Mrs. Fiebelkorn), Anny Seitz (Minchen Fiebelkorn), Ilse Buhl (Friederike Fiebelkorn) Jacob Tiedtke (Konsistorialrat), Else Elster (Mistress of Süß); Emil Heß (Hans Bogner), Käte Jöken-König (Mrs. Bogner); Ursula Deinert (Primaballerina).

THE STORY

Jud Süß is set in 1733, the year Süß Oppenheimer, an ambitious Jewish businessman, becomes treasurer to the Duke of Württemberg by showering him with gifts. As the Jew's schemes grow more elaborate and his actions more brazen, the dukedom nearly erupts into civil war. Persuaded by Süss Oppenheimer, the Duke ignores the constitution and alienates the assembly by lifting the local ban on Jews in Stuttgart. In a display of his power, Süß rapes a young German woman and tortures her father and her fiancé. When the Duke succumbs to a sudden heart attack, the assembly of Elders tries Oppenheimer and sentences him to death for having had "carnal knowledge of a Christian woman."

BACKGROUND

The character Jud Süß is based on Joseph Süß Oppenheimer, a German Jew born in Heidelberg in 1692, and one of the most famous members of the wide-spread Oppenheimer family. After being trained by his Viennese uncle, Süß became a wealthy banker in Frankfurt, and in 1732, the Württemberg Duke Carl Alexander made him his Court and War Financier, a position comparable to that of a state treasurer. Like Süß, Carl Alexander had spent his early years in Vienna, where he had learned to admire the splendor of the Hapsburg Empire. After becoming Duke of Württemberg, Carl Alexander wanted to make Stuttgart into a provincial Vienna, but the Protestant Württemberg gentry, suspicious of the Duke's conversion to Catholicism, refused any such changes through their advisory board. Eventually the Duke used the money from Süß's banking operations to bypass the gentry's refusal. After Carl Alexander's death, Süß was arrested and tried for Carl Alexander's political ventures of aspiring to turn Württemberg into an absolutist state. An accusation of "cohabitation with Christian women" was dropped from the charges against him to protect the names and reputations of twenty six women of society who were recorded as having had sexual relations with Süß. He was found guilty of conspiring to change the constitution and received the death-sentence on December 13, 1737. On February 4, 1738, Süß was hanged in Stuttgart.

The movie is not simply "a visual expression of National Socialist ideology," as the comments on the video case suggest, but rather represents an escalation in the propaganda war against the Jews. During the thirties, Germany gradually increased the denial of rights to its Jewish population, culminating in passing the Nuremberg Laws, which stripped them of citizenship. Such animosity toward the Jews led to the 1938 pogrom known as the "Night of Broken Glass," an action orchestrated by if not officially sanctioned by the Nazi government. By 1940 the Nazis moved to the second phase in the propaganda war against the Jews. Several movies were made to suggest the notion of the Jews' inability to live among civilized people. The most virulent of these was the pseudo-documentary *The Eternal Jew*, which used newsreel footage, reenactments, and clips from German and American feature films to construct a theory that Jews wanted to dominate the world. Perhaps even more powerful was *Jew Süss* which as a fictional film had a more visceral effect on viewers' emotions. In order to achieve this end, the movie mixes several aesthetic and political programs; it interweaves elements of the historical chronicle with elements of a love story, which together create a binary world: on one side there are Germans, family values, love, sacrifice, and good; on the other Jews, anti-family values, sex, selfishness and evil. The film portrays Süß's execution as a revolutionary act; an historical and historic event that began cleansing Germany of its Jewish population. The film thus prepares viewers to accept or overlook the on-going disappearance of the Jews into concentration camps as finishing a process that their Württemberg forefathers had begun with Süß's hanging on the Stuttgart market-square. The movie wants viewers to conclude that by killing the Jew, the country was ridding itself of people intent on harming Germany.

The relationship between Süß and Dorothea is modeled after well-known German classical plays, e.g. the Gretchen-tragedy in Goethe's *Faust*-drama, Friedrich Schiller's *Kabale und Liebe*, and in particular Lessing's *Emilia Galotti*. Süß takes on characteristics of Lessing's villain, Marinelli, the prince's executive officer. Lessing's drama, an 18th century bourgeois tragedy, contrasts the code of virtues of the bourgeoisie or middle class with the egotism of the aristocracy. The conflict between the two codes of conduct leads to the play's tragedy. By modeling Süß after Lessing's courtier Marinelli, Harlan is able to copy the relationship between Marinelli and the Prince in his film, showing how Carl Alexander is misguided by the Jew. The most striking similarities between Lessing and Harlan can be found in the figures of Harlan's Dorothea and Lessing's Emilia. In Lessing's play, Emilia, influenced by her mother, is attracted by the life at the absolutist court; Harlan transfers what the play sees as a character flaw to his female lead, Dorothea.

A new interest in the Süß case was created during the Weimar Republic when Jews became free from the restrictions of the ghettos. As they moved into the centers of power, the public attitude towards Jews generally changed to acceptance. In the story of the Jew Süß Oppenheimer trying to gain access to political life in Württemberg many saw parallels to the political scene in the Weimar Republic, and thus the Jewish novelist Lion Feuchtwanger chose it as the basis of a 1924 novel. In *Jud Süß* he shows parallels between the Süß figure and a modern emancipated Jew like the Weimar politician Walther Rathenau. Both Süß and Rathenau acted as enlightened and emancipated men in societies that were not ready for change: 18th century Württemberg towards absolutism, Germany of the 1920s towards democracy.

In Süß, Feuchtwanger showed a modern, enlightened Jew ready to leave ghetto restrictions in order to assimilate into modern society, the way 20th century Jews were ready to forget their Jewish heritage and assimilate into German culture. Feuchtwanger carefully avoids glorifying or romanticizing Süß's Jewishness. Rather he portrays a common human being with weaknesses and strengths. Feuchtwanger's book is intended to warn Jews about the pitfalls of public life, which Feuchtwanger saw as a brutal arena, where Jews could lose out. Feuchtwanger preferred to see Jewish intellectuals stay out of the political arena altogether and limit their influence to that of educated philosophers who contemplate rather than act. In this way, Jews would not compromise their attained emancipated position in the Weimar Republic. Feuchtwanger suggests that they should very cautiously proceed into public positions, once the status quo had been accepted by everybody.

From this account it is apparent that the Nazis changed Feuchtwanger's pro-Semitic book into an anti-Semitic narrative. In 1934, Lothar Mendes had made a more understanding film of Feuchtwanger's story, in keeping with the author's positive portrayal of Jews.

EVALUATION

Jud Süss is the ultimate propaganda film whose purpose was to stir up anti-Jewish hatred. Its effectiveness as propaganda comes from its value as entertainment, as a way to deliver its message under the cover of German culture. As a propaganda film, *Jud Süß* represents an authentic document of how Nazi irrationalism and hatreds subverted traditional German values to realize Hitler's and the Nazi's own perverted agenda. The film makes modern viewers intensely aware of the deformation techniques the Nazis employed. It heightens their analytical perception regardless of their background and increases their awareness of how political propaganda may be used in contemporary commercial films.

The movie was conceived and produced at a time, 1940, when the last preparations to kill millions of Jews in concentration camps were being made. Produced with money from Goebbels' propaganda-office, it served together with similar, less-known films like *Die Rothschilds* (*The Rothschilds*, Erich Waschneck 1940) to prepare the German population for the coming "final solution," as the Nazis phrased it. Veit Harlan's (the movie's scriptwriter and director) claim that he knew nothing about the Nazis' propaganda plans seems hardly believable. Harlan was one of the best-known film directors in Nazi Germany, and like so many other artists of that time, after the war he attributed his actions to naiveté, political unawareness, and personal fear. However, Harlan's complicity in the making of the film is easily detected if we compare the original sources with the eventual movie. He altered the reason for Süß's condemnation from the political conspiracy portrayed in the novel to the personal crime of raping a young German woman portrayed in the film, equating the rape to a crime against the Nuremberg race laws. Harlan's journeys to the occupied Polish territories offer further evidence that he actively supported Goebbels' propaganda machine. In Poland he studied Ghetto Jews and selected more than one hundred for his movie, telling the participating Jews that they were acting in a documentary about Jewish customs, not in an anti-Semitic feature film. In a war crimes trial in 1949, Harlan was acquitted of all charges on the grounds that he was coerced, a reason advanced by most war criminals in West Germany.

The film is a notorious representation of anti-Semitism, attempting to rewrite German history as a continuous battle against Jewish domination, as a battle of good against evil. The difference between "Aryans and Jews" is seen as an eternal antagonism in creation and therefore becomes the movie's structuring device. This polarity becomes a leitmotif, as in the alternating lines of the German folksong "All meine Gedanken" ("All My Thoughts") and a disharmonious Jewish Sabbath melody that repeatedly interrupts the German song. This principle of antagonistic composition continues throughout the film; it shows Süß as an ever-increasing threat that culminates in his vicious attack on Dorothea and her ultimate death. Thus the Nazi idea of the separation of the races is transformed into aesthetic categories in the movie.

Süß is the ultimate villain as played by Ferdinand Marian, an attractive actor and thirties matinee idol. Süß wants to use his position to marry into the gentry by courting Dorothea. This element adds to the intended realism of his character since he can be regarded as an example of the emerging bourgeoisie. Süß is portrayed in the film as a modern, enlightened man who serves his Duke Carl Alexander well in his attempt to lead Württemberg into the modern absolutist age. This foreign absolutist element (foreign because it was seen as French) is not only rejected by the Württembergians in the movie, but also by Süß's fellow Jews, whose traditions he violates. Rabbi Loew, a representative of Orthodox Jewry, warns Süß: "God's wrath is harsh when Jews forget who they are." Süß wants to help other Jews and defends himself against Rabbi Loew's criticism of his modern dress. Süß knows that he would "open doors" for other Jews in places like Stuttgart that had been off-limits to Jewish businessmen. This loyalty to his fellow Jews is Süß's main virtue and represents the Jewish version of the Nazis' dedication to fatherland, Führer and people. But the film makes clear that Süß's loyalty serves only the Jewish world in support of the Anti-Christ.

The character of Dorothea (played by Kristina Söderbaum, a native Swede and Veit Harlan's wife) brings the film an element of beauty, which it otherwise lacks. In many scenes Harlan draws the viewers' attention to Dorothea's body. The rape scene in particular reveals how Harlan's direction and camerawork create erotic tension in the film. Filmed in slow motion (the only part of the film that is), Dorothea's rape creates an element of sexual violence that feeds the film's major subtext, "Jews are a danger to German values." This scene reinforces the Nazis' ideology, which viewed the Jews as having an infinite sexual appetite. The Jew according to this view cannot control his emotional and physical self nor is he able to control his emotional desires for money and his greed, very much like the Prince, Emilia's corrupt suitor, in *Emilia Galotti*. As depicted in the film, Jewish morals, just as the values of the Prince in *Emilia Galotti*, are detrimental to middle class people. Dorothea embodies the virtuous, innocent and sentimental German woman. Casting Kristina Söderbaum, known to movie-goers for her melodramatic and naive female characters, added to the message of innocence defiled that the film wanted to send.

The tragic elements in Dorothea's character are reinforced in the relationship to her fiancé, played by Malte Jäger, an actor who resembled images of the German classical writer Friedrich Schiller, who for most Germans embodies nationalism. Thus, both Dorothea and Faber represent the German element in this film; they have to defend themselves against the evil represented by the Jew. Dorothea in her naiveté cannot see through the deceit of Süß's character. Faber, on the other hand, who is clearly aware of his German ethnicity and understands what it means to be German, sees intuitively that Süß is a Jew when he meets him for the first time: "But that is a Jew!" Another scene of contrast between German and Jewish values occurs when Dorothea talks with Süß about his home, and he describes the whole world as his home. This idea of cosmopolitanism impresses the naive German girl, who has never gone much beyond the city walls of Stuttgart, but it also stamps Süß as non-German, foregrounding the anti-Semitic stereotype of the Wandering Jew.

Heinrich George plays the Duke, the person responsible for Oppenheimer's rise. Harlan introduced the person of the Duke into the movie to represent a person who, like Germany, was helpless in the face of the onslaught of the Jewish threat. His guilt according to Harlan's and the Nazis' ideological representation consists in not realizing the permanent threat Jews pose to Aryans; he becomes guilty mainly because of his elaborate lifestyle for which he requires constant sexual pleasures, which Süß provides. The Duke's violent death is an intended warning against anyone who might consider cooperating with Jews. The Nazis, however, reluctant to show a bad German character, instead portray Carl Alexander as a weak and undetermined figure, a characterization achieved by the outstanding performance of the actor Heinrich George. Incidentally, the actor bore a resemblance to the Weimar President Hindenburg, reinforcing the intended political parallels.

George died in 1946 in the Sachsenhausen concentration camp under Soviet supervision where he had been taken for his role in *Jud Süss*. (RZ)

QUESTIONS

1. Describe Veit Harlan's style as director, paying attention to camerawork, editing, and mise-en-scène. Name some of the techniques that Veit Harlan uses.

2. Summarize briefly Nazi policy towards the Jews from the time they take over the German government.

3. What are Dorothea's mistakes in her relationship with Oppenheimer?

4. Develop profiles for how the Nazis saw Jews and Germans on the basis of portrayals in this film.

5. Ferdinand Marian was a matinee idol. Why cast him in such a negative role?

RELATED FILMS

Der ewige Jude (*The Eternal Jew*, Fritz Hippler 1940). Banned to this day in Germany, this virulently anti-Semitic pseudo documentary was required viewing by students and the armed forces at the time of its release. Using film clips, staged and documentary footage, and newsreels, Hippler constructs a world of Jewish intrigue intent on destroying Germany.

Ich klage an (*I Accuse*, Wolfgang Liebeneiner 1941). The film's theme of euthanasia focuses on a wealthy German woman with an incurable illness. Coming at a time, however, when Germany was engaging in euthanasia of the mentally and physically severely disabled and also preparing to murder millions of Jews, the film was intended to engage viewers in discourse on the desirability of government-sanctioned killing.

Baron Münchhausen (*The Adventures of Munchhausen*, Josef von Báky 1943). For the most part the film offers an excellent example of a purely entertaining film, lacking overtly propaganda messages. However, Ferdinand Marian's characterization of Graf Cagliostro, a magician, carries a strong anti-Semitic subtext because of the manner in which he plays the part. Moreover, viewers will hardly have forgotten his role of the Jew in Veit Harlan's *Jud Süß*.

Kolberg (Veit Harlan, 1945). Goebbels wanted his film to be a German *Gone with the Wind* (Victor Fleming 1939). Telling of a lost battle during the war with Napoleon, the major theme is that even though Germany loses a war, it will never be defeated. No sacrifice is too great for the German fatherland.

INFORMATION

Jud Süß (1940), VHS, in German w/subtitles, b/w, 90 minutes, International Historical Film.

Feuchtwanger, Lion: *Jud Süß*: Roman. Frankfurt am Main: Fischer-Taschenbuch-Verlag, 1990.

Hull, David Stewart. *Film in the Third Reich: A study of the German Cinema 1933-1945*. Berkeley and Los Angeles: U of California P, 1969; reprint New York: Simon and Schuster, 1973.

Hollstein, Dorothea: *"Jud Süß" und die Deutschen: antisemit. Vorurteile im nationalsozialist. Spielfilm.*—Ungekürzte, durchges. u. um d. Vorw. zur Taschenbuchausg. erw. Ed. Frankfurt/M; Berlin; Wien: Ullstein, 1983.

Knilli, Friedrich *"Jud Süß": Filmprotokoll, Programmheft und Einzelanalysen.* Friedrich Knilli. Berlin: Spiess, 1983. (Reprints zur Medienwissenschaft; 2).

Rentschler, Eric. *The Ministry of Illusion: Nazi Cinema and Its Afterlife*. Cambridge, MA: Harvard UP, 1996.

Taylor, Richard. *Film Propaganda: Soviet Russia and Nazi Germany*. London: I.B. Tauris, 1998.

Welch, David. *The Third Reich: Politics and Propaganda*. London and New York: Routledge, 2002.

CHAPTER 9

Die Mörder sind unter uns

(The Murderers Are among Us, **also** Murderers among Us **1946**)

Susanne Wallner (Hildegard Knef) and Hans Mertens (Ernst W. Borchert) look out the window of their apartment. Staudte reveals his indebtedness here to the films of German Expressionism in the high contrast lighting, the broken shards of glass in the window pane, and the intersecting vertical, horizontal and diagonal lines. The external elements reflect the inner demons of the characters, in particular of Hans, whose face is partially obscured by the cross lattice of the window pane.

CREDITS

Director .... Wolfgang Staudte
Screenplay .... Wolfgang Staudte
Director of Photography .... Friedl Behn-Grund and Eugen Klagemann
Music .... Ernst Roters
Producer .... Herbert Uhlich
Production Company .... DEFA
Length .... 85-91 mintues; b/w

Principal Cast

Ernst W. Borchert (Hans Mertens), Hildegard Knef (Susanne Wallner), Arno Paulsen (Ferdinand Brückner), Robert Forsch (Mondschein), Albert Johannes (Bartolomaeus Timm).

THE STORY

Time and place are clearly specified at the outset of the film: 1945, Berlin, after Germany's capitulation. The surgeon Dr. Hans Mertens had already returned to Berlin after having served in the war. Traumatized by his wartime experiences, he is by no means ready to resume his profession, to start a new life, or to help with the rebuilding of Germany. Having found living quarters in an abandoned apartment, he spends his waking hours discharging cynical statements to anyone willing to listen and attempting to drink himself into oblivion in one of the many places of amusement that had sprouted up in Berlin at the end of the war. But Susanne Wallner, a concentration camp survivor, interrupts his self-destructive lifestyle when she returns to the apartment as its rightful inhabitant. Allowing Mertens to stay, she slowly helps him to overcome his aversion to all humankind and succeeds in gaining his love.

The film is well on its way before the cause of Mertens' trauma comes to light: the execution of the innocent population of a Polish village on Christmas Eve of 1942 ordered by his commanding officer, Ferdinand Brückner—an execution Mertens had tried to prevent. Accidentally discovering that Brückner was still alive and living in Berlin, Mertens pays him a visit. He finds Brückner in prosperous surroundings in the midst of a loving family, successful in postwar Germany as the head of a factory that turns war helmets into cooking pans. Resentful and angry that Brückner shows no signs of remorse at his unjustified wartime order, Mertens makes two attempts to kill him, the second one on Christmas Eve 1945. But, when Susanne, who had read his diary and had surmised his intent, arrives at the scene of the potential murder, Mertens drops his gun, conceding that individuals have no right to personal acts of revenge. He emphasizes it is the individual's duty to raise accusations but the province of the court system to enact justice. The film ends with Brückner behind the bars of the factory gate looking as if he were behind the bars of a prison cell.

BACKGROUND

Wolfgang Staudte's *Die Mörder sind unter uns* (*The Murderers Are among Us* 1946) is the first German film produced after the Second World War and also the first German film to confront issues of guilt pertaining to the Nazi era. That a German was allowed to produce a film so soon after the war was in itself a minor miracle. Even several months before the final German capitulation—in November 1944—the four Allies (France, Great Britain, the Soviet Union, and the United States) had released Law 191 of the Military Government intended for Germany, which stipulated that Germans halt production of printed media, news broadcasts, and all forms of entertainment, including films and music. On May 12, 1945, four days after the unconditional German surrender, the Allies amended Law 191 to allow the licensing of print media and film production, specifying that each of the four occupation zones was to determine its own licensing system. In practice, this meant that films approved in one occupation zone could be shown in another only if the licensing board of the other occupation zone also gave its approval.

Since film had been the medium most instrumental in transporting Nazi ideology, whether with its flood of carefully controlled images or propagandistic narratives, it had turned into the most suspect Nazi art form and thus also the one initially most guarded by the Allies. Wolfgang Staudte, for example, may have received a license for film production from the British (he lived in the British sector of Berlin), but he was unable to receive either permission or money from the British to produce *The Murderers Are among Us*. He was equally unsuccessful in the French and American sectors of Berlin. Particularly the words of Peter van Eyck, the German-American who headed the U.S. Film Section of the Information Control Branch (later he was to become a well-known actor in German films) stung Staudte the most. Treating Staudte like a Nazi as he mustered him from head to toe, Peter van Eyck declared that in the foreseeable future no Germans would be allowed to produce films (film critics quoting this conversation, all basing their comments on recorded interviews or conversations with Staudte, vary as to the number of years van Eyck had predicted for the exclusion of Germans—five, ten, and twenty years are the figures related most often).

Daunted, but not enough to give up, Staudte turned to the remaining occupying power. Unexpectedly, the Soviets treated him in friendly fashion and agreed to read his script. When Staudte returned after three weeks, the Russian in charge of film licensing astonished him by being able to quote many parts of the script verbatim. Staudte then received permission to film—on the condition that he change the ending of the film from one emphasizing personal retribution to one placing decisions of guilt and subsequent acts of justice under the jurisdiction of the court system. The Russian insisted that the chaotic times called for constructive filmmaking, a view Staudte readily embraced. Thus he also changed the film title from the original *The Man I Will Kill* to *The Murderers Are among Us*, the title Fritz Lang had initially planned for his film *M* (1931). No other compromises were expected from Staudte. The ideological strictures imposed on films in the eastern part of Germany began only after his first postwar film.

It is in retrospect not at all surprising that the Soviets were the ones to first grant a German permission for filming. The Americans, for instance, subscribed most fervently to the tenet of collective guilt—that all Germans were guilty and all had to be reeducated before being allowed to rejoin the family of nations. On the one hand, the documentaries they had produced of the death camps became obligatory viewing for those in the American sector. On the other hand, however, they flooded their occupation zone with American films, regardless of type or quality, trusting that any American film would turn into a democratizing force. As the Americans often did not bother to dub their films into German or to provide German subtitles, enthusiasm for watching American films understandably began to wane, and there were fewer films to watch anyway, since Hollywood began to send fewer films to a market by no means considered lucrative.

Thus the Americans turned to German films of the past to help meet the demand for entertainment and escapism so prevalent in the German postwar population. Oblivious to hidden propaganda, the American control board set up to evaluate films from the past approved particularly many of the Nazi entertainment films. Films of concentration camps and Nazi entertainment films—this combination often became the filmic fare in the American sector. With the start of the Cold War (1947) and the attendant American wish to draw Germans to the capitalist side, the collective guilt tenet faded from policymaking and denazification measures too were largely abandoned. This also meant that the

German film industry was allowed to revive, but in decentralized fashion—that is, instead of promoting one major studio to represent German film, as the UFA had in the Weimar and Nazi periods, the Americans, along with the other western Allies, encouraged the establishment of a wide spectrum of smaller German film studios in all of the western occupation zones.

Like the Americans, the Soviets were convinced of the need to reeducate Germans. But they relied on the communist German émigrés to Russia during the Nazi era to initiate the necessary cultural reeducation of Germans upon their return to Germany in the postwar period. In keeping with Lenin, who had considered film the most important art for influencing the masses, the Soviets and the communist German émigrés agreed at the outset to reestablish the German film industry as soon as possible. Rather than banishing Germans from important roles who—like Staudte—had remained in the German film industry during the Nazi era, they actively sought humanistically inclined Germans for leadership roles.

In November 1945, filmmakers, writers, and others active in the field of culture met in Berlin's famous Hotel Adlon, still severely damaged, to discuss the establishment of a German film industry in the Soviet sector—at that time a film industry meant to serve all Germans rather than merely the ones living in the Soviet occupation zone. Speakers stressed the need for German films clearly committed to humanism, antifascism, and democratic principles.

The official founding of DEFA (Deutsche Film AG/German Film Company) occurred on May 17 in Potsdam-Babelsberg—not on the grounds of the severely damaged UFA-studios that were to be turned into the DEFA-site but in a nearby studio. Representatives of all occupation powers and film enthusiasts from all occupation zones were present at the official ceremony that highlighted the moral mission of the German films to come. Films were to give answers to essential questions of life; they were to proclaim truth, awaken conscience, drive out all remnants of Nazism and militarism, and—above all—to educate youth in democracy and humanism. After the ceremony, the guests—Peter van Eyck among them—were invited to observe Staudte directing a scene for *The Murderers Are among Us* in a nearby studio (Staudte had been permitted to start filming for DEFA several days before its official founding).

By openly confronting questions of German guilt and focusing on integrating a surgeon, plagued by wartime nightmares, in postwar life so that he would be useful in the process of rebuilding Germany according to humanistic principles, Staudte's film clearly exemplified the ethical ideological concerns of DEFA's founding fathers. Yet the pacifistic Staudte had been prompted to write his screenplay not by postwar developments but by an unpleasant chance meeting with a pharmacist acquaintance during the last weeks of the war. The pharmacist, a fanatic Nazi, had discovered that Staudte was in hiding, attempting to the end to avoid army service. With the film industry at a standstill, Staudte was no longer relieved of war duties—as he had been when he acted as an extra in several films, among them the infamous *Jud Süß* (*Jew Süss*, Veit Harlan 1940) and when he was directing minor comedies during the Nazi era. Later Staudte openly admitted to having been an opportunist in the Nazi period, avoiding army service at practically any cost. When the somewhat intoxicated pharmacist was apprised of Staudte being in hiding, he angrily directed a gun at him. Though the pharmacist refrained from pulling the trigger, Staudte was angered, silently vowing retribution at the end of the war. This translated into the screenplay for *The Murderers Are AmongUs*, finished even before Germany's official surrender.

Staudte's film was the first of several so-called "rubble films" produced in Germany until the currency reform of 1948. While Germans soon tired of this genre, wishing the cinema to distract them from their bleak existence rather than reenacting it on the cinematic screen, there is no question that *The Murderers Are among Us* succeeded in touching the nerve of the times. Its premiere date, Oct. l5, 1946, was the night before the day on which sentences pronounced at the Nuremberg Trials were to be carried out. In fact, the newspaper *Sonntag*, produced in the eastern zone, carried reviews of Staudte's film in the same issue that reported on the execution of Germany's top war criminals.

There was much at stake with the first postwar German film. Its importance was underscored at the premiere, attended by whatever celebrities there were in occupied Germany, film lovers from all German-speaking areas, and high military officials from the American, French, and Soviet occupation zones (the British absence was due to a protest against the male lead). The first German film was expected to answer many questions, among them the following: Was it possible for a German who had remained in Nazi Germany to produce a film untainted by Nazi cinematography and Nazi ideology? Could Germans be trusted at all in democratizing cinema? Was it realistic to hope for the revival of the German film industry? Could a German film project any humanistic values at all? Could it resurrect any from the past? Could a completely new German film language be created? If not, what filmic conventions would be chosen to bridge past and present? A comedy as the first German postwar film would be wrong, many sensed. But, could a German film provide substance without being overbearing? Would a topical German film end in escapism? How would a German depict the end of the war and the occupation forces governing most areas of life? How would a German portray other Germans? Was any German capable of producing a film that could act as an effective tool for educating the young? Would Staudte's film initiate the rebirth of the German individual and, by implication, of the German nation?

With so many questions and so much accumulated tension preceding the premiere, it is understandable that the first postwar German film fell short of universal acclaim. Yet, as a whole, the film garnered far more praise than negative comments. The general consensus was that it indeed represented the rebirth of the German film industry. By 1951, viewer numbers in eastern Germany alone topped the five million mark. Though it reached mainstream movie theaters in West Germany only in 1959 (until then only film clubs, film festivals, and educational institutions received permission to show it), it again received unstinting praise. Curiously, by that time, DEFA had withdrawn it from circulation in the GDR, regarding it as too individualistic and too decadently aesthetic for its socialist population, but continued to export it avidly.

EVALUATION

Flourishing after the First World War in film as in other arts, German Expressionism seemed to Staudte the best mode for portraying German sensibilities after the Second World War as well. In his attempt to circumvent the filmic language of the Third Reich, Staudte linked the first postwar German film with the golden age of German cinema, resurrecting for the present the best German cinematic tradition rather than developing a new filmic language but thereby also reenacting some of the past traumas. Strong contrasts, tilted camera, precariously slanted surroundings, labyrinthine stair cases, doors seemingly opening and closing by themselves, mysterious gazes through many windows, menacing shadows—Staudte drew amply on these hallmarks of German expressionist cinema to portray the chaotic postwar world and the turbulent psychic condition of many Germans. Also like the Expressionists, Staudte favors foggy weather and prefers to film at dusk and at nighttime. Given the lack of sufficient film stock and hundreds of other impediments to filming, Staudte's reliance on the filmic language of Expressionism, much of it needing technical expertise more than additional materials, can easily be justified.

Staudte frequently uses dissolves to underscore the simultaneity of harshly contrasting events rather than to signal time changes, the more common purpose of dissolves. In the establishing shots of the film, for example, the image of Mertens entering the amusement locale in order to be distracted and entertained dissolves slowly into the rushing train transporting people not comfortably seated inside but precariously hanging on to the outsides of the train cars. Much like the train in *Berlin: Die Symphonie der Großstadt* (*Berlin: Symphony of a Great City*, Walther Ruttmann 1927), Staudte's train needs to reach Berlin, its goal, as quickly as possible. It contrasts sharply with Mertens' aimless meandering in the sequence of the establishing shots devoted to him. Yet the train too is disorienting, for it first rushes from left to right, tilted upward at a dangerously steep angle, then abruptly changes its course to proceed from right to left and then again from left to right, suggesting similar jolts in the lives of the people it is transporting. Susanne, however, is not easily disoriented. Exiting from the train station in the midst of a crowd, she walks straight ahead toward the eye of the camera. Not seeking distraction, her gaze fastens on the war wounded, two of them flanking an old, crookedly placed poster with the inscription "Germany." The Germany-poster depicts the market square of a romantic-looking German town.

The next dissolve is from the poster to eerie silhouettes of bombed buildings. The camera lingers on them. The violin music that had accompanied Susanne abruptly halts. Now there is utter silence. The sight of this non-poster-book Germany presumably jars Susanne as much as the spectators. The violin music resumes only when Susanne reenters the frame to continue the walk to her home. Another dissolve occurs soon—when the horizontally walking Susanne, proceeding purposefully from the left of the screen to the right, turns into the drunken Mertens weaving vertically upward on a poorly lit roundabout staircase to the apartment he has made into his own. These dissolves, though clearly delineating Susanne and Mertens as opposites, underscore the simultaneity of their activities and thus interrelate the two protagonists. This type of dissolve technique is used throughout the film. When Mertens, for example, applies for work in the hospital, the frame dissolves into the sequence of Susanne visiting the Brückner family, and from there back to the hospital where a child's crying triggers in Mertens the war traumas that connect Brückner to him. And, when a flashback recreates the events in the Polish village of Christmas Eve 1942, it dissolves into Susanne seated in the apartment—by now comfortably refurbished, reading the description of the same event out loud from Mertens' diary from the point where the flashback left off. That Susanne has gained access to the same thoughts as Mertens, and is in a sense thinking them the same time as he, enables her to rush to his rescue in time.

In the final images of the film, the camera zooms in and out on a Brückner behind bars—presumably prison bars—as Mertens finishes his sentence on the citizens' duty to tender accusations of war crimes on behalf of millions of

Ferdinand Brückner (Arno Paulsen), stands facing his executioner Hans Mertens (Ernst W. Borchert), whose shadow threatens to engulf Hans's former superior officer. Staudte's mise-en-scène borrows from German Expressionism and film noir, styles which relied heavily on shadows and threatening imagery

innocent victims. A faint image representing the innocent women and children is briefly superimposed on Brückner's figure as he continues to deny his guilt in an increasingly desperate voice. The subsequent image of male victims soon dissolves into a medley of crosses dissolving into ever more crosses to suggest the death of countless innocent people and the futility of Brückner's protestations of innocence. Senseless death provides the frame for the entire film: The movie starts with a single cross in front of two mounds in the rubble landscape; the movie ends with focus on a single cross. Unlike the first cross, this last cross can no longer be ignored, for the camera zooms in on it and then expands the image to take up the whole screen. This exaggerated focus on Christian symbolism to depict deaths seems misplaced, for surely crosses are more appropriate for Christian Germans who had died as soldiers than for the Jews who had comprised the highest number of innocent victims. Created largely through the final dissolves, the symbolism ending the film seemed to be an escapist device for several reviewers in 1946, mainly because it offered no concrete guidelines for accusations and convictions in everyday life. But the wish for an alternate ending, such as a realistic court trial, with Brückner held accountable for specific crimes and receiving a specific punishment, seems unrealistic as well, since the German court system was still a shambles in 1946 and since the Allies did not trust Germans to arbitrate guilt and innocence.

The use of shadows to express danger, fear, uncertainty, insecurity, or inner turmoil occurs in the film with a rate of frequency comparable to that of the dissolves. Significantly, parts of Mertens's face are often obscured by shadows, and his is the body most prone to being duplicated as a shadow. His presence on the apartment's staircase almost always provides a reason for casting his shadow onto the wall (Susanne's shadow is shown only once, as she is walking up the staircase with Mertens). When Mertens is first seen in the apartment, rummaging for the camera in the drawers of a cabinet, his shadow is projected onto the cabinet, suggesting that nothing good could come of his attempt to steal the camera. When he looks at a puddle, his shadow reflected in the muddy water soon ominously dominates the frame. Even when he starts to operate on the girl, his shadow appears on the wall, for the girl's mother is holding a lantern to provide at least some light for the operation. As Mertens's confidence during the operation increases, the shadow disappears—in concert with the medium close-up of Mertens filmed from a low angle to indicate his competence and at least the momentary disappearance of his doubts. Still, the expressionist shadow at the beginning of the operation distracts somewhat from the important task at hand, and certain shadows, such as the lingering, exaggerated, sharply delineated silhouette-faces of two gossiping apartment house inhabitants, merely retard the development of the narrative.

Yet the concluding segment of the film exploits the visual potency of shadows in a particularly creative fashion. Arguably Mertens's shadow on the white wall of the factory hall slowly incorporating Brückner's entire figure the more Brückner denies his guilt and the more frightened he becomes of Mertens has become one of the most memorable visual images of the film, the one that tends to locate the film as Staudte's *The Murderers Are among Us* in documentary retrospectives of postwar German cinema. With Susanne's appearance at the scene, the danger of death subsides, visually represented by Brückner leaving Mertens's enveloping shadow. Possibly this episode would have been less effective if shadows had not been employed throughout the film.

A somewhat odd fact emerges from the film reviews written in the wake of the October 1946 premiere: in the course of the film showing, the audience repeatedly clapped in appreciation—not at any of the messages the film was conveying but at particularly impressive shots of the stone rubble Berliners encountered plentifully in their everyday lives. Apparently there was painful silence in the movie theater when Mertens accuses Brückner of having murdered the innocent, and applause was slow in coming at the end of the film. But there was admiration for the camera's ability to turn bombed Berlin into aesthetically pleasing, expressionistic ruins. Several reviewers particularly criticized, however, the abundance of staged ruins in the film, complaining that Staudte's concern with aesthetics was often escapist, or that the aesthetic filming was pursued at the expense of the narrative.

Several of the ruins indeed often seem inserted only for their visual power. During the filming, Staudte often spent days at a time to find the most expressive bombed buildings. Even then his cameraman did not simply photograph them. Floodlights—in immense quantities—lit up the ruins or the skies behind them, indeed staging the bombed buildings as if they had been in a studio. Before Susanne starts to walk among the ruins of Berlin, spectators see a lingering shot of somewhat lit-up ruins against the background of a gray sky sprinkled with clouds. In the next shot, Susanne begins to walk, but now the sky has become completely white, enveloped by clouds, accentuating the pitch-black remnants of facades that seem to be sending variously shaped accusatory gestures into the skies.

Yet, in genuine expressionist fashion, most of the ruins depicted in the film not only represent the general inner devastation of the characters but also illustrate specific feelings or foreshadow specific events, even when they seem inserted into the film haphazardly. In one instance viewers see a close-up of Susanne, a side view, in which she is upset at the drunk Mertens's denigration of her poster and at his refusal to seek work. Suddenly viewers hear dramatic musical chords that extend to the next image—one of beautiful ruins dramatically caving in. Since Susanne remains inside, the ruin seems inserted for no reason other than to show its beautiful demolition. But it actually foreshadows the stormy nature of Susanne's and Mertens's next meeting with each other, the scene in which Susanne informs Mertens of having found the letter meant for Mrs. Brückner. Mertens's anger at Susanne turns this episode into the major crisis in their relationship. In fact, like the building caving in, their relationship could now end, for the patient and understanding Susanne is angry enough to leave the house. Mertens of course follows her. They now meet in the midst of splendidly shaped and romantically lit ruins that seem more like castles in a fairytale than the ravaged buildings they in reality are.

At this point, the film seems to slip into the kind of melodrama associated with Nazi entertainment films. When Susanne and Mertens walk toward the camera instead of embracing, not looking at each other but into the nebulous sky, and Susanne says that she will wait for the day when Mertens will be able to love her, it is difficult not to be reminded of the last scene in *Die große Liebe (The Great Love*, Rolf Hansen 1942). There Zarah Leander and her pilot interrupt their intent to kiss and look instead into the sky, implying that they will defer their love until the country's missions have been accomplished.

Considering that Susanne and Mertens had just spent an extended period in the midst of splendid ruins, it is at first puzzling that yet another impressive outline of a ruin soon follows. When they return to the apartment building and reach the door to their apartment, the two human figures are immediately replaced by the image of this additional ruin. Again the music highlighting the image is the same music that had accompanied Susanne and Mertens to the apartment door. What, then, does this ruin have to say about their relationship? Though a slanting ruin like most of the others in the film, its empty rectangles, suggesting where the windows had once been, seem especially symmetrical, as if their frames had been chiseled with particular care. Each rectangle, moreover, allows an unhampered view of the clear sky beyond the ruin. Contrasting markedly with the ruin that had caved in, this harmonious ruin reflects the harmonious state of affairs that had ensued between Susanne and Mertens. Still, this ruin merely reinforces the obvious.

Unquestionably, Staudte lavished great care on each image of ruins. Though his aim was to use them in the manner of Expressionists highlighting and distorting objects for specific psychological purposes, his ruins are memorable for their isolated dignity and beauty. They actually approximate what Albert Speer, Hitler's architect, had envisioned for Germany: grand, indestructible architecture that remains impressive even as ruins. (MS)

QUESTIONS

1. Staudte had difficulty getting permission to film in the English, French, and American sectors of occupied Germany but received permission from the Soviet (Russian) sector. Why might the Allies have refused and the Soviets consented?

2. Describe the role the city plays in the film.

3. Imagine being a German seeing this film in 1946. How would your reception of the movie be different from your reception today?

4. Explain the title.

5. Discuss Staudte's cinematic style.

RELATED FILMS

In jenen Tagen (*In Those Days*, Helmut Kautner 1947). Käutner tells the story of a car and its owners during the Third Reich from the perspective of the car.

Irgendwo in Berlin (*Somewhere in Berlin*, Gerhard Lamprecht 1946). Lamprecht's rubble film looks to the future. It was also filmed in the eastern or Soviet sector.

Germania Anno Zero (*Germany Year Zero*, Roberto Rossellini 1948). This rubble film by the famed Italian neo-realist Rossellini follows a boy through the rubble of postwar Germany.

Land der Väter, Land der Söhne (*Country of the Fathers, Country of the Sons*, Nico Hofmann 1988). A son confronts his father about crimes he may have committed in Eastern Europe in the Second World War.

Fußgänger (*The Pedestrian*, Maximilian Schell 1973). A son confronts his father for atrocities he committed during the Second World War in Greece.

Rama dama (Joseph Vilsmaier 1991). Vilsmaier sets a romance in this latter day rubble film set in Bavaria. The title is dialect for "we're cleaning up."

INFORMATION

The Murderers Are among Us (1946), DVD, in German w/subtitles, b/w, 91 minutes, First Run Features, released, 2002.

Bandmann, Christa and Joe Hembus. *Klassiker des deutschen Tonfilms*. Munich: Goldmann, 1980.

Byg, Barton. "DEFA and the Traditions of International Cinema." In *DEFA. East German Cinema, 1946-1992*, edited by Sean Allan and John Sanford, 22-42. New York and Oxford: Berghahn Books, 1999.

Fehrenbach, Heidi. *Cinema in Democratizing Germany. Reconstructing National Identity after Hitler*. Chapel Hill: U of North Carolina P, 1995.

Kannapin, Detlef. *Antifaschismus im Film der DDR. DEFA-Spielfilme 1945-1955/56*. Hochschulschriften 21. Cologne: PapyRosa Verlag, 1997.

Ludin, Malte. *Wolfgang Staudte*. Reinbek bei Hamburg: Rowohlt, 1996.

Mückenberger, Christiane. "The Anti-Fascist Past in DEFA Films." In *DEFA. East German Cinema, 1946-1992*, edited by Sean Allan and John Sanford, 58-76 New York and Oxford: Berghahn Books, 1999, 58-76.

Orbanz, Eva and Hans Helmut Prinzler, eds. *Staudte*. Berlin: Wissenschaftsverlag Volker Spiess, 1991.

Ott, Frederick W. *The Great German Films*. Secaucus NJ: Citadel Press, 1986.

Reimer, Robert C. and Carol J. Reimer. *Nazi-Retro Film: How German Narrative Cinema Remembers the Past*. Boston: Twayne Publishers, 1992.

Shandley, Robert R. "*Die Mörder sind unter uns* and the Western." *The German Quarterly* 74:2 (Spring 2001), 132-147.

_____. *Rubble Films: German Cinema in the Shadow of the Third Reich*. Philadelphia: PA Temple UP, 2001.

Weckel, Ulrike. "The Mitläufer in Two Postwar German Films: Representation and Critical Reception." *History and Memory* 15:2 (Fall/Winter 2003) 64-93.

CHAPTER 10

Berlin – Ecke Schönhauser

(*Berlin – Schönhauser Corner*, **Gerhard Klein 1957**)

CREDITS

Director ....Gerhard Klein
Screenplay ....Gerhard Klein and Wolfgang Kohlhaase
Director of Photography ....Wolf Göthe
Music...Günter Klück
Producer .... Erich Albrecht
Production Company .... DEFA
Length...80 minutes; b/w

Principal Cast

Ekkehard Schall (Dieter), Ilse Pagé (Angela), Ernst-Georg Schwill (Kohle), Harry Engel (Karl-Heinz), Manfred Borges (Dieter's brother), Raimund Schelcher (Police officer/Volkspolizei Kommissar)

THE STORY

As *Berlin – Schönhauser Corner* opens a young man rushes into a police station and announces that "Kohle is dead." The film then flashes back to the story that got us to this point. Three men in their late teens or early twenties and a girl, age 16, hang out on their neighborhood street corner, playing tough and acting bored with the life around them. One of them breaks a street lamp on a dare, and all are hauled off to the police, where the officer in charge assumes a role toward them more like a wise father or older brother than a policeman. Unable to thaw their mean-street demeanor, however, he sends them home.

At this point the film introduces the bleak home life of the four. Angela, the only girl in the gang, lives with her mother, who is having an affair with a married man that requires that the daughter leave the small flat so that the couple may have privacy. Kohle, the boy whose death was announced as the movie opens, lives with an understanding mother who is unable to stop her second husband from beating his stepson. Karl-Heinz is from a well-off family that lives in hope that the East German regime will collapse. His father turns off the money spigot from which until now the son has been spoiled. Dieter lives with a brother who is a police officer and who is also prone to lecture his brother on the virtues of being a good socialist.

To replace the loss of his parents' money, Karl-Heinz participates in illegal activities in the West, unable to convince his friends to join him. After accidentally killing a man during a botched robbery, Karl-Heinz returns home only to be confronted by Kohle and Dieter who want him to make good on a bet he had made with them. Kohle accidentally knocks him unconscious. Believing he has killed Karl-Heinz, Kohle, together with Dieter, flees to the West. Discovering not everything there is for the better, Kohle poisons himself in an attempt to gain his freedom from the relocation camp into which western authorities have placed him. Dieter escapes from the camp and goes home to East Berlin. It is at this point that the story comes back to the opening scene. The police officer tells Dieter that Karl-Heinz has been arrested and convicted on manslaughter, and that Angela is pregnant and is looking forward to his return.

BACKGROUND

After the Second World War, Germany was divided by sectors among the Allies: America, France, Britain, and the Soviet Union. Berlin, in the middle of the Soviet sector, was likewise divided into four zones among these same countries. In 1949 the American, French, and British sectors became the Federal Republic of Germany (West Germany) and the Soviet sector became the German Democratic Republic or East Germany. In the early fifties, East Germany established heavy security on its border with the West intending to keep immigration to the Federal Republic under control. The border between East and West Berlin remained open with travel checked at official border crossings. However, it was possible to cross from East to West illegally by avoiding checkpoints. It was not until the completion of the Berlin Wall in 1961 that East and West became almost impenetrably divided.

Berlin – Schönhauser Corner was made in 1957, the year in which the story is also set, at a time that is halfway between a populist uprising against the East German regime in 1953 in East Berlin and the building of the Wall. The conditions that had led to workers' unrest: poor central planning, consumer shortages, and increased work requirements, had not been entirely eliminated. Judging from scenes in the film, apartments were small, and opportunities for youth for training in fields attractive to them were not readily available. Moreover, based purely on material satisfaction, East German youth were behind their counterparts in the West. Young people, however, did have clubs to visit which played contemporary, youth oriented music, and consumer items from West Berlin were available through a grey market.

In spite of having a healthy outlet for their rebellious energy, the youth of the film represent a threat to East German society. Even the youngest of the film's protagonists would have been in their formative years during the 1953 uprising, perhaps even had parents who took part, and the older among the characters, Dieter for example, would have been at an age to have participated on his own. Thus Dieter, Kohle, and Karl-Heinz, the young men who engage in seemingly meaningless acts of rebellion, like their counterparts in films from Hollywood and West Germany, add a political and urgent subtext to the film: take care of our youth or there will be more unrest in the future.

EVALUATION

Critics cite *Berlin – Schönhauser Corner* as an example of neo-realism in East German film. Neo-realism, a film movement characterized by grainy film images, location shooting, loosely structured stories, and non-professional actors is associated mainly with Italian film, where the style reached its peak between 1945-55, producing classic examples of the style such as *The Bicycle Thief* (Vittorio de Sica, 1948) and *Rome Open City* (Roberto Rossellini, 1945). Although the film is shot partly on location in the streets around Schönhauser Corner, to label the film neo-realist is to misunderstand both neo-realism and the film. In actuality, the film is an excellent example of classical German cinema, as practiced at different periods in German film history: in Weimar, during the Third Reich, and after the war in both West and East Germany. Visual style, characterization, music and themes echo material from German predecessors rather than Italian, and when the film does borrow from elsewhere, it borrows from Hollywood not Italy.

Similar to the films of his German predecessors and contemporaries, Klein gives his film a formal structure, framed by the opening and closing sequences to the film's main story, which is told in flashback. Scenes are not simply found, as in neo-realism, nor is the camera simply filming, using available light. That is, Klein strives for state-of-the-art production values. When Dieter first enters the screen, we see him running toward the camera, eventually capturing our full interest as he passes by a sign that reads: "You are now leaving the western zone." Klein is careful to show the sign from both sides, either the West or East, whenever characters cross the border. Or as an alternate means of signaling change in political locale he will include hawkers of western newspapers that comment on political events that have resonance with the characters personal situation. One such newsboy, for example, sells papers announcing West Germany's plans for armament. Another announces that Persian Princess Soraya (a favorite subject of the tabloids in the fifties) is expecting a child, this item is inserted shortly after the seduction of Angela, the film's teenage female lead.

Klein also uses lighting to dramatic ends, similar to the films of Helmut Käutner and Wolfgang Staudte, both directors of films for the Third Reich and both with successful postwar careers. Lighting is likewise reminiscent of classical German cinema, as practiced in film eras since the twenties. Thus the film at times plays like a film noir, with dramatically lit scenes as when Dieter and Kohle confront Karl-Heinz in an attic, shining a flashlight at their prey. The scene's chiaroscuro lighting (a term borrowed from art that refers to dramatic contrasting of light with shadow), reminds us of the trapped murderer in Fritz Lang's *M*, a Weimar film , or Staudte's *The Murderers Are among Us*, a postwar film.

There are times, though, that the film is similar to neo-realism in style. This is particularly true in street scenes captured from a distance: The opening shot, for instance, or the gathering of a crowd after Kohle, one of the male teens, has vandalized a light provide examples of neo-realism's style to spontaneously capture everyday life. The scene in the club is likewise loosely structured after a young woman accuses Dieter of complicity in stealing an ID out of her purse. The camera reveals the entire scene, allowing us to find its meaning rather than directing our attention to specifics. Such scenes are the exception in the film and not the rule. For the most part, Klein controls his subjects, framing and lighting scenes in classical style. More importantly he tells a structured story with classical cinematic devices of framing, foreshadowing, symbolic mise-en-scène, and music.

Characters are drawn from stock characters in movies of that time and are hardly the non-professionals of neo-realism, even if they represent contemporary youth in East Germany. Dieter, a young man in his late teens or early twenties, is clearly the leader of a group of alienated youth who hang out on the corner of their neighborhood. Seen by the neighbors as rowdies because they prefer listening to rock and roll to finding work, the young men seem destined for trouble. Dieter clearly relishes his role as eldest, as the one the other boys all look to for their actions. He has a job, appears independent, and has a more sophisticated presence than the others, which ensures he has plenty of girls. But he too has trouble coming to terms with living in the German Democratic Republic, a country engaging in a social experiment that seemingly stresses the individual's responsibility to the group. Dieter is unwilling to join any youth organizations and is reluctant to listen to his elders, neither his brother, nor the police, nor the head of the youth organization at his place of work. Dieter postures in threatening situations, assuming a tough-man attitude whenever confronted by or confronting authority.

The camera delights in capturing Dieter in poses reminiscent of Marlon Brando's bad biker in *The Wild One* (László Benedek 1954) or James Dean's nascent hoodlum in *Rebel without a Cause* (Nicholas Ray 1955). And like both of these models, Dieter too is confused, hurting inside, and ready to fall in love. Dieter likewise resembles young rebels in two West German films, Freddy in *Die Halbstarken* (*The Hooligans*, also known as *Teenage Wolfpack*, Georg Tressler 1956) and Hans in *Die Frühreifen* (*The Rowdies*, Josef von Báky 1957). As Tressler's and von Báky's heroes are modeled after Brando's and Dean's portrayal of troubled youth, the resemblance is hardly surprising. The films also resemble each other in the way they portray the first postwar generation to critique the socio-political situation or climate of their respective countries. Youth becomes a voice of protest against the values of the older generation. Unlike the Hollywood and West German films though, which end without the youthful protagonists embracing the values of the adult world, *Berlin – Schönhauser Corner* ends with its hero finding a place in East German society.

Gerhard Klein, the director, and Eckehard Schall, the actor playing Dieter, together create Dieter's look of defiant vulnerability. Schall has a half smile that easily morphs into a smirk or grin or full laugh depending on his attitude to the situation. His eyes are equally as expressive, and often when being lectured by authoritative figures, the actor glances down, avoiding the look of his interlocutors but also precluding communication with the viewer. When he does then glance up, the effect on the statement being made at the time and the comment on the situation he finds himself in is all the more meaningful. Klein's camera contributes to the subtle messages by slow pans from other characters to Dieter's face, by lingering on his facial expressions longer than another director might, and by situating his expressive facial responses in a context of personal trouble within a social problem. And ultimately, Dieter learns from the context that he is part of a whole that precludes individual rejection or avoidance of others.

Karl-Heinz is Dieter's counterpoint in the film. He too is an individual, he too opts out of the great social experiment. But here the similarities end. He is not an existentialist loner, as is Dieter, but a sociopath (someone who rejects the rules of the social order), for whom individuality is means to material gain. Karl-Heinz combines character traits and appearance of the heroes and secondary characters in the West's rebel films. The actor's dark hair and features remind one of Horst Buchholz, the rebel star of *The Hooligans* (the West German equivalent). His penchant for criminality also brings him closer to Buchholz's character, Freddy, than Schall's character. His hairstyle meanwhile resembles that of James Dean. His antisocial attitude could also be borrowed from Dean's character Jim Stark, as Jim also could be described as a spoiled adolescent with no reason for rebelling. In addition his behavior resembles the behavior of Freddy in *The Rowdies*, who has a similar reaction to privilege. Since *The Rowdies* was being filmed before *Berlin – Schönhauser Corner* was released, however, this suggests the similarities are coincidental and not referential.

Kohle is the youngest of the gang; he is also the most vulnerable. Living in a fantasy of western action films, he dreams of being able to strike back at a world that picks on him. He longs to escape from the abuse he receives from his stepfather. If not as sensitive as Sal Mineo's character in *Rebel without a Cause*, he is nonetheless related in the manner in which he is exposed to the torments of others. And like Mineo's character he is befriended by the hero, his death providing the denouement that leads to the hero's growth. His death also reflects a convention of the young rebel genre, which generally ends with the death of a friend of the hero in order to bring about a learning experience.

Angela's character remains undeveloped. It is almost as if the film wanted to focus only on men as the builders of the new socialist state. Thus Angela never moves beyond love interest for the hero and being a symbol of his responsibility. When Dieter gets her pregnant, the film makes clear that he will return and take care of her. Moreover, before he returns, his brother and the state look after her until she reconciles with her mother. Thus her pregnancy serves a dual purpose in the film: it supports the traditional value that men have responsibility for taking care of the family. It also highlights the fact that the socialist state looks after those in need. Klein films Ilse Pagé, the actor playing Angela, as a passive on-looker in the drama that is unfolding. Whether she is defying her mother, being part of the gang, or walking with Dieter, she is passive. She leans against walls, moves to the background, makes big eyes when Dieter talks back to people in authority, and in general responds to questions with a shy mumble.

Three sets of parents portray various aspects of absentee caregivers in the film. Angela's mother has more interest in her affair with a married man than in being with her daughter. In an opening conversation introducing the relationship the two have with each other, the camera circles around a small room as the mother makes up in a mirror. Admonishing her daughter to not run around, she is more intent on getting her lipstick on straight than being present for her daughter and is happy that she can get the girl out of the small apartment when her lover arrives. The scene is reprised a short while later when the mother, trying to talk with Angela about her friends and attitude, is ignored as the daughter preens in front of a mirror, making up as the mother forbids her to do so. Karl-Heinz's parents are wealthy. Having indulged their son with money, they are surprised to discover how selfish and demanding he has become. The camera moves around the large apartment creating distance between the son and parents. Kohle's family life is equally dysfunctional. His mother has remarried in order not to be alone and the stepfather is abusive, as well as an unemployed heavy drinker. Only Dieter seems to have an unencumbered home life, perhaps because his parents are dead and the brother he lives with, although older, is well-intentioned in his admonitions, thinking of his brother and not of himself.

Dieter's brother, one of his co-workers, and the main police official represent enlightened authority. Each in turn tries to talk Dieter into accepting his role in the task of rebuilding Germany as a socialist state. In line with their positive role in the movie, camera shots of the three are never exaggerated. Lighting shows them fully lit, the camera captures them at eye level, not from above or below, and their proxemic relationship with Dieter is always neutral, never turning completely away from him but also never forcing their presence and hence their ideas on him. It is as if they know he will come around to their way of thinking. Meanwhile, representatives from the West are portrayed as a menacing presence. The black marketers leer; they are in close, threatening proximity to Karl-Heinz, their contact in the East. The officials who run the relocation camp, to which Dieter and Kohle temporarily flee, are filmed often from below, giving them a threatening demeanor. They sit behind desks or stand directly next to Dieter as they interrogate him. Their manner of speaking, as well as their way of holding a cigarette, suggest stereotypes of Nazis from Hollywood films.

The musical score of *Berlin – Schönhauser Corner* reinforces the visual elements, highlighting the story of a lost generation looking in vain for love. As the credits roll, discordant sounds segue into an orchestral melody, heavy on brass. The visuals are of a Berlin street and of a young man running who enters a room exclaiming, "Kohle is dead." In this opening Klein has introduced the opposition his music will show throughout the film, discordant jazz and or swing sounds (sometimes rock music) and an orchestral melody. Interestingly though, swing and jazz don't necessarily comment negatively on the action, although sometimes they do. More importantly, the movie's signature melody also comments both negatively and positively.

Klein allows the situation to determine the music's use. Thus as Angela meets her mother's lover on the stairs, a jazz melody indicates friction. On the streets rock music comments ambivalently, depending on a viewer's taste in music. One could assume parents or adults in the audience might see the music as characterizing a lost generation, while young people would appreciate its freshness and coolness. In the club, swing has mainly a positive note as we see young people, for the most part well behaved, enjoying a night out.

Klein uses the movie's signature melody to support a story telling of youth looking for love they cannot find at home. The melody is introduced during the scene at the club, when the non-diegetic (the music only the audience can hear as it is not a part of the world being depicted on screen) melody we have been hearing behind some of the scenes enters the screen world. The singer also introduces us to the words, "Everyone speaks of love, longs for love." Here in the club, the music and words reflect the scene, young people out on a date with their special friend. As background though, the music tells a different story. For example, as Kohle asks his sister what will happen to him if she leaves, the signature melody appears as a discordant jazz refrain. When Dieter and Angela walk silently through their neighborhood, slowly falling in love, the melody played by violins and then full orchestra ends on a slightly discordant note after the two have consummated their love, a foreshadowing that Angela has conceived a child. In a later scene, as Karl-Heinz is carried injured into his parents' apartment, the melody again sounds, this time plaintively, underscoring the son's need for love and the lack of it in the family. The melody plays as Angela argues with her mother and moves out. It comes back as she is found wandering the streets by Dieter's brother, who offers her a place to live. It plays again in truncated form at the home for asylum seekers, and finally its full orchestral sound at the end supports the film's heavy message that everyone is to blame for the state of affairs (Kohle's death), for "when we aren't together, you will find our enemies."

Berlin – Schönhauser Corner is on the one hand an exposé of the reasons behind the alienation in the postwar generation. In this respect the film resembles its American and West German counterparts as all these films focus on the generation which was born early in the war years and thus had no part in the war or its immediate aftermath, the cold war. We can see this alienation in the aimless lives the young protagonists occupy, the music they listen to, the disrespect they show parents and authority, and in their selfishness. The world centers exclusively on what they want at the moment. Dieter best expresses this viewpoint. Even though he works, and is the only one of the group who does so, he remarks that what he does after work is his business. He thus chooses not to join any organization intent on building a new socialist state. This is hardly different from the attitudes of his contemporaries in Hollywood and West German films whose philosophy is that they did not make the world the way that it is, so why should they help fix it? The problems that have brought about the state of malcontent among the young are similar in all the films of youthful rebellion. Parents do not understand their children and moreover have little time for them. Economic conditions are constant reminders of the war, at least in the German films. Parents seem intent on making up for deprivations of the war at the same time they seem to want to forget the past. Young people in general are afraid of joining adult society, of becoming like their parents.

On the other hand, *Berlin – Schönhauser Corner* is about the unique situation in East Germany in 1957. In 1953, four years before the film was released, workers in East Germany had rioted, demanding reforms in the government. In 1956, workers had rioted in two other Soviet block countries, Poland and Hungary. In East Berlin, the proximity of the West was a constant reminder of the consumer society, highlighted by the degree to which West Germany supported the more appealing and spectacular aspects of capitalism. The subtext of dissatisfaction with both the political system and one's personal situation is thus always present in the film. The apartment in which Angela and her mother live is so small that Angela must leave in order for her mother to have privacy for an affair. Dieter and his brother share a small room. Only Karl-Heinz and his parents live in luxury, awaiting a day when they can either escape to the West or greet a new government.

Whether dealing with the alienation of youth or attributing youthful rebelliousness to parents, economy, or politics, *Berlin – Schönhauser Corner* also proposes solutions, thus setting it apart from the social problem films in the West. In the films from Hollywood and West Germany young people die, but the denouement brings about no change in the characters. Instead the films close with enigmatic questions such as: "where will the events we have just witnessed lead or end?" Thus the Hell's Angels-like rowdies ride off at the end of *The Wild One*. *Rebel without a Cause* closes with Sal Mineo's character being held by his friends, played by James Dean and Natalie Wood, a substitute for his missing parents. *The Hooligans* closes with a shot of motorcyclists riding down a quiet city neighborhood, signifying trouble ahead. The ending of *The Rowdies* most closely resembles the close of *Berlin – Schönhauser Corner*. As the movie ends, the hero and the girl to whom he has gone back walk off toward a tower that represents the mine where he works, an indication that the couple is joining the adult world. The final shot of *Berlin – Schönhauser Corner* shows Dieter slowly walking through the spacious hallway toward the light of an open door of an apartment complex. When he gets to the doorway, he leans up against the side of the door contemplating the words of a police detective uttered in the previous scene. "Where we aren't together, you will find our enemies." In brief, the existential angst of the teenage rebel movie has been replaced by the idealism of social realism. (RCR)

QUESTIONS

1. Relate this film to more recent films of rebellion with which you might be familiar.

2. What role does the scene of the bomb scare play in characterizing Dieter but also characterizing the period?

3. Describe in detail the scenes of Dieter's interrogation at the asylum home, comparing them with the scenes of his interrogation by the East German officer.

4. Describe all the ways in which Klein portrays the West as negative.

5. How does the film characterize East German ideology?

RELATED FILMS

Vergiss Amerika (*Forget America*, Vanessa Jopp 2000). Vanessa Jopp sets her coming-of-age film after the fall of the Berlin Wall and the unification of Germany. While her characters don't rebel in the sense of the youth rebel films of the fifties, they nonetheless are beset with similar problems of dysfunctional home lives, unemployment, and petty criminality.

Die Halbstarken (*The Hooligans*, Gerog Tressler 1956). Tressler's film was a popular success in the fifties although the critics did not always know what to make of sympathetic petty criminals. The film made a star of Horst Buchholz who went on to also have a brief career in Hollywood.

Die Frühreifen (*The Rowdies*, Josef von Báky 1957). Wanting to capitalize on the success of films of youthful rebellion, von Báky's film emphasizes the impatience of youth in West Germany to raise living standards for all.

The Restless Years (Helmut Käutner 1958). Successful German director Helmut Käutner came to Hollywood to make this film of teenage angst and rebellion.

INFORMATION

Berlin – Schönhauser Corner (1957), VHS, in German w/subtitles, b/w, 82 minutes, DEFA Film Library (U. of Mass.).

Feinstein, Joshua. *The Triumph of the Ordinary: Depictions of Daily Life in the East German Cinema 1949-1989*: Chapel Hill, NC: U of North Carolina P, 2002.

Claus, Horst. "Rebels with a Cause: The Development of the *Berlin Filme* by Gerhard Klein and Wolfgang Kohlhaase." *DEFA: East German Cinema, 1946-1992*, edited by Seán Allan and John Sandford, 93-116. New York: Berghahn, 1999.

Kohlhaase, Wolfgang. "DEFA: A Personal View." *DEFA: East German Cinema, 1946-1992*, edited by Seán Allan and John Sandford, 117-130. New York: Berghahn, 1999.

-----. "Some Remarks about GDR Cinema." *Studies in GDR Culture and Society, 7. Selected Papers from the Twelfth New Hampshire Symposium on the German Democratic Republic*, edited by Margy Gerber, 1-6. Lanham, MD: UP of America, 1987.

CHAPTER 11

Hunde wollt ihr ewig leben?

(*Dogs, Do You Want to Live Forever?*, **Frank Wisbar 1958**)

CREDITS

Director .... Frank Wisbar
Screenplay .... Frank Dimen, Heinz Schröter, Frank Wisbar
Director of Photography .... Helmut Ashley
Music.. Herbert Windt
Production Company .... Deutsche Film Hansa
Length .... 97 minutes; b/w

Principal Cast

Joachim Hansen (Lieutenant-colonel Wisse), Ernst Wilhelm (General Friedrich Paulus), Wolfgang Preiss (Major Linkmann), Carl Lange (General von Seydlitz), Horst Frank (Sergeant Böse), Peter Carsten (Private Krämer), Sonja Ziemann (Katja), Gunnar Möller (Lieutenant Fuhrmann), Alexander Kerst (Chaplain Busch).

THE STORY

Oberleutnant (lieutenant-colonel) Wisse is schedule to go to the Russian front, but before leaving, he meets a woman of Russian German background, for whom he tries to get papers so that she may stay in Germany. Before their relationship can develop, he leaves for the front. Wisse is idealistic and supports the offensive in the East without reservations about the objectives or doubts about the eventual outcome. Soon after his arrival, however, he has an encounter with Major Linkman, an officer who masks his cowardice behind a harsh façade, dispensing orders without regard to military morale. Although Wisse is able at this time to ignore Linkman, as he is not under the Major's direct command, the situation changes when everyone is ordered closer to the front. Discovering he is now under Linkman's command, Wisse must use his sense of honor and decency to countermand the Major's irrational orders. As the situation in the Battle of

Stalingrad deteriorates, Linkman is exposed as a coward. Eventually Wisse and his men are forced to kill him when he tries to desert to the enemy. Although the men continue to fight bravely in spite of low to no rations and inadequate clothing, their unit, the Sixth Army, surrenders, succumbing to weather, hunger, and superior forces. The story is framed by a prologue in which men march off to war and an epilogue in which they march to prisoner-of-war camps.

BACKGROUND

Fritz Wöss's autobiographical novel *Hunde wollt ihr ewig leben?* (1958) on which Frank Wisbar based his movie, was one of many works that attempted to come to terms with the Battle of Stalingrad, one of the major defeats for Germany in the Second World War. Indeed even before the battle took place, Stalingrad was part of the political discourse. In a history of the literary legacy of the Battle of Stalingrad, Michael Kumpfmüller asserts that German military propaganda began preparing the public for the importance of Stalingrad in the summer of 1942. As German troop build-up continued along the eastern front, newspaper reports discussed the strategic importance of the city as a center for raw materials. Left unsaid but certainly an important reason for the Battle of Stalingrad was that the city carried the name of the Soviet Union's leader. Regardless of the reasons for the advance on the city, the Battle of Stalingrad remains one of the more bloody conflicts ever fought with casualties in the scores of thousands. Moreover the battle marked the turning point in the war which until then had been going in Germany's favor. In actuality, the war may have already turned against Germany, but psychologically, the battle produced a pessimistic mood in the populace that is reflected in the frame that opens and closes the movie.

At the time *Dogs, Do You Want to Live Forever?* was released in 1958, reminders of the war were still ever present throughout Germany. Foreign troops from America, France and England in the West and The Soviet Union in the East were a double reminder of Germany's past. They represented the victors in the war while ostensibly remaining in Germany to keep the peace, that is, to protect their respective regions from the other side. At the same time they were a constant reminder of the past, in the same way that pock-marked buildings and cold war rhetoric were a presence of the past. In a sense, even the economic miracle, which had begun in the mid-fifties, was a reminder of the war, as old, unsafe buildings were replaced with modern construction and as the new prosperity reminded the populace of how far the country had come since defeat.

Reminders of the war were also present in the political situation in the West, where the film was made, which saw the Federal Republic of Germany (West Germany) becoming an ever stronger member of NATO. Beginning in 1954 Konrad Adenauer, West Germany's first chancellor, began a campaign to persuade Germans of the need to enter into an agreement with western nations in a defense league against the nations of Eastern Europe under control of the Soviet Union. Shortly thereafter he lobbied the public strongly for the need to rearm Germany as part of the NATO defense alliance.

The strongest reminder of the war was found in the absence of the men who died and the presence of those who had survived. That is, there were significantly fewer men in the age category that would have fought in the war and now would have been between 35 and 50 years old. Those who were that age had probably fought in the war, and even though they may not have talked about their experiences, their very presence was a reminder of the past.

Dogs, Do You Want to Live Forever? belongs to a series of war films released in Germany between 1954 and 1960. Contrary to what is often written about films made in the fifties, German filmmakers did not avoid the subject of the Second World War. Indeed the subject of fighting and being a soldier in the Third Reich forms the background of a number of films made during this time. As mentioned earlier, few wanted to talk about the war, but there were some who wrote about their experiences, and these memoirs were now being filmed, offering the public a glimpse of the war from the enlisted man's point of view.

Thus the problem is not that the war was not present in the films but rather in the way that it was presented and represented. For rather than engaging the material critically, examining the fighting man's role in the war, not to mention in the Third Reich, the films propagated a myth of military values unrelated to the cause of the National Socialists. Rather than help German viewers come to terms with their country's recent past by helping them confront their history, they helped viewers avoid that history by relocating the war to a non-historical sphere. Thus, rather than forging a new national identity that included the citizenry's involvement in Nazi Germany, the films resurrected an old identity that excluded implication in the Third Reich.

Paul May's trilogy *08/15* (1954-1955) may serve as a paradigm of the German War film during the decade after the war. Replete with bumbling, cowardly, and cynical captains and majors and competent, heroic, and sincere lieutenants and non-commissioned officers, the three films by May, influenced by novels about the Second World War, draw a clear distinction between those who commanded and those who fought the war. Without ambiguity, the films exonerate the fighting men, who are never brutal and who never act arbitrarily when facing the enemy. On the warfront, they fight with dignity, courage, and above all, a sense of military ethics. Away from the front they show comradeship, humor, and a healthy libido. And even though they never overtly question the fighting of the war, there are enough instances of rebelliousness to suggest they are uncomfortable in their role as soldiers. In contrast, the officers above the rank of lieutenant have little regard for human life (including the lives of the men under their command), show poor strategic planning, and are void of understanding, courage, and initiative, the qualities that make good leaders. The films leave an indelible impression that enlisted men were just doing what soldiers do, following orders; that they had no interest or involvement in National Socialism; that they were totally innocent of Nazi Germany's crimes. Films that followed this formula include *Kinder, Mütter und ein General* (*Children, Mothers, and a General*, László Benedek 1955), *Haie und kleine Fische* (*Sharks and Small Fish*, Frank Wisbar 1955), *Nacht fiel über Gothenhafen* (*Darkness Fell on Gothenhafen*, Frank Wisbar 1959) and *Dogs, Do You Want to Live Forever?*

To be sure, not all films followed the formula. Bernhard Wicki's *Die Brücke* (*The Bridge*, 1959), treated elsewhere in this book, offers a different paradigm, avoiding the question of responsibility, by focusing on a group of 15-year olds who are drafted into fighting at the end of the war. East German war films such as *Ich war 19*, and *Mama, ich lebe* also offer a variation of the paradigm by relocating the division of officers and enlisted men into fascist soldiers and enlightened socialist soldiers, who, although being German, support the Soviet cause.

One of the most recent films to look at the role of the ordinary German soldier in the Second World War is Josef Vilsmeier's *Stalingrad* (1993), a film which anticipated by two years a major examination of the Wehrmacht. Vilsmaier's film for the most part adheres to the formula of the war film in the fifties, in which the enlisted men are depicted as merely doing their duty while the higher officers are the cause of the atrocities. His recruits escape history's judgment by deserting or otherwise refusing to follow orders. A major exhibition on the Wehrmacht which toured Germany from 1995 to 1998 and opened in New York City in 1999 told a different story about the role of the military during the Third Reich. Through photographs, the exhibition implicates ordinary soldiers in the atrocities that occurred, not allowing individuals to hide behind claims of "only following orders." The debate that followed the exhibit wherever it opened revealed the tension that still accompanies discussions of the military. On the one hand, the exhibit and its supporters were hoping to revise an image of the military as victims by showing their involvement in acts of atrocities. On the other hand, detractors of the exhibit were claiming that the exhibit besmirched the reputation of men who were merely following orders.

EVALUATION

Dogs, Do You Want to Live Forever? follows the German war film formula described earlier that exonerates the ordinary enlisted men and makes them victims of their superior officers. Lieutenant-colonel Wisse, the hero of the film and thus the character we come to identify with, is an enthusiastic young officer who relishes getting to the front to join the Sixth Army. Assigned as an adjunct to the Bulgarian troops allied with the Germans in the siege of Stalingrad, he awaits orders in German-occupied Poland. We see his good character and integrity in the way he reacts to a Russian woman threatened with deportation if she does not find work. He offers to help her, and when he receives orders to go, he assigns a friend to finishing the task. That he also has a dog further characterizes him as man of good character.

Wisse undergoes a maturation process, once at the front. His naiveté gives way to cynicism, his enthusiasm to resignation. But he never loses his integrity. He refuses to recruit men out of a hospital in a last effort by his leaders to augment troop size, and after surrender, he organizes help for the one superior officer who had acted with integrity during the ordeal. In a sense, Wisse is an early example of a war film cliché found also in Hollywood movies: he is the honest, but unseasoned, officer who earns the respect of his men through heroic actions and decent treatment. Yet he differs from his Hollywood counterparts in that he has to prevail against cowardly, incompetent, or unfeeling senior staff, even in times of battle. While Hollywood films also show how recruits and young officers engage in a battle of wits with military brass, they seldom do so during the fighting itself. Wolfgang Petersen's *Das Boot*, discussed elsewhere in the book, combines the German and Hollywood clichés. During a brief docking in Gibraltar, the naturalness of the men of the submarine contrasts with the arrogant officers on shore. Yet once back at sea, the men forget their dislike of their superiors and bravely undertake what they perceive to be a suicide mission.

Major Linkman is Wisse's main opponent, at least as dangerous as the Russian fighters. Linkman's name, which contains the root of the German word for sneaky, *link*, reveals his role in the film, as a coward obsessed with escaping from Stalingrad and willing to sacrifice any or all of his men to get away. When he is killed by his own men as he tries to go over to the Soviet side, his characterization has been so completely negative that one cheers an act (the major's murder) that one might otherwise feel compelled to condemn.

The other characters in the film fall into two groups, fictional and historical. The fictional characters, such as the chaplain or the men under Wisse's command, represent types found in other war movies, including those made outside of Germany. The chaplain must reconcile his calling as a man of God with the inhumanity he witnesses all around. The non-commissioned officers and enlisted men offer brief respite from the horrors of war with mildly humorous banter and also offer an opportunity for Wisse to show his prowess as a commander. The Russian woman, seen briefly in the opening and again briefly later in the movie, has little bearing on the story and seems motivated solely by a desire to have a female presence in the film, regardless of how insignificant it might be.

The historical characters have a clearly political purpose. They remove the onus of fighting an unjust war and place the blame for Nazi criminality on the leaders. Thus in the military hospital, Hermann Göring's speech heard on the radio contrasts with the suffering of the men. Hitler's admonition not to bother him with sentimentalities such as news of the Sixth Army's defeat places all blame for the suffering of millions on one man alone. And General Paulus's refusal to allow an advance of German troops (that the movie, without any evidence, suggests could have saved the Sixth Army) deflects criticism of the battle to criticism of how it was fought.

Shot mostly on studio lots with scenes of stock footage of the actual war, *Dogs, Do You Want to Live Forever?* evokes a sense of safe reenactment rather than a sense of real fighting. Although the statistics of dead and wounded, the military parade at the beginning, and the scenes of prisoners marching to camps at the end suggest the horrors of the Battle of Stalingrad, they do not capture the enormity of the suffering on both sides in this war. Only the scene in the hospital, in which men lie dying as they wait for treatment of amputated limbs and eviscerated bowels, suggests the historical tragedy that Stalingrad represents.

As in many early war films, much of the film plays without musical background, making the use of music during battles and other strategic scenes more noticeable and more effective, even if more clichéd. Martial music accompanies the parade scenes of the opening, calling attention to the narrator's cynicism that dead men aren't much moved by the pomp of military marching. Likewise as tanks roll over bodies and cannon fire explodes, music underscores the intensity of the fighting. Wisbar likewise uses on-screen music to clichéd effect. Thus the Christmas hymn "Silent Night" plays as the men gather around a makeshift tree to celebrate the solemn day before going off to die in battle. The scene suggests a contrast in values between Christianity and Nazism, at the same time that it distances the men from the Nazi ideology by positioning them within the Christmas spirit. A feeling of humanity is reinforced later in the film when, during a cease fire called to collect the dead, one of the German soldiers plays Bach on a piano that he has found in the middle of a battle area.

Dogs, Do You Want to Live Forever? has an ambivalent relationship to the history it represents. Wisbar's use of a frame within which he tells the story of the battle raises the film above its formulaic origins and creates a reenactment of the events. Through the film's prologue and epilogue the director offers some distance to the film and leaves room to contemplate the film's antiwar message. Yet the film avoids engaging in any meaningful debate with Germany's past. The prologue of *Dogs, Do You Want to Live Forever?* introduces an image of a dead soldier in snow, German troops marching under a banner proclaiming victory, and a voiceover commenting that victory does not matter if you are dead. Its epilogue shows a shot of soldiers marching in the snow to a prisoner-of-war camp, followed by a close up of two of the soldiers wondering if history will learn from their defeat. Left unsaid is what history is supposed to teach, whether never again to unleash a horror like the Second World War on the German people and the world, or whether to fight differently next time. To be fair, the film wants viewers to recognize the horrors of the Battle of Stalingrad as a micro-event representing Germany's defeat and the misery its war unleashed on the world. The problem lies not in the well-meaning intent of the movie but in the way the story of Germany's defeat is told. For within the clearly politicized and somewhat preachy frame lies a conventional war narrative in which viewers are asked to identify with the men fighting for Nazi Germany. Through clichéd images of bravery, comradeship, and sacrifice, viewers identify closely with the men and are thus denied critical perspective from which to judge their cause.

Rather than documenting history, *Dogs, Do You Want to Live Forever?* offers yet another war movie cliché. For, paradoxically, as the frame distances viewers from the historical events unfolding, it also allows them more involvement with the classically told narrative. On the one hand viewers experience the events as having occurred in the past; they have no immediacy and thus should allow for contemplation of the politicized message that war causes needless death and suffering. The frame tells us this, as do dramatic reenactments within the film, such as Hitler's cold response upon hearing of the many deaths at Stalingrad: "Then put together a new army." On the other hand, viewers receive no historical information beyond the insertion of Hitler's callous reaction and the radio address by Hermann Göring to place the story in perspective. In place of history, the movie offers the clichés of a war movie: potential love story, soldiers who fight bravely, injustices perpetrated on enlisted men, and a magical moment of truce to focus on the true meaning of humanity as reflected in music. And in addition, as mentioned earlier, it offers the clichés of a German war movie by depicting soldiers with no obvious involvement in Nazism fighting for officers who mismanage the war. As a result, viewers forget about the historical war and the history behind it and instead become involved in a private war of individuals with no basis in history.

A later film, Vilsmaier's *Stalingrad*, as mentioned earlier, corrects the more egregious errors of fifties war films. While he left unchanged the paradigm that separated enlisted men, the good Germans, from Nazi leaders, the bad Germans, Vilsmaier addressed the more basic problem of the ahistorical nature of the earlier films. By adding scenes of the devastation of Stalingrad, the hunger and hardships of the Russian people, and horrific scenes of death in war, he situates his film within an historical context that allows viewers to judge the men and the events, even while identifying with them. (RCR)

QUESTIONS

1. Identify all instances when history breaks into the film and describe how these historical inserts affect our reception of the story.

2. Characterize Lieutenant-colonel Wisse and the cowardly major.

3. Discuss the effect the incomplete love story has on the narrative.

4. Compare the movie with other war films you have seen. What similarities do you see? What differences are there? Why do you think these similarities and differences exist?

Related films

08/15 (Paul May 1954/55). Comprising three films, this series ends with the admonition to never again let the military way of thinking control politics.

Haie und kleine Fische (*Sharks and Small Fish*, Frank Wisbar 1957). This submarine epic is a precursor to Wolfgang Petersen's *Das Boot* (*The Boat* 1981)

Kinder, Mütter, und ein General (*Children, Mothers, and a General*, László Benedek 1955). Benedek looks at high school-aged boys on the front several years before Bernhard Wicki's better known *Die Brücke* (*The Bridge* 1959)

Stalingrad (Joseph Vilsmaier 1993). Vilsmaier remade *Dogs, Do You Want to Live Forever?* with more realistic fighting and dying. He also augmented the romance only hinted at in Wisbar's film.

Enemy at the Gate (Jean-Jacques Annaud 2001). Annaud tells the story of the Battle of Stalingrad from the perspective of a Russian sniper and a German marksman. The film was an American/German co-production and directed by one of France's top directors.

Das Boot (*The Boat*, Wolfgang Petersen 1981). Petersen's film is arguably the best known and perhaps also best executed of any of the many submarine epics.

Die Brücke (*The Bridge*, Bernhard Wicki 1959). Wicki's cinematic statement against war still affects viewers in its depiction of teenage boys who die as the war comes to a close while protecting a bridge that has no strategic value.

Information

Stalingrad — Dogs, Do You Want to Live Forever? (1958), DVD, in German w/ subtitles, b/w, 97 minutes, released 2001.

Beevor, Antony. *Stalingrad: The Fateful Siege, 1942-1943*. New York: Penguin, 1999.

Gerlach, Heinrich. *The Forsaken Army: The Great Novel of Stalingrad*. London: Cassell, 2002.

Reimer, Robert C. "Picture-Perfect War: An Analysis of Joseph Vilsmaier's *Stalingrad* (1993)." In *Light Motives: German Popular Film in Perspective*, edited by Randall Halle and Margaret McCarthy, 304-325. Detroit: Wayne State UP, 2003.

Reimer Robert C. and Carol J. Reimer. *Nazi-Retro Film: How German Narrative Cinema Remembers the Past*. New York: Twayne Publishers.

Wöss, Fritz: *Hunde, wollt ihr ewig leben?*: Roman. Frankfurt/M; Berlin: Ullstein, 1995.

CHAPTER 12

Die Brücke

(The Bridge, **Bernhard Wicki 1959)**

Hans (Folker Bohnet) is wounded during the battle of the bridge.

CREDITS

Director .... Bernhard Wicki
Screenplay .... Michael Mansfeld, Karl Wilhelm Vivier
Director of Photography .... Gerd von Bonin
Music.. Hans-Martin Majewski
Producer .... Hermann Schwerin
Production Company .... Fono Film
Length .... 105 minutes; b/w

Principal Cast

Karl Michael Balzer (Karl Horber), Folker Bohnet (Hans Scholten), Fritz Wepper (Albert Mutz), Frank Glaubrecht (Jürgen Borchert), Michael Hinz (Walter Forst), Günther Hoffmann (Sigi Bernhard), Volker Lechtenbrink (Klaus Hager), Guenter Pfitzmann (Cpl Heilmann), Wolfgang Stumpf (Stern, the teacher), Cordula Trantow (Franziska), Edith Schulze-Westrum (Frau Bernhard).

THE STORY

Die Brücke (*The Bridge*, 1959), directed by Bernhard Wicki, is the story of seven teenage boys who are drafted into the German army in a futile effort to stop the enemy Allies' invasion. All but one die.

The film is set in Germany in late April 1945. As *The Bridge* opens, a group of teenage boys from a small town, friends and schoolmates, are impatiently waiting to be drafted. Fiercely patriotic, they believe that to fight for their fatherland is the ultimate honor. When the boys are finally called to duty, they are elated, but their teacher secretly appeals to the company sergeant to spare them from the war. The company sergeant gets permission to have the boys watch a strategically useless bridge, which is going to be blown up anyway. Not aware of this, the boys take their orders very seriously. They refuse to leave their posts even when fleeing German troops retreat across the bridge. As dawn breaks, American tanks suddenly appear and try to cross the bridge. The boys fight bravely, and the Americans finally retreat. When German soldiers arrive to blow up the bridge, the boys realize that their friends' deaths were senseless and open fire on their countrymen. Another of the boys dies, leaving only one survivor.

BACKGROUND

On June 6, 1944 the Allies landed at Normandy to begin the offensive against Germany on the western front. Meanwhile, the Soviet army was advancing along the entire 2,500-mile eastern front. By the end of the year it stood poised on the eastern frontiers of prewar Germany. In the west, British and American troops stood ready to attack across the western borders. On the German home front, 1944 became a year of acute suffering. On July 20 an officers' plot to assassinate Hitler, part of a long-simmering opposition to Hitler from within German military and civilian circles, was carried out, but Hitler managed to escape the dramatic attempt on his life practically unharmed. He attributed his survival to his having been selected by fate to succeed in his mission of restoring Germany to greatness. Fate did not again intervene on Hitler's behalf. In mid-January of 1945 he withdrew underground into his bunker in Berlin where he remained until his suicide on April 30.

By late April 1945 Soviet soldiers were streaming into Berlin. All that remained of the Reich was a narrow wedge of territory running southward from Berlin into Austria. With the Soviet army in control of Berlin and the western Allies within striking distance to the west and the south, there was no prospect of dividing them. Nonetheless, when Hitler's successor, Grand Admiral Karl Dönitz, sought to open negotiations in order to surrender a few days after Hitler's death, he still hoped that a separate surrender to the British and Americans in the west might allow the Reich to rescue something from the Soviets in the east. The western Allies, fearful of any move that might feed the suspicions of Stalin, refused to consider the German proposal, insisting that a German surrender be

A young soldier lies dead on the bridge. The photo gains its power from the youth of the victim and his placement in the frame, which emphasizes how alone he is and reminds viewers of how pointless his death is.

signed with all of the Allies at the same time. Early in the morning of May 7, 1945, a German delegation came to U.S. General Dwight D. Eisenhower's headquarters in Reims, France, and at 2:41 AM signed the surrender documents. Despite the fact that a Soviet major general signed for the Soviet Union, Stalin insisted that a second surrender ceremony be arranged in Soviet-occupied Berlin. This second surrender was signed in a Berlin suburb the following afternoon.

The film is based on a book by Manfred Gregor (pseudonym of Manfred Dorfmeister), who was drafted into the Volkssturm in April 1945. As did the seven schoolboys in his novel and in the film, Dorfmeister had to defend a tiny bridge across the river Loisach near his hometown of Bad Tölz in Bavaria where three of his friends were killed by the advancing Americans. After retreating, or perhaps running away, from the Americans, Dorfmeister was drafted again into defending yet another bridge, the Isar bridge in Bad Tölz, his home town. After two of his friends were killed, Dorfmeister realized the futility of the enterprise and deserted his post to meet his father. Although Wicki made considerable changes to Dorfmeister's story, their works contain a common focus with their message of pacifism and the futility of war.

EVALUATION

The Bridge, a film about the Second World War, tells a shocking war story. It is one of the few German films to include battlefield engagement of American and German soldiers. Its gruesome images of death expose the inhumanity of war and move viewers to fundamental questions about the validity of war. Bernhard Wicki sees the action in idealistic war films as cartoon-like, where fast cuts avoid drawing the viewer into the painful truth of war. Those films, Wicki stated, tend to emphasize the heroic and spectacular and serve as mere propaganda devices. War, on the other hand, is boring and tedious, where waiting for death is the main activity. Death itself is a slow and agonizing process, as in *The Bridge*. Wicki focuses on the painful death of six of the seven schoolboys and the traumatized reaction of the lone survivor.

Wicki's film builds suspense through its dramatic structure. It is divided into two almost equal parts. The first shows the lives of the seven schoolboys—Jürgen, Walter, Karl, Klaus, Sigi, Hans and Albert—before they enter military service. The second follows them into battle. One of the movie's few flaws stems from the fact that these seven boys seem rather similar, in spite of the hour-long introductory glance at their "civilian" lives that is meant to introduce their individuality. This introduction does, however, reveal the boys' child-like mindset – they are just typical likeable boys who are more interested in pranks and girls than in the reality of war. War to them has an aura of glory, which is in contrast to the reality and harshness of life that the adults see. The boys still live in their romantic idealism of war.

We discover Jürgen's aristocratic background—his father was killed in battle, and the son wants to continue his legacy by joining the army as an officer, with his mother's approval. She even hands Jürgen his father's pistol after he enters military service. One of the other boys, Walter, is the son of the town's Kreisleiter, the local Nazi boss. He sends his wife away so he can be with his mistress, as his son suspects and later finds out to be true. Karl, a third member of the group, is the son of the local barber shop and beauty parlor owner. He discovers that the girl he loves is his father's mistress. One could probably argue that Walter and Karl are motivated by their fathers' extra-marital affairs to escape a society that is falling apart as the war nears its end. But they are as much motivated by patriotism and defending the fatherland as the other five boys, whose home life gives no reason to want to escape. A fourth youth, Klaus, has an innocent and platonic love with his girlfriend Franziska who is overjoyed when he gives her his watch as a farewell present, but is crushed when he asks for his present back from her after realizing that it would be of more use to him than to her. A fifth boy, Sigi, has an overly protective mother, played by Edith Schulze-Westrum. In a bow to Hollywood cliché, Sigi is the first one killed in battle. After they receive their enlistment papers, the boys' English teacher Stern helps them receive orders to guard the bridge in their town, which has no military importance and should thus keep them safe from harm.

After the film's rather lengthy exposition to introduce the boys, but also to build suspense, we witness the unfolding of the horrors of war in stages. Induction of the boys into the military begins with their training in the local barracks. The corporal, who is in charge of the teens, feels responsible for their welfare, as he is also their high school teacher. He thus understandably wants to prevent their death and accompanies them to the bridge, much to their disappointment, for they see others take off to what they perceive as more glorious battles, the ones they were taught to dream about in their Nazi-inspired education. In the end, though, the Nazis, who created the spirit of nationalism that causes the boys to defend their country, are also responsible for destroying their idealism, as the Nazi military had already decided to blow up the bridge in order to stop the U.S. advances. The boys don't discover this until it is too late.

The film portrays the final days of the war as chaotic, laying the blame for the boys' death on the errors in communication resulting from the chaos. Ironically, the Corporal's desire to save the boys is thus what kills them. We see the Nazi soldier's death, the death of two American soldiers, and the death of the boys: Jürgen, Walter, Karl, Klaus, Sigi and Hans. We hear the horror of the advancing tanks before they are seen, making the sound of the advance one of the most frightening experiences in the movie. (In the film *Das Boot* (*The Boat*), treated elsewhere in this book, Wolfgang Petersen uses sonar probes in a similar fashion). Wicki limits the scope of his theater of war to a manageable space, thus creating scenes of realism that capture the feeling of entrapment in battle and the inevitably of a tragic outcome.

The film's power comes from Wicki's emphasis on point of view shots. Most scenes are filmed from the perspective of the boys with the camera dug into the ground and filming at the level from which they see the action. The film offers no wide-angle shots, that might show more than the boys could see. Only in the final scene, when the battle is over, does Wicki take in the entire scene of battle, allowing the futility of the effort to become clear. Albert staggers home and collapses on the doorstep. To underline the futility of the boys' efforts in the last days of the war, the film closes with the directors' comment: "The events in this story happened in 1945. Two days later the war in Europe ended."

Part of the appeal of the story derives from its symbolic quality, the symbolic complexity of the bridge. As in literature the bridge functions on a number of levels. It is a bridge across a river, yet it is also a bridge from known territory into unknown. Moreover, it not only links but also divides the boys' hometown from the enemy. The bridge also exposes people's fear as well as highlighting their sense of adventure. Wicki's *Bridge* further refers to the bridge between youth and adulthood, something the teenagers were never to experience.

The story itself is a perfect old-fashioned story line that shows the inability to give meaning to the absurdity of modern-day war. The notion of a noble war disappeared in the twentieth century with the brutal futility of modern warfare. Wicki is not alone in presenting the bridge as a key symbol—other examples are *Die letzte Brücke* (*The Last Bridge*, Helmut Käutner 1954), *The Bridge on the River Kwai* (David Lean 1957), *The Bridge at Remagen* (John Guillermin 1969), and *A Bridge Too Far* (Richard Attenborough 1977).

The Bridge is clearly influenced by Lewis Milestone's *All Quiet on the Western Front* (1930). Just as in that film, emphasis is on the destruction of youth at a time when it should be at its most vital. Based on the novel by Erich Maria Remarque about a teenage German soldier in the First World War, who experiences death after entering the army directly out of the Gymnasium (German high school), the film captured the horrors of war as depicted in the book, and both book and film were eventually banned by the Nazis for their pacifist message. In turn, *The Bridge* has also influenced other movies. The dark tone of *Das Boot* and the claustrophobic nature of the climactic scene in *Saving Private Ryan* remind one of *The Bridge*. (RZ)

QUESTIONS

1. Describe the lives and home situations of the boys and compare them with their brief military careers.

2. How does Spielberg's movie *Saving Private Ryan* use the bridge as a symbol?

3. How does sound enhance the horror of this film?

4. What positive effect does the film's use of black and white (rather than color) have on the way we experience the movie?

5. Relate the multiple meanings that the bridge can symbolize in the film's story.

RELATED FILMS

Kinder, Mütter, und ein General (*Children, Mothers, and a General*, László Benedek 1955). Benedek looks at high school-aged boys on the front several years before Bernhard Wicki's better known *Die Brücke* (*The Bridge* 1959)

Das Boot (*The Boat*, Wolfgang Petersen 1981). Petersen's film is arguably the best known and perhaps also best executed of any of the many submarine epics.

INFORMATION

The Bridge (1959), DVD, in German w/subtitles and dubbed, b/w, 105 minutes, Belle and Blade Studios, released 1998.

Bandmann, Christa and Joe Hembus. *Klassiker des deutschen Tonfilms*. Munich: Goldmann, 1980.

Gregor, Manfred: *Die Brücke*. München: Heyne, 1992.

Gregor, Manfred. *The Bridge*. London: Cresset, 1962.

Ott, Frederick W. *The Great German Films*. Secaucus, NJ: Citadel Press.

Reimer, Robert C. and Carol J. Reimer. *Nazi-Retro Film: How German Narrative Cinema Remembers the Past*. New York: Twayne Publishers, 1992.

CHAPTER 13

Aguirre, Der Zorn Gottes

(*Aguirre, the Wrath of God,* **Werner Herzog 1972**)

One of the rafts carrying the expedition down the Amazon gets caught in a deadly whirlpool. The archetypal circular imagery of entrapment and futility repeats itself throughout Aguirre, the Wrath of God *as well as in many of Herzog's other films.*

CREDITS

Director ....Werner Herzog
Screenplay ....Werner Herzog
Director of Photography ....Thomas Mauch
Music.. Popol Vuh
Producer ....Werner Herzog
Production Companies..... Hessischer Rundfunk, Werner Herzog Filmproduktion
Length ....100 minutes; color

Principal Cast

Klaus Kinski (Don Lope de Aguirre), Daniel Ades (Perucho), Peter Berling (Don Fernando de Guzman), Justo González (González), Ruy Guerra (Don Pedro de Ursua), Del Negro (Brother Gaspar de Carvajal), Alejandro Repulles (Gonzalo Pizarro), Cecilia Rivera (Flores), Helena Rojo (Inez).

THE STORY

In 1561 Gonzalo Pizarro and his party of conquistadors arrive in Peru in search of El Dorado, the legendary city of gold. Descending down the Andes mountains the group encounters trouble when some of their food and military equipment falls into the river below. Believing it best not to travel with the entire group before knowing what lies ahead, Pizarro sends out an advance party of forty men and two women, including Don Lope de Aguirre and his daughter, Don Pedro de Ursua and his wife, Don Fernando de Guzman (the highest ranking of the nobles on the journey), Brother Gaspar de Carvajal (whose journal is the source of the story), and Peruvian Indians. The party has one week to find a way to El Dorado or to return to the main group, should this prove impossible.

Before long, the party gets into difficulties because of the impenetrability of the jungle, the unforgiving rush of the waters, and the hidden danger of the Indians on land. After one of the rafts is caught in a whirlpool and is unable to escape, Aguirre, Ursua's second in command, disagrees with Ursua, the leader, that the men should be rescued, and secretly arranges that the men on the raft be killed. As difficulties of travel increase, Ursua wants to return to Pizarro and the main party. Aguirre, the more charismatic of the two potential leaders, wants to continue. Slowly, through intrigue, murder, and persuasion, he wins the men over to his side as the party continues down river, ever deeper into the jungle. During the increasingly more perilous journey, Aguirre arranges Ursua's murder, names Guzman as king of the area the Spaniards are traveling through, and reveals his increasing state of madness. As their numbers dwindle because of internal killings as well as death at the hands of the Indians, Aguirre becomes more and more insane until he is the only one left on the raft as the film ends.

BACKGROUND

Aguirre, der Zorn Gottes (*Aguirre, the Wrath of God* 1972)) is one of the iconic films of New German Cinema, a film movement that roughly spans the years from 1962, when young German filmmakers declared in the Oberhausen manifesto that they rejected the films then being made in Germany, to 1982, the year Rainer Werner Fassbinder, the most prolific of the filmmakers, died. Although Werner Herzog, who directed *Aguirre, the Wrath of God,* no longer holds the rank of one of the leading directors of New German film, at the beginning of the movement he was as significant to the reputation German film enjoyed as were Fassbinder, Wim Wenders, and Volker Schlöndorff, whose films are treated elsewhere in the book. Indeed, the striking beauty of Herzog's visual imagery and the often extreme nature of his characters created some of the most memorable films of New German Cinema.

Werner Herzog tells stories about eccentric individuals facing extreme situations. His films can be understood as psychological case studies of these individuals as they cope with or are destroyed by forces outside their control, or they can be understood as critiques of the socio-political climate that exploits individuals until they crack. Often choosing his protagonists from legend and literature, Herzog shows them beset by an environment which, because of their eccentricities, they are unable to master. In *Jeder für sich und Gott gegen alle* (*Every Man for Himself and God against All* 1974), for example, his protagonist, Kaspar Hauser, has lived the first eighteen years of his life in a cellar, fed through a hole in the wall. One day he is freed and must begin acquiring those cultural tools of life that have been denied or withheld from him until now and which allow individuals to function within society: language, music, writing, and an understanding of social custom and human relationships. In *Nosferatu* (1979), Herzog pays homage to F. W. Murnau's film, where the vampire is a hideous monster longing to die but condemned to live alone forever. And as Murnau's film comments through its story and visuals on the state of Germany after the First World War, in familiar fashion Herzog's film equates Germany after the Second World War with the soullessness of his monster. In *Stroszek* (1977), Herzog looks at a mentally diminished young German who, with his girl friend, emigrates from Germany to America, only to be engulfed in a consumer society that destroys him. Although the film takes place in America, the film is condemning the economic exploitation taking place in most of the West.

Klaus Kinski, a noted German actor with an edgy persona from the fifties, plays an especially important role in Herzog's output, reprising again and again the role of outsider. His Aguirre is a megalomaniac whose physical deformity reflects the increasingly deteriorating state of his mind and soul. He again plays a psychopathic loner, whose eccentric nature leads him to murder in *Woyzeck* and *Nosferatu*. But whereas Woyzeck kills his lover in a jealous rage, and Nosferatu kills because of his vampiric nature, Aguirre kills (or instructs others to kill) for power. His lust for power also differentiates him from another Kinski/Herzog collaboration in the South American jungle, *Fitzcarraldo*(1982). The title character Fitzcarraldo is also a megalomaniac, but channels his insanity into bringing opera to the jungle. Fitzcarraldo too exploits the indigenous culture to the point of death.

Playing Aguirre, Woyzeck, and Nosferatu contributed to Kinski's already established type as murderer, outlaw, and monster. But if he was typecast before the series of films he made with Herzog, his association with the director of extreme outcasts created a legend, for the reputed fights that the director and actor had while making films together, some of them at gunpoint, filled tabloids. And when Herzog tried to revive his film career, he did so with a biography/autobiography of his relationship with Kinski, *Mein liebster Feind – Klaus Kinski* (*My Best Fiend* 1999).

EVALUATION

Aguirre, the Wrath of God derives its impact from the tension created between madness and exploitation. Visuals, music, setting, and characterizations all serve to emphasize the fragility of humanity when at the mercy of social order, nature, or political power. Aguirre's madness reflects the state of the expedition throughout the movie. Although Aguirre appears normal when first introduced in the film, his mental wellbeing deteriorates as the expedition goes down the Amazon. In addition, his mental deterioration mirrors the worsening of his physical deformity. That is, the deeper into the Amazon jungle the raft takes Aguirre and his party, the more insane he becomes, and the more insane he becomes the more noticeable are his stoop and slope to the right. Moreover his physical and mental metamorphosis mirrors the strength of his belief in himself as conqueror and savior of the New World. He sees himself as creating first an empire in the New World and finally, with his daughter, a new dynasty to rule over El Dorado. Like Kurtz in Joseph Conrad's 1902 novella *Heart of Darkness*, the jungle has driven him mad, and he proclaims a new dynasty while first holding his dead daughter in his arms, and then a monkey.

As a tale of madness, *Aguirre, the Wrath of God* explores the effect that the extreme situation of the jungle, combined with desires for wealth and power, has on various characters in the movie. As the title character, the main focus is, of course, Aguirre. At the start of the trip down the Amazon, he still has the wits to proclaim that from that starting point their trip will be downhill. By the end he has become consumed by his madness so that he cannot recognize that his daughter is dead and the expedition defeated. Other characters also succumb to madness. Pizarro's right hand man reflects the mental deterioration enveloping the trip as he repeatedly mumbles "la, la, la," a chant-like mantra generally indicating ineffectuality or even madness. The monk Gaspar, whose main focus should be teaching God's word, is obsessed with the gold of El Dorado. Herzog also uses madness of characters to add humor to the film. As they are pierced by arrows, characters make jokes about long arrows coming into fashion or of arrows not being real.

Brother Gaspar de Carvajal, although seemingly a minor character in the story, has a major role in the film's text. Carvajal is not only the source through which we learn the story of the fate of the expedition, he is the voice of Western Europe in South America, representing the ostensible reason Spain has come to the New World. He espouses the official Spanish program that the conquistadors have come to convert the indigenous peoples to Christianity. Carvajal's actions, however, expose the hypocrisy of the church's role in the expedition. He admits to Flores, Ursua's wife, who has asked him to intervene on her husband's behalf, that the church has always been on the side of the strong, not necessarily the deserving. Moreover, he is more willing to shoot the Indians for not immediately converting to Christianity than he is in attempting to teach them God's word.

Other characters likewise reflect and mirror themes of madness and exploitation, regardless of how minor their roles might be. Aguirre's chief opponent, Don Pedro de Ursua, is a decent leader whose main concern is for the safety of his men. He fails to understand how dangerous Aguirre is to him. Aguirre exploits his naiveté to carry out his treason. The two women, Ursua's wife Flores and Aguirre's daughter Inez, represent the incursion of western civilization into the New World. As they are seated in sedan chairs and dressed in Spanish finery, both seem distinctly out of place in the jungle. At the same time, their purity suggests the purity of the New World that is being defiled by Aguirre and the conquistadors. Don Fernando de Guzman, the highest-ranking nobleman on the expedition, is an arrogant, corpulent, intellectual lightweight. Aguirre easily manipulates him by playing to his ego and eliminates him when his actions endanger the plans for mutiny. The Indians with speaking roles mouth platitudes about the native culture that they are losing, and Aguirre's henchman represents the strongman's deranged sidekick, willing to do all of his boss's messy work.

The setting for *Aguirre, the Wrath of God* reinforces the film's emphasis on madness and not being in control of one's situation. Herzog sets his film in the Peruvian Andes and Amazon jungle, revealing an environment that is both beautiful and frightening. Cinematographer Thomas Mauch captures the mystery of the fog-shrouded mountains but also the dangers in the steep grade of the decline. Likewise he reveals the lushness of the jungles enclosing the river on either side, suggesting that there is no avenue of escape. The Andes and Amazon play a significant role in the film's ultimate meaning. Herzog believes that he has seen things others have not and that it is his mission to show others his visions through his films. In *Aguirre, the Wrath of God* he films the Amazon jungle as an impenetrable wall of lush green that swallows up the blues, reds, and yellows of the conquistadors. The thick growth of trees and bushes provides the Indians with refuge and cover to the same degree

An insane Aguirre (Klaus Kinski) holds the body of his dead daughter (Cecilia Rivera) as he proclaims he will found a dynasty in El Dorado.

that it proves an insurmountable obstacle to the Spaniards. The river meanwhile rushes forward or meanders, trapping the Spaniards in its fast waters or holding them prisoner in its languid pools, all the while exposing them to the Indians as targets to be killed with poison darts. The sounds of the jungle likewise enter into the setting as threat. The conquistadors often don't know if the sounds they hear are the sounds of birds or of natives announcing the approach of the Spaniards to other tribes. In spite of the danger the jungle and river pose for the Spaniards, the environment provides a reminder of the magnificent beauty of the New World. From the mist-shrouded mountaintop where the film begins to the quiet river where it ends, the film shows off the Amazon River and its basin as much as it champions any of its characters.

Visuals continuously reflect the tale of madness and exploitation being told by the narrative voice and dialog. In turn music and sound effects underscore the insanity and loss of control. As the film opens, the camera shoots from a distance as the conquistadors come down a fog-enshrouded mountain. They are like gods descending from above, a visual homage to the opening sequence of Leni Riefenstahl's *Triumph of the Will*, which shows Hitler descending through clouds as he arrives in Nuremberg. The party serpentines down the mountain, the circular motion suggesting the ordeal ahead and also its futility. The circular imagery introduced at the beginning is mirrored throughout the film by objects and the environment, which reinforce the sense that the expedition will fail. This feeling of going nowhere is underscored by the film's non-diegetic background music (the off-screen music that is not a part of the world depicted on screen), mostly a minimalist electronic score that repeats its motifs as the visuals repeat the circular motion. The diegetic music provided by Peruvian Pipes mirrors the circularity of the sound of the off-screen music.

The visual and musical imagery continues to be dominated by circular and downward movement. Once descended from the mountains, the party gets into rafts which float swiftly downstream in the rushing currents of the Amazon. One of their boats is lost to a whirlpool. Others are swamped by the rising waters. But as the Amazon basin is reached, the river slows and the large raft the conquistadors have built drifts aimlessly. Whether in the early scenes on the rushing river or in later ones on the sluggish waters, the boat is caught between the dense foliage of the trees on shore. Moreover the sounds of birds and natives and the suggestion of hidden Indians on shore add to the feeling that the Spaniards are trapped in the Amazon jungle. As the movie ends, the camera pulls up and away, showing Aguirre holding a monkey and standing in the middle of a raft going in circles. Even without his monologue, one understands that he is mad and that the expedition has failed.

The history of Pizarro's party of conquistadors offered Herzog the story, environment, and eccentric characters he preferred in order to explore his theme of madness. But the film is more than a story of madness. By basing his story loosely on Conrad's *Heart of Darkness* he turns the tale of a madman into a statement on exploitation of the weak by the powerful; in short *Aguirre, the Wrath of God* becomes a film about colonialism, cataloging a list of transgressions by colonial powers against the inhabitants of the New World. These include enslavement, conversion, and even killing. Herzog uses members of actual tribes to play roles of Indians kidnapped from their homes to serve the Spaniards on the expedition. In one extended sequence he has an Indian prince, who has been kidnapped from his home, lament that he is forced to serve where once he was served. In another episode, the party forces a black slave to undress and run ahead of them through the jungle, believing his blackness will frighten the Indians. Finally, in another sequence, the party invites two natives on board their raft but then shoots them when the pair does not immediately accept the word of God.

Trappings of colonization appear from the beginning of the film. The Europeans stride down the mountain dressed in their Spanish glory. The women, carried in sedan chairs, are immaculate in beautiful European dress. The men wear armor and carry weapons more suited to fighting in Europe than here in the jungle. But their superiority nonetheless is apparent. Aguirre's crazed monologues also allude to colonization. He stresses the fact that more Europeans will come after them if they do not find El Dorado and that they will succeed in conquering the continent. But as the film continues, the sedan chairs become useless, the cannons fall down the mountain and are destroyed, the horse they have brought is pushed off their raft, the women shed the heavy outer layers of their cloaks, and the veneer of European mores vanishes. Aguirre's descent into madness likewise suggests that the Old World conquerors may not be successful after all. In the end, it will be the native culture that subsumes the European, and colonization will be defeated. (RCR)

QUESTIONS

1. Describe the characterization of the indigenous inhabitants of the New World.

2. Locate as many circular images in the film as you can.

3. Locate and describe the humorous elements of the film. Why do you think Herzog has included these?

4. Identify those elements of the film that characterize Spanish colonization as negative.

RELATED FILMS

Stroszek (1977). Herzog studies what happens when a young German immigrant in Wisconsin with minimal skills in English gets into economic difficulties because of easy credit.

Woyzeck (1979). Based on a nineteenth century play by Georg Büchner, the film gives Klaus Kinski, the star of many Herzog films, an opportunity to explore the limits of insanity.

Nosferatu (1979). Herzog remade the 1922 *Nosferatu* as an homage to F. W. Murnau, one of the leading directors of Germany's silent film era.

Mein liebster Feind - Klaus Kinski (*My Best Fiend - Klaus Kinski* 1999). This documentary of the love/hate relationship between Kinski and Herzog documents the eccentric behavior, bordering on madness, of both men.

Apocalypse Now (Francis Ford Coppola 1979). As Herzog in *Aguirre, the Wrath of God*, Coppola finds in Conrad's *Heart of Darkness* the perfect metaphor for conquest, war and madness.

INFORMATION

Aguirre, the Wrath of God (1972), DVD, in German with English subtitles, color, 100 minutes, Anchor Bay Entertainment, released 2000.

Franklin, James. *New German Cinema: From Oberhausen to Hamburg.* Boston: Twayne Publishers, 1983.

Galster, Ingrid: *Aguirre oder die Willkür der Nachwelt : die Rebellion des baskischen Konquistadors Lope de Aguirre in Historiographie und Geschichtsfiktion* (1561 - 1992). Frankfurt am Main: Vervuert, 1996.

Peucker, Brigitte. "Werner Herzog: In Quest of the Sublime." In *New German Filmmakers: From Oberhausen through the 1970s*, edited by Klaus Phillips, 168-194. New York: Frederick Unger Publishing Co., 1984.

Sandford, John. *The New German Cinema.* London: Oswald Wolff Ltd., 1980.

CHAPTER 14

Die Legende von Paul und Paula

(*The Legend of Paul and Paula***, Heiner Carow 1973)**

Paul (Winfried Glatzeder) displays the picture of his final triumph over Paula (Angelika Domröse). The black and white photo within the old fashioned oval frame in this otherwise contemporary color film recalls the emphasis placed on family and tradition during one of the film's magical love scenes.

CREDITS

Director	Heiner Carow
Screenplay	Ulrich Plenzdorf
Director of Photography	Jürgen Brauer
Music	Peter Gotthardt
Producer	Erich Albrecht
Production Company	DEFA/Berlin
Length	106 minutes; color

Principal Cast

Angelica Domröse (Paula); Winfried Glatzeder (Paul), Fred Delmare (Herr Saft, Paula's suitor), Heidemarie Wenzel (Paul's wife).

THE STORY

Die Legende von Paul und Paula (*The Legend of Paul and Paula*) directed by Heiner Carow, became the most popular film in the GDR ever produced by DEFA. The film, whose screenplay was written by the successful GDR novelist Ulrich Plenzdorf, starred Winfried Glatzeder as Paul and Angelica Domröse as Paula. It portrays everyday life in East Berlin in a love story between a passionate single mother and a complacent married bureaucrat. The movie shows an unusually private story for the GDR, where apolitical love stories caused concern among the authorities. Paul, a student, meets a beautiful woman ("die Schöne"), the daughter of a carnival entertainer, and marries her because she admires his academic background and his possibilities for career advancement.

Paul also runs into Paula at the same carnival, where Paula, a single mother, falls in love with a carousel worker and has yet another child. Paula longs for a more stable life to escape her job as a supermarket worker. Herr Saft, an elderly respectable tire salesman, offers this opportunity, yet Paula isn't passionate about Saft at all. While Paul completes his mandatory military service of three years, his wife, whose only redeeming quality seems to be stunning beauty, has an affair with her dance instructor.

The Legend of Paul and Paula very much depends on coincidence, suggesting that Paul and Paula are destined for each other in this romantic representation of love. More than a year after their first encounter at the carnival, Paul and Paula meet again in a disco where Paul wants to escape from his bourgeois conventional family life and Paula wants to live it up one more time before she finally will settle down with Saft in his *dacha*. By the end of the evening they are passionately in love. Paula decides to change her life, while Paul believes he cannot have a divorce; as a respectable citizen of the GDR establishment, "you can't always do what you want to do, at least up to now that's been the case, especially at the expense of others." ("Keiner kann nur immer das machen, was er will, vorläufig ist das so. Bloß nicht auf Kosten anderer.").

After Paula's son is killed in a car accident, she feels guilty because Paul and their love diverted her attention. She will no longer see Paul, although he now realizes the mistake he made in letting her go earlier, and decides to camp outside her apartment until she changes her mind. The novel on which the film is based, *The Legend of Happiness without End*, speaks of an entire summer of Paul's camping out in the apartment complex. Only with Paul's perseverance are the two of them finally able to fulfill their destiny, when Paul borrows an ax to break into Paula's apartment and kidnaps her. The neighbors applaud upon witnessing this ultimately romantic scene.

But this fairy tale ending continues to a less than happy conclusion. Paula is warned by her gynecologist not to have any more children. Ignoring his warning, she decides to have a child with Paul. Paula's doctor anticipates for the viewers the film's unsatisfactory conclusion when he remarks, "The ideal and reality can never merge, there will always be something left over, a residue." ("Ideal und Wirklichkeit gehen nie übereinander. Ein Rest bleibt immer.") Paula dies at the end of the film.

Paula (Angelika Domröse) applauds between movements at a concert of classical music, much to Paul's (Winfried Glatzeder) dismay.

BACKGROUND

The ensuing calm that resulted from the restrictions after the building of the Berlin Wall in 1961 led to a new GDR confidence among the Communists that they would finally be able to build socialism without interference from the West, which resulted in a new official literature. 1961 could be seen as the beginning of the GDR as an independent state, with its own identity. After 1961 a new generation of writers took over, eager to help with building socialism and thus taking up true GDR topics for the first time, as in the novels of Hermann Kant (*Die Aula*), Karl-Heinz Jakobs (*Beschreibung eines Sommers*), Erwin Strittmatter (*Ole Bienkopp*), and Erik Neutsch (*Spur der Steine*). These new writers were interested in overcoming the thousands of contradictions in the socialist system of the GDR, but they did not want to attack the fundamental flaws in their society. This short period of relative peace and prosperity lasted until the end of the Ulbricht period in 1971 when GDR literature had attained a new self-confidence that made it attractive to western readers.

Confident of the social progress made in the nineteen-sixties reflected in the new GDR national literature, Honecker began further liberalization and permitted free expression of different opinions, as in one of the most popular GDR texts, Plenzdorf's *Die neuen Leiden des jungen W*, (*The New Sufferings of the Young W*. 1972). The year *The Legend of Paul and Paula* was produced was 1973, after the transition of power from Walter Ulrich to Erich Honecker. With Honecker's declaration that no cultural restrictions would be enforced if the artist appeared to be on firm socialist ground, East Germans believed their time for cultural liberalization had begun. *The Legend of Paul and Paula* is a result of this policy change, a story that focuses on love and family, not on political issues.

Ulrich Plenzdorf was the author of the book and also the film script to *The Legend of Paul and Paula*. Plenzdorf was the main advocate for the cultural freedom granted by the Honecker government. Plenzdorf was born October 26, 1934 in Berlin. His father was an active member of the Communist Party and a photographer for the *Arbeiter-Illustrierte Zeitung*. Plenzdorf attended a school alternative to the state-run school system, then studied philosophy in Leipzig. From 1955-58 he worked as a stagehand at the DEFA studios. After completing military service he studied screenplay writing at the Film Academy in Bablesberg, then began working as a scriptwriter in 1964. Plenzdorf became one of the best-known GDR writers, recognized for his youthful, biting criticism in screenplays, novels, and short stories.

The movie music sound track is produced by the Puhdys, the legendary GDR band which in thirty years produced more than twenty LPs and CDs and sold more than eighteen million of them in twenty countries of the world. Twelve times they were chosen the most popular band of the GDR. They played concerts in about twenty countries, among them Poland, Czechoslovakia, the Soviet Union and West Germany, where they played to a full house at the commercial Berlin open air venue Waldbühne. The Puhdys participated in five DEFA and TV productions, among them the cult film *The Legend of Paul and Paula*, which includes two of their most popular hits.

EVALUATION

The Legend of Paul and Paula centers on Paula. She is a messenger from a past believed long gone but which has come back to haunt modern sanitized GDR, represented by Paul. In this light *The Legend of Paul and Paula* must be seen as a snapshot of the GDR in the early nineteen-seventies, an era that represents an important turning point in the country's history. Plenzdorf wanted to shake his fellow-citizens' and the governing clique's conscience not to fall into a regulated complacency. In this vein, Paula's outrageous behavior can be seen as shock therapy, waking the establishment up to problems in the country.

But Paula's protest is not merely a protest against the establishment; it is also a desire for unconditional fulfillment of her own interests. Paula's love must be seen as a protest against the established order of politics and science, since her gynecologist warns her against having another child. Since science was the ultimate authority for the Communists, Paula's romantic love must also be seen as a protest against the established order of the party. In that sense Paula is subversive or anarchist. As the motor of the story, her desire kindles Paul's passion. He is much more rational and bourgeois, a GDR "Spießer" (a narrow-minded bourgeois), vs. Paula's free spirit. Paula's fight for Paul is a fight to introduce not only romantic ideas but also introduce the notion to GDR society that although socialism has come to a standstill, it can still reinvent itself.

One of the most touching moments in the movie comes when Paula attends her first classical music concert with Paul. Just as Paul's pedantry shows him trying to educate his wife, he also wants to educate Paula to all that is good, all that he learned to appreciate through education, and in Paul's mind, Beethoven is part of a good education. Paula, reluctant at first, agrees to go to the open-air concert with Paul and, in her naiveté, applauds after the first movement, to the utter embarrassment of the middle-class Paul. The audience at the concert, however, understands Paula's inexperience and happily claps along. While the viewer hears the music playing, the camera focuses on Paula's face as she is transformed from the initial reluctant listener to an intense and passionate appreciator of music. While tears are flowing down her cheeks she looks at Paul, whose love she only now is able to understand with the help of this music. This scene, beautifully acted by Angelika Domröse, blends Paul's traditional approach to life with Paula's spontaneous appreciation of creativity and shows how state limitations can lead to something new.

The director Heiner Carow emphasizes Paula's anarchism by enclosing her more bizarre moments in a fantasy world, much like the magic realism of Latin American fiction. Paula's daydreams are treated as real. For example, when she and Paul are making love, the bed changes into a floating barge and her relatives appear applauding their affair. This dream symbolism occurs also in images of the surrounding city, where old buildings are constantly torn down while new ones go up. The GDR viewed itself as the legitimate heir to German history, just as Paula's ancestors applaud her and her lifestyle as a continuation of the family's traditions. The movie's symbolism of the GDR as constantly rebuilding itself is further evident in the contrast between the stable Paul's modern slick apartment in a GDR *Plattenbau* (a modern high rise), which was seen as the way of the future, and the eccentric Paula's apartment in a soon to be torn down building across from Paul's place.

Audiences in the GDR recognized Paula's role as a thorn in the side of modernizing East Germany; her free-spirited nature, almost an aberration in East Germany in 1973, made *The Legend of Paul and Paula* the biggest success in GDR film history. Modern audiences in Germany and the U.S. might have a problem with its seventies style, a blend between romantic comedy and art film. Today's audiences also will find the bellicose style of communicating unattractive – it seems unbelievable that people would have treated each other with such an intense degree of nastiness in their daily lives, but this is meant to be understood as a result of continuous irritation in everyday life. (RZ)

Questions

1. What are some examples of magic realism in the movie? How do they further the audience's understanding of Paul and Paula's relationship and their lives?

2. How does the director Heiner Carow use music throughout the film?

3. Discuss Paula's death as symbolic of the political and social situation in East Germany.

Related Films

Sonnenallee (Leander Haußmann 1999). The title refers to a street in Berlin that begins in West Berlin and ends in East Berlin. Playing at about the time *The Legend of Paul and Paula* was made, *Sonnenallee* pays homage to Heiner Carow's films through characterizations and casting.

Der Traum vom Elch (*The Dream of the Elk*, Siegfried Kühn 1985). This melodrama looks at the limited choices for love of two women in East German society.

Bürgschaft für ein Jahr (*On Probation*, Herrmann Zschoche 1981). This is one of many films made in the seventies and eighties depicting the problems of single mothers in East Germany.

INFORMATION

The Legend of Paul and Paula (1974) DVD, in German w/subtitles, color, 105 minutes, First Run Features, released 2002.

Das war die DDR (*That Was the GDR*, Gitta Nickel and others). This compilation film using newsreels and interviews to reconstruct the history of the GDR offers a good introduction to East Germany.

Die Legende von Paul und Paula. Based on the novel by Ulrich Plenzdorf *Legende vom Glück ohne Ende*. Frankfurt a/M: Suhrkamp, 1981.

Hake, Sabine. *German National Cinema*. London: Routledge, 2001.

Naughton, Leonie. *That Was the Wild East: Film, Culture, Unification, and the "New" Germany*. Ann Arbor: The U of Michigan P, 2002.

CHAPTER 15

Angst essen Seele auf

(*Ali: Fear Eats the Soul*, **Rainer Werner Fassbinder 1974**)

Emmi (Brigitte Mira) and Ali (El Hedi ben Salem) reprise their dance to the "Black Gypsy" and reconcile before Ali's collapse.

CREDITS

Director ....Rainer Werner Fassbinder
Screenplay ....Rainer Werner Fassbinder
Director of Photography ....Jürgen Jürges
Music...Rainer Werner Fassbinder
Producer ....R. W. Fassbinder
Production Company .... Tango Films
Length...93 minutes; color

Principal Cast

Brigitte Mira (Emmi), El Hedi ben Salem (Ali), Barbara Valentin (Barbara), Irm Hermann (Krista), Elma Karlowa (Mrs. Kargus), Gusti Kreissl (Paula), Lilo Pempeit (Mrs. Munchmeyer), Hark Bohm (Doctor), R. W. Fassbinder (Eugen)

THE STORY

As *Angst essen Seele auf* (*Ali: Fear Eats the Soul* 1974) opens, Emmi, a cleaning lady in her mid-fifties, walks into a bar frequented by immigrant workers and meets Ali, a Moroccan in his late thirties. They begin an affair which leads to marriage and to Emmi's abandonment by family, neighbors, and co-workers. The high point in their relationship to each other is contrasted with the low point in their relationship to others. Finally, unable to cope with the hateful behavior of the people with whom they have contact, they go on holiday, hoping people at home will get over their initial objections to the relationship. When they return, family, neighbors, and co-workers have indeed decided to renew their relationship with Emmi and to accept her choice of husband. Their decision is based more on their need for Emmi's help than on any change in attitudes toward immigrants. Just as before the holiday her closeness to Ali was contrasted with her distance from others, so now her reestablishment of friendly relations with others is contrasted with the disintegration of her relationship with Ali. At the moment when she and Ali seem to have reconciled their differences, he collapses from an ulcerated stomach attack and the film closes with Emmi promising to nurse him back to health.

BACKGROUND

Fassbinder's films play on multiple historical levels. They recreate not only the period in which they are set and the time in which they are being created, but they also reflect Germany's history, in particular its Nazi past. To be fully understood, they must be seen within a framework that includes German radical politics contemporary to the filming of the movie, reaction or overreaction of the German government and its citizens to protest, a conservative media conglomerate headed by Axel Springer that encourages overreaction to events, and the changing profile of the German ethnic population

Germany's changing ethnic profile can be illustrated with some statistics. The country's present population of 80 million includes over 7 million non-ethnic Germans. Many of the non-ethnic Germans immigrated to Germany between 1955 and 1973, the years when an official policy of recruiting guest workers to fill an employment gap was in effect. More have come since 1973, as relatives of the immigrants already in Germany. In its early years, the program attracted workers from Italy, Greece and Yugoslavia. But in 1961 the majority of workers were coming from Turkey and other Muslim countries, including Morocco. In 1973, the period in which *Ali: Fear Eats the Soul* takes place, there were over three million foreign workers in the Federal Republic of Germany (West Germany), about 5 percent of the population, estimated at about 60 million. In *Ali: Fear Eats the Soul* Fassbinder focuses primarily on discrimination against Moroccans, but he also includes a scene in which an immigrant from Herzegovina, then a region in Yugoslavia, is excluded from the German majority. In *Katzelmacher*, one of Fassbinder's first films, the object of German racial hatred was a Greek worker.

Although racial prejudice creates the film's dynamic tension, it does so in tandem with Fassbinder's preoccupation with history and radical politics. Beginning in 1968 West Germany experienced student and radical protests that had escalated by 1977 to terrorist violence. In the early years of protest, students demonstrated for university reform, against American involvement in Viet Nam, and against the conservative policies of the Springer Publishing House. Such protests, however, form merely the background of a more deeply located anti-establishment and anti-government mood represented by the radical and eventual terrorist activities of the Baader-Meinhof group, later to become the Red Army Faction. Popular slogans in those years such as "wer zweimal mit derselben (demselben) pennt, gehört schon zum Establishment" ("he who sleeps twice with the same person belongs to the establishment") and "alle Macht den Rätern" ("all power to the Soviet") hid the dangerous undercurrents flowing through German youth culture. The government's immediate reaction to protest was ambivalent. On the one hand, it restricted personal freedoms in the name of protecting the republic form of government that Germany had enjoyed since the end of the Second World War. On the other hand, the government moderated its measures because of memories of the Second World War and also because of the vocal and surprisingly large support radical politics had among Germans, between 10 and 15 percent. Such moderating tendencies are most evident in the initial response of the police to the attack on the Israeli Olympic team by Palestinian terrorists, a response which seemed to be more low key than the situation required. In *Ali: Fear Eats the Soul*, this liberalized attitude turns up in Fassbinder's ironic characterization of the two Munich police officers.

Seldom has the setting of a film been as important as Fassbinder's choice of Munich for *Ali: Fear Eats the Soul*. On the surface it would seem that the film could have been set in any German city with a large immigrant worker population, and for many viewers the choice of Munich might have little obvious impact as the city is difficult to recognize in the movie. Yet, no other city would have suggested the weight of Germany's history and the impact of that history on the present as much as Munich, except of course Berlin. But the choice of Berlin would have taken the film into a geo-political direction, looking outward, as there was still a divided Germany in 1973. Fassbinder, even though concerned with historical events that had worldwide impact, prefers to focus his films inward. In *Ali: Fear Eats the Soul*, he uses Munich, the city of Hitler's beerhall putsch in 1924 and of the Palestinian attack on the 1972 Olympics, to focus on immigrant workers in contemporary West Germany. Bavarian conservatism makes the city ideal for portraying the constant struggle between past and present, at least in the minds and films of the New German Cinema, of which Fassbinder came to be the body, intellect, and soul.

EVALUATION

As with many of Fassbinder's films, *Ali: Fear Eats the Soul* is a perfect blend of cinematic form and thematic content. Indeed, the film's text and characterizations come as much from Fassbinder's use of camera, mise-en-scène, and historical references as they do from dialog and situation. Moreover, framing, movement, and staging tell us who the characters are, how they feel, and what motivates them. Given the simplicity of the story told in the screenplay, it is surprising how complex a narrative Fassbinder has crafted.

In the opening sequence Emmi, a widow in her mid to late fifties, enters a bar frequented by immigrant workers, setting up the film's premise of outsider.

Although she is German and should be in a position of power, the camera captures her discomfort in this environment. Emmi is separated from the guest workers in the bar in a shot that exaggerates the distance between the individual and the group. The camera lingers longer than is customary for an establishing shot, focusing in turn on Emmi at a table and then the immigrant workers standing statically at the bar. The duration emphasizes her misgivings at having entered the bar and their mistrust of the outsider.

In an inspired twist of subversive irony, Fassbinder has made the German the outsider and the immigrants the majority. Fassbinder prevents reading his irony as a conservative's complaint of being a stranger in one's own land by making Emmi an outsider among Germans as well. She hardly ever sees her children. She was a member of the Nazi party and yet is free of prejudice as evidenced by her marriage to a Pole. Moreover, she came into the bar because the strange music attracted her, evidence of an accepting and inclusive outlook. Like Ali, the true foreigner in the film, she is a positive character. She redeems whatever weakness her temporary rejection of Ali's Moroccan culture reveals with her understanding and acceptance of his infidelity and her determination to support him through his illness.

Emmi's status as outsider extends to the German community as well, at least for the first half of the movie. In a dialog sequence between Emmi and her co-workers about the habits of foreign workers, Fassbinder uses a series of edits that create spatial isolation for Emmi that in reality does not exist as she is sitting near her colleagues. In fact a different camera angle could have emphasized their proximity. Similarly when Emmi and Ali are in a restaurant and again later at an open-air café, camera placement shows the two of them isolated from the Germans who are occupying the same area, within speaking distance. Additionally, once Emmi is reintegrated into the majority (German) group, the camera comments unfavorably on her willingness to see foreign culture merely as an exotic object, or worse, to exclude it altogether. Thus in a reprise of the scene in which Emmi eats lunch at work, the camera now shows a young woman from Herzegovina behind the slats of a staircase, separated from the majority Germans. In a sense even as Emmi integrates into the German community she remains an outsider, for by this time viewer sympathies are with Ali. Emmi, who voices an objection to cous cous, a traditional Mideastern dish, with the comment "this is Germany," is outside the view the film projects.

When Emmi voices her objection to cous cous, she flirts with succumbing to the prejudices of her children, neighbors, and co-workers. Played mostly by Fassbinder's ensemble troupe, they represent the clichés of the lower middle class. For example Emmi's daughter and son-in-law (Irm Hermann and Fassbinder) are constantly quarreling, intentionally hurting one another with verbal barbs. The son-in-law further represents the German worker who feels displaced by the influx of immigrant workers and resents especially their work ethic that gets them promoted ahead of Germans into supervisory roles. The grocer, played by Walter Sedlmayr, embodies stereotypical prejudicial reluctance to believe foreigners can communicate in German. Indeed, all of Emmi's family, friends, and neighbors are bigoted, but they are also pragmatic enough to accept Ali when their self-interest requires they do so. The only Germans in Emmi's sphere who display no prejudice against foreigners are the police and Emmi's landlord, an ironic twist for Fassbinder, whose movies generally reserve harsh criticism for authority and the wealthy.

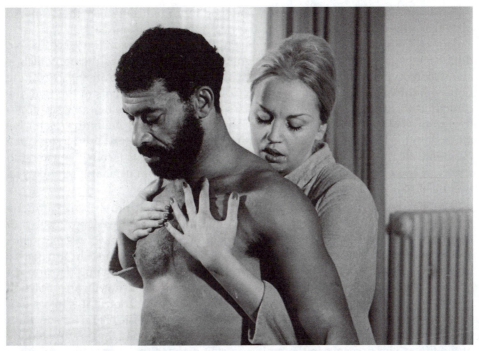

Ali (El Hedi ben Salem) seeks cous cous and comfort from Barbara the bar owner (Barbara Valentin) after he and Emmi quarrel.

As important as Emmi and her cohorts are to the film's criticism of racial prejudice, Fassbinder's true focus is Ali (El Hedi ben Salem), whose physical presence dominates the movie. Camera, music, and staging merge the political and personal texts of the film to become not only Fassbinder's homage to El Hedi Ben Salem's body but also a commentary on making the other into an object to be exploited for its usefulness and displayed for its beauty. Ali combines traits that are both stereotypical and counter the stereotype of the German guest worker: he endures poor housing, poor health, and discrimination; he embodies animal magnetism, muscular body, heavy accent, poor grammar, and existential outlook; and he exposes the irrationality of Germans' prejudices about the personal hygiene, sexual appetite, and motivation for working of the guest workers. Finally, Ali's personal philosophy of shrugging off offenses against his person — he uses the phrase "kif, kif" to show he is not bothered — works only on the surface. His ulcerated condition belies the calm demeanor he presents to the world.

Ali is one of the most positive characters Fassbinder ever created, perhaps because the actor playing the part was his lover, and perhaps because he based the character very loosely on Rock Hudson's Ron Kirby (but also Jane Wyman's Carrie Scott) in Douglas Sirk's *All That Heaven Allows*, one of Fassbinder's favorite movies. Like Ron Kirby, Ali is philosophical, attentive, and respectful of others. Unlike Ron, he has vices, alcohol and gambling, but these result from personal disillusionment as his marriage dissolves rather than from moral weakness. Also unlike Ron, he is unfaithful. His infidelity also stems from his disillusionment when Emmi seems to reject him and his culture. Ali is also like Carrie Scott in that he is passive and unsure of his worth. These traits endear Ali to the viewer, an infrequent reaction to a Fassbinder character.

From the opening sequence and continuing throughout the film Ali dominates the screen. In the bar at the beginning of the movie "Du schwarze Zigeuner" (Black Gypsy), a tune popular in the fifties, plays on the juke box. No doubt the song is meant as an ironic comment on the movie's theme, which is about stereotyping the other. Yet the film also turns Ali into the other by equating him with the exotic black male of the lyrics. At various moments in the film, the camera captures him in the shower, gazes at his physique as he makes muscles for Emmi's colleagues, and peeps at him from a distance as he undresses for his affair with the barmaid (Barbara Valentin). Moreover it captures him in negative moments also, as for example when he repeatedly slaps his face while gazing in a mirror, when he doubles over on the dance floor from an ulcer attack, and as he lies unconscious in bed as Emmi talks with the doctor.

That the film is indeed about Ali and not just workers' problems in Germany is clear from the way Fassbinder treats Ali's cohorts. Required for purposes of the plot, Ali's circle of friends and workers are for the most part unremarkable, and when they do project themselves into the movie, they do so in a negative rather than positive way. The women in the bar, for example, appear jealous of Emmi's relationship with Ali, which seems an irrational if not bizarre reaction given Emmi's age. Only the bar owner (Barbara Valentin) contributes in a major way to the film's text. But in this case it is Valentin and not the character she plays who makes the contribution. For Barbara Valentin is an icon of the bosomy blonde of the fifties. Her presence in the movie pays homage to the very movies the New German Cinema was reacting against, but they would also be the movies with which Fassbinder grew up. In addition, by casting a star from the fifties Fassbinder gives the film an arc from the Nazi period to the present time, thus showing an uninterrupted thread running from the Nazi past through the Adenauer years to the present of the film. Fassbinder has emphasized this relationship in many of his films, most notably *Der Händler der Vierjahreszeiten* (*The Merchant of Four Seasons* 1972) and *Die Ehe der Maria Braun* (*The Marriage of Maria Braun* 1979).

The last scene in particular shows the degree to which Fassbinder uses cinema technique to create the text. In this scene Emmi and the doctor converse about the hopelessness of Ali's condition, as Ali lies in the background in the last bed of the ward. Emmi wants to be optimistic; the doctor tells her that although Ali may recover, he will be back within the year, continuing to suffer ulcers, a stress-induced condition that befalls, he tells her, many guest workers. Emmi's refusal to accept the doctor's pessimistic prognosis is placed into question as the doctor leaves and the camera zooms in on a mirror reflection as Emmi goes to Ali's bedside. The reflected or virtual world they are in may have a happy Hollywood end. The last scene of its model, *All That Heaven Allows*, frames a worried Carrie at the injured Ron's bedside, behind them a large picture window opening onto a blue sky and snow covered landscape into which a deer wanders. In *Ali: Fear Eats the Soul*, when the camera cuts from the virtual image to the actual one, we see Emmi at Ali's bedside, behind them a small closed window out of which one sees the gray German sky, suggesting there is little reason for hope. To underscore the pessimism, the sweet sadness connoted by a melodic leitmotif that accompanies more intimate moments of the film reminds us of the motto with which the film began, "Happiness is not always fun." (RCR)

QUESTIONS

1. Fassbinder made his movie to address the prejudice many Germans had against guest workers at the time the film was made. Keeping this in mind, analyze the opening five minutes of the film (up to the time Ali and Emmi begin dancing), discussing in particular the prejudices being addressed in this scene.

2. The movie is divided into two parts: before the marriage and after. Describe how relationships between the characters (between Emmi and Ali, but also between these two and the others) change from the first part to the second.

3. Analyze the mise-en-scène (the way Fassbinder places objects and characters in the frame) in the restaurant, when Ali and Emmi are having their wedding meal.

4. Identify the instances where Fassbinder turns individuals into the object of someone's stare. Why do you think he does this? Give some examples of when this occurs.

5. Do you find the end of the film optimistic or pessimistic? Be able to defend your answer with filmic evidence.

RELATED FILMS

Katzelmacher (1969). Through static tableaux, Fassbinder studies the boredom and aimlessness of Germans in their twenties and their prejudices toward guest workers.

Der Amerikanische Soldat (*The American Soldier* 1970). In this film, Fassbinder first introduces the story of an older woman married to a Moroccan that became the basis for *Ali: Fear Eats the Soul.*

Deutschland im Herbst (*Germany in Autumn* 1977). The film, which Fassbinder made with a number of other directors, serves as New German Cinema's response to the government's reaction to political radicalism.

Der Händler der Vierjahreszeiten (*The Merchant of Four Seasons* 1972). As he does in *The Marriage of Maria Braun* and to a lesser extent in *Ali:Fear Eats the Soul*, in this film Fassbinder conflates history, showing the relationship between Germany in the Third Reich, in the fifties, and in the seventies, the time the films are being made.

Die Ehe der Maria Braun (*The Marriage of Maria Braun* 1979). The film represents Fassbinder's most critically and commercially successful film.

All That Heaven Allows (Douglas Sirk 1954). German director Detlev Sierck emigrated to Hollywood and turned out a series of melodramatic movies in the fifties, which had an influence on Fassbinder's style. This film served as the model for *Ali: Fear Eats the Soul.*

Far from Heaven (Todd Haynes 2002). Todd Haynes remade the story of a May-December romance combining elements of Sirk's and Fassbinder's films.

INFORMATION

Ali: Fear Eats the Soul (1974), DVD, in German with English subtitles, color, 93 minutes, Criterion Collection, released 2003.

Elsaesser, Thomas: *Fassbinder's Germany: History, Identity, Subject*. Amsterdam: Amsterdam UP, 1996

Franklin, James. *New German Cinema*. Boston: Twayne Publishers, 1983.

Haunschild, Jessica: *The Perception of Foreign Films by American College Students: Two Films of Rainer Werner Fassbinder*. Stuttgart: Ibidem, 1997.

Hayman, Ronald. *Fassbinder: Film Maker*. London: Weidenfeld and Nicolson, 1984.

Jansen, Peter W. and Wolfram Schütte, eds. *Rainer Werner Fassbinder*. Munich: Carl Hanser Verlag, 1979.

Rayns, Tony, ed. *Fassbinder*. London: BFI, 1976.

Reimer, Robert C. "A Comparison of Douglas Sirk's *All That Heaven Allows* and R. W. Fassbinder's *Ali: Fear Eats the Soul*: or How Hollywood's New England Dropouts Became Germany's Marginalized Other." *Literature/Film Quarterly*. (Vol. 24, No. 3, 1996), 282-287.

CHAPTER 16

Die verlorene Ehre der Katharina Blum

(*The Lost Honor of Katharina Blum*, Volker Schlöndorff, Margarethe von Trotta 1975)

Katharina (Angelika Winkler) meets Ludwig (Jürgen Prochnow) at the party.

CREDITS

Director	Volker Schloendorff, Margarethe von Trotta
Screenplay	Volker Schlöndorff, Margarethe von Trotta
Director of Photography	Jost Vacano
Music	Hans Werner Henze
Producers	Willi Benninger, Eberhard Junkersdorf
Production Companies	Bioskop, Paramount-Orion Filmproduktion, Westdeutscher Rundfunk
Length	106 minutes; color

Principal Cast

Inspector Beizmenne (Mario Adorf), Architect Blorna (Heinz Bennent), Werner Tötges (Dieter Laser), Angela Winkler (Katharina Blum), Jürgen Prochnow (Ludwig Götten).

THE STORY

The story of Schlöndorff's and von Trotta's movie *Die verlorene Ehre der Katharina Blum* (*The Lost Honor of Katharina Blum* 1975) has become a timely subject again. Americans are discovering that Germany also had a terrorist problem with the Marxist Baader-Meinhof group's assassinations of prominent politicians. Since Heinrich Böll, the author who wrote the story that the film is based on, can speak from experience – he had been accused of being a sympathizer as well – the movie has a distinct air of authenticity. It is not a documentary, however, since the incriminated criminal Götten (Jürgen Prochnow) is either a regular criminal or a member of a terrorist organization–that choice is left open deliberately. In some reviews Götten is called an anarchist, in some a bank robber, but never a terrorist, a term that was not commonly used then.

The story begins with the innocent Katharina (Angela Winkler) falling in love with Ludwig Götten at a Carnival party in Cologne. She asks him to stay at her apartment in her highrise condominium. The next morning a police "anti-terrorist unit" breaks into her apartment to arrest Götten, who has disappeared. Inside, the police chief Beizmenne (Mario Adorf) arrests Katharina as Götten's accomplice and interrogates her at the police station. She is kept in a cell and exploited by a tabloid newspaper, generically titled *ZEITUNG* (literally, *The Paper* but in the translation of Böll's novel, *The News*). Within days, Blum's life is turned upside down. The police read her mail, examine her reading and spending habits, record her phone conversations and keep constant surveillance on Götten and anyone he contacts.

The movie portrays these tactics themselves as a form of terrorism. The same is true of exploitative media, embodied in the irrepressibly pompous, sensationalist reporter Werner Tötges (Dieter Laser). He questions Blum's neighbors about her sex life and interviews her ex-husband about their separation. In daily articles, *The Paper* accuses Blum of being radical and irreligious, and fabricates statements from her employer about Blum's predilection for crime. It even accuses her late father of being a Communist. In other words, the media convict Blum before the state does, their motivation as corrupt as their practice; after Tötges puts words in the mouth of Blum's dying mother, he remarks, "We must help simple people express themselves." Katharina invites Tötges to her apartment. In arriving he fantasizes she wants to have sex with him. The entire scene is shown in one long take from Katharine's perspective: she pulls out a gun and shoots Tötges, as a response to institutional violence from the press.

The film tries to stay close to Böll's novel and adds only a final scene at the cemetery where a politician (Achim Strietzel) utters stereotypical oily phrases about the freedom of the press—a cynical comment on violence and the irresponsible role of the media.

BACKGROUND

Böll's *Die verlorene Ehre der Katharina Blum* (1974) is one of his most personal stories since it shows his involvement with the left and terrorism. After Böll had received the Nobel Prize for Literature in 1972, the first German writer after World War II to receive this award, his public reputation began to rise as he was praised by the Left as the "conscience of his age" and attacked from the Right as a writer without any real aesthetic values. Those opposed to Böll claimed that the best writers never received the Nobel Prize. Böll responded that, as a German, he could not afford not to accept the Nobel Prize, since Germany had not had many people to whom the world could look up after the Second World War. He subsequently became more involved in political causes such as Chancellor Brandt's successful reelection campaign.

In 1972 Böll published an article in *Der Spiegel* defending Ulrike Meinhof and the terrorist Baader-Meinhof Group. In reaction to this article, the papers controlled by the conservative Axel Springer (who also owned the *BILD-Zeitung*) published a letter written by *Ministerpräsident* Filbinger of the State of Baden-Württemberg and others asking for Böll's resignation as president of the International PEN (an organization of writers). On June 1, 1972, Böll's house was searched by the police, and on June 7, in a debate in the West German Federal Parliament in Bonn, the Christian Democratic Union concluded "fellow travelers" like Böll were more dangerous than the Baader-Meinhof Group itself.

The critic Dorothee Sölle is credited with giving the most reasonable assessment to both the Meinhof debate and Böll's *The Lost Honor of Katharina Blum* (Sölle 1974, 885-87). The main assumption of Sölle's review is the claim that Böll wrote a "realistic *1984*" for the Federal Republic, where the police are in charge of external control, and the press, especially ZEITUNG (Böll's novel version of the *BILD-Zeitung*) is in charge of the internal control, of ideas and emotions as well as wishes (Sölle 1974, 886). Thus Katharina's rebellion is largely a linguistic resistance against a prescribed language where the sexual act can only be called *ficken* (fucking) and words like *gütig* (kind) are censored and replaced in the minutes with *sehr nett* (very nice) or *gutmütig* (gentle).

Springer's newspapers were outrageously conservative. Owned by Lord Axel Springer, the Springer Press controlled almost half of the newspaper circulation in West Germany, among them the *BILD-Zeitung*, Europe's largest circulation tabloid paper and Böll's model for *The Paper*. Springer was an avowed anti-Communist. During a time when other corporations were leaving West Berlin in droves (fearful of the tenuous political situation that barely kept the city out of East German hands), Axel Springer chose to put the headquarters for his publishing empire in Berlin, mere yards away from the Berlin Wall (a block away from Checkpoint Charlie), and put a huge reader-board on the side facing East Berlin. The board would flash the news of the free world to the Germans that Springer characterized as enslaved on the other side of the wall. The sheer size of the building was intended as a constant reminder to East Germans of the superiority of the capitalist system.

Springer's paper empire was held responsible for escalating violence against leftist groups, a claim the Baader-Meinhof Group took very seriously. The Group came into existence on April 2, 1968, when Andreas Baader and his girlfriend, Gudrun Ensslin, firebombed Frankfurt's Kaufhaus Schneider department store. Two years later the famed left-wing journalist Ulrike Meinhof helped to break

Baader out of prison custody in Berlin, on May 14, 1970. The name Baader-Meinhof Group certainly didn't come into usage, of course, until after Meinhof helped Baader escape from custody and the German press was looking for a suitable moniker to attach to the Group. The Group never used the term to describe themselves (they called themselves the Red Army Faction). Liberals and moderates would never call them a *Bande* (Gang), but were instead careful to refer to them as a *Gruppe* (Group). Conservative Germans were equally careful to do the exact opposite. In 1971 millions of wanted posters appeared in store windows across the Federal Republic in an effort to find the members of the elusive Baader-Meinhof Group.

The second irony of the term "Baader-Meinhof" is that it described a leadership within the Group that in reality did not exist. Baader was unquestioningly the leader of the Group, but his girlfriend Ensslin was more of a co-leader than Meinhof ever was. And Baader and Meinhof were certainly never lovers. The Baader-Meinhof Group ceased to exist in May and June of 1972, when Baader, Meinhof, Ensslin, Jan-Carl Raspe, and Holger Meins (the five core members of the Group) were captured. Early in the morning of November 18, 1977, Baader, Ensslin, and Raspe committed suicide in prison (Meinhof had committed suicide the previous year and Meins had died from a hunger strike in 1974). Their own name for their urban terrorist organization, the Red Army Faction, continued to be used by the successive generations of terrorists that continued the cause after the original leaders were captured.

EVALUATION

The Lost Honor of Katharina Blum starts out as a thriller, with music that was familiar to German audiences from the thriller TV series *Tatort*. In the opening scene, a detective watches Ludwig Götten through his camera. The camera lens becomes the screen, which turns into a black and white movie. This visual change divides the movie into the perspective of the detective's camera surveillance, black and white, and of the action itself, Katharina's and Götten's world (their reality) in color. The spectator is forced to move into the voyeur position with the policeman–the spectator becomes the policeman, the controlling force. The voyeuristic position of the spectator becomes increasingly clear with the frequent switches from color to black and white photography, which corresponds to Böll's monotonous style of narration in the novel. While Böll's novel reads like a badly written police report, parts of the movie look like a poorly edited documentary by a bungling film maker, which is supposed to indicate that we are watching a police report. Böll's emulated police-report style of the novel corresponds to the flatness and graininess of the pseudo-documentary part of the movie.

The headlines of *The Paper*, shown in black and white, make visual this division between the police state supported by the press on the one hand and Katharina and reality on the other. After the murder of her mother, Katharina finally articulates the central thought of this movie: "These people are murderers, all of them. It is their very business to rob innocent people of their honor and often to take their lives. Otherwise nobody would buy their paper," to which the attending physician replies, "Are you a Marxist?" This sentence is contrasted with the final scene added by the authors (not included in Böll's book) where a journalist defends the freedom of the press as "our last bastion of freedom," a sentence that sounds utterly cynical after what the viewer has witnessed.

The film is thus profoundly biased in that it presents a visual division between "them" and "us," between the press and the police on one side and the viewers on

*Beizmenne (Mario Adorf)
prepares to raid Katharina's
apartment.*

the other, showing Germany as a police state where "we" are all endangered. In this perfect blend of content and film technique, *The Lost Honor of Katharina Blum* is one of the best political movies ever to be produced in Germany.

In this complex, evocative portrayal of a woman struggling to make sense of the perplexing yet subtle brutality against her, Blum expresses her feelings only sporadically; more often she stares, apparently blankly, into space. She's internalizing her profound, increasing alienation, and, in the moments when she lashes out, she is not exhibiting weakness, but, instead, understandable and complicated responses to the destruction of individual identity. This tragedy is compounded by the fact that Blum is a threat to no one. All the resources assembled against her are completely out of proportion to their target, evidenced early in the film when Blum, alone in her apartment, prepares breakfast as a massive array of men and armor descend on her doorway. Contrasting Blum's innocence with the state's authority, the scene is darkly humorous but also horrifying. As an Orwellian commentary on the abuse of power and information, *The Lost Honor of Katharina* Blum is terrifying.

Katharina starts out as an apolitical woman whose political conscience is awakened through her treatment by the sensationalist press. Tötges is a sort of Kafkaesque figure of power who, along with the police machine whose representative is Beizmenne, degrades the naïve Katharina. Violence is presented in a very subtle, civilized manner, building very slowly in the movie where she is interrogated as a witness first, and increasingly is treated as an accused who is caught in the machine. Language is a revealing factor to show the differences between Katharina and Beizmenne when they discuss the difference between "Zudringlichkeit" ("advances"), Katharina's version, and "Zärtlichkeit" ("tenderness") as Beizmenne wants to write in the report. His complete lack of interest in these subtleties demonstrates his insensitivity (and the insensitivity of the state) towards Katharina's private rights as a citizen, and as a woman. The word "tenderness," which she defines as a two-way feeling, contains her (and Böll's) view of the world, human and democratic. Thus denying her that use of the word takes away her humanity, her honor and her pride. This simple dialog shows the heartlessness of the police and *The Paper* and opens up Katharina's character to the viewer who begins to understand her ordeal as a process of self-realization. The transformation is shown in Angela Winkler's face, which increasingly shows how deeply her personality has been wounded, and finally flinches only briefly when she kills Tötges.

Katharina's transformation from a naïve single woman without a relationship to men to a self-determined modern individual who kills because her honor has been violated is at the core of the film. She is the only real protagonist in this movie and fights with the political machinery of police and press, an individual alone against the state. The movie shows us in its bias the perverted signs of a police state that leftist Germans saw looming on the horizon. But true to its intention of showing Katharina's transformation to a modern woman, the film depicts how Katharina learns to rely on her friends, who surprisingly agree with her on most political principles: her aunt, her former boss Blorna and his wife, nicknamed the "red Trude." Thus the film is telling us that the police and the repressive press can only manipulate society to a certain point, since well-meaning people have a solid core to counter slanderous attacks. Since her life is now ruined, by killing Tötges Katharina frees herself from the societal demands he represents: money, subjugation of women, and her domesticated status. Katharina becomes herself.

Schlöndorff's and von Trotta's adaptation of Böll's novel belongs to a specific cinematic tradition. It is part of the New German Cinema, which represents socially conscious movies and was led by Wenders, Fassbinder, and Herzog, among others, who assaulted both movie convention and the established political order. (RZ)

QUESTIONS

1. Argue for or against the proposition that freedom of the press is so important that it should outweigh human rights and personal character.

2. What are the political implications of the film?

3. Give examples of police supervision in *The Lost Honor of Katharina Blum*.

4. What was the significance of the epilogue at the time the film was released and what is its significance today?

RELATED FILMS

Deutschland im Herbst (*Germany in Autumn*, Consortium of Directors 1979). The film presents several short films that attempt to come to terms with the heightened political situation in Germany after the kidnapping and murder of businessman Hanns Martin Schleyes, the suicides of three members of the Red Army Faction (Baader-Meinhof Group), and the hijacking of a Frankfurt-bound plane in Mogadishu.

Die dritte Generation (*The Third Generation*, Rainer Werner Fassbinder 1979). A comedy, in which Fassbinder looks at radical groups after the RAF (Red Army Faction) and concludes that the younger generation terrorizes for the sake of terror and not out of conviction.

Messer im Kopf (*Knife in the Head*, Reinhard Hauff 1978). A man accidentally enters the scene of a police raid on radicals and is shot in the head, causing brain trauma. As he pieces his life back together, the police accuse him of killing a police officer and the radicals exploit his injuries as resulting from police brutality.

INFORMATION

The Lost Honor of Katharina Blum (1975), DVD, in German w/subtitles, color, 106 minutes, Criterion Collection, released 2003.

Böll, Heinrich: *Die verlorene Ehre der Katharina Blum oder wie Gewalt entstehen und wohin sie führen kann*: Erzählung. - Köln: Kiepenheuer und Witsch, 1974.

Böll, Heinrich. *The Lost Honor of Katharina Blum: How Violence Develops and Where it Can Lead*. New York: McGraw-Hill, 1975.

Franklin, James. *New German Cinema: From Oberhausen to Hamburg*. Boston: Twayne Publishers, 1983.

Hehr, Renate. *Margarethe von Trotta: Filmmaking as Liberation*. London: Edition Axel Menges, 2000.

Moeller, Hans-Bernhard and George Lellis. *Volker Schlöndorff's Cinema: Adaptation, Politics, and the "Movie-Appropriate."* Carbondale and Edwardsville: Southern Illinois UP, 2002.

Schlöndorff, Volker and Margarethe von Trotta. *Die verlorene Ehre der Katharina Blum*. Transcript von Andrea Park. Tübingen: Narr, 1981.

CHAPTER 17

Die Ehe der Maria Braun

(*The Marriage of Maria Braun*, **Rainer Werner Fassbinder 1979**)

Hermann (Klaus Löwitsch) and Maria Braun (Hanna Schygulla) in their new house.

CREDITS

Director .... R. W. Fassbinder
Screenpay ....R. W. Fassbinder, Peter Märthesheimer, Pea Fröhlich
Director of Photography ....Michael Ballhaus
Music.. Peer Raben
Producer ....Michael Fengler
Production Companies............ Albatros Produktion, Fengler Films, Filmverlaf der
                    Autoren, Tango Film, Trio Film, Westdeutscher Rundfunk
Runtime ....120 minutes; color

Principal Cast

Hanna Schygulla (Maria Braun), Klaus Löwitsch (Hermann Braun), Ivan Desny (Karl Oswald), Gisela Uhlen (Mother), Elisabeth Trissenaar (Betti Klenze), Gottfried John (Willi Klenze), Hark Bohm (Senkenberg), George Byrd, aka Greg Eagles (Bill), Claus Holm (Doctor), Günter Lamprecht (Hans Wetzel), Anton Schiersner (Grandpa Berger), Sonja Neudorfer (Red Cross nurse), Volker Spengler (Train conductor), Isolde Barth (Vevi), Bruce Low (American at conference).

THE STORY

In a registry office that has just been hit by a bomb, Hermann (Klaus Löwitsch) and Maria (Hanna Schygulla) Braun are married during the Second World War. After the war, as Maria waits for Hermann's return, a friend returning from the front brings the news that Hermann is dead. Then Maria becomes Bill's (George Byrd) lover, an American soldier whom she meets in a GI bar where she works. When Hermann unexpectedly returns home from a POW camp, Maria kills Bill with a bottle. Hermann confesses to the crime and is sent to jail. On a train Maria meets the manufacturer Oswald (Ivan Desny), and he offers her a job as personal assistant in his company. She becomes indispensable to his textile firm because of her knowledge of English, her sense of business, and her physical attractiveness.

Oswald falls in love with Maria. Although Maria returns his affection and enters into an affair with him, she refuses to become dependent since she only lives for the day when Hermann will be released from prison. When the moment comes, he disappears without a trace (later in the film we learn that he went to Canada for a few years) and reappears suddenly after Oswald's death. At the reading of Oswald's will, Maria discovers that Hermann had made an agreement with Oswald to leave Maria alone as long as Oswald was alive. Because of this arrangement, Oswald had willed his fortune to the couple, half to Maria and half to Hermann. On July 4, 1954, while the reporter Herbert Zimmermann describes the final moments of a championship soccer match between West Germany and Hungary in Bern, the house explodes. Maria had not properly turned off a gas jet. The film leaves open whether it was deliberate or by accident and ends with a series of photos of past West German chancellors once the credits have rolled.

BACKGROUND

Rainer Werner Fassbinder, who was born in 1945 and died in 1982, was the most significant director of New German Cinema. In just thirteen years, between 1969 and 1982, he made 44 films about social and political issues, including movies about hatred of foreigners, *Katzelmacher* (1969) and *Angst essen Seele auf* (*Ali: Fear Eats the Soul* 1973), films about infidelity, *Der Händler der vier Jahreszeiten* (*The Merchant of Four Seasons* 1971), a trilogy about women in the 1950s, *The Marriage of Maria Braun* (1979), *Lola* (1981), and *Die Sehnsucht der Veronika Voss* (*Veronika Voss* 1982); and movies about gays, *Faustrecht der Freiheit* (*Fox and His Friends* 1975) and *Querelle* (1982).

Fassbinder was a child of the second generation after Germany's collapse in 1945, the generation that tried to rebuild Germany after it had lost its place in the world. While the fifties had been relatively peaceful and apolitical in German political life, with the majority of citizens concentrating on reconstruction and producing the much acclaimed *Wirtschaftswunder* (economic miracle), their sons

The family gathers to celebrate a birthday. From left Hans (Günter Lamprecht, Mother (Giesela Uhlen), Willi (Gottfried John), Grandpa Berger (Anton Schiersner), Maria (Hanna Schygulla), Betti (Elisabeth Trissenaar). Note how Fassbinder has staged the mise-en-scène as if to call attention to each character's artifice.

and daughters, tired of the older generation's reluctance to confront Germany's past, began to criticize their parents. The younger generation's criticism became more vocal in the 1960s with the introduction of the *Notstandsgesetze*, emergency laws which reminded many of the absolute power handed over to the government at the end of the Weimar Republic, before the Nazis took control of the government.

Subsequently, West Germany, including West Berlin, exploded in violence and witnessed thousands of demonstrations. The birth of West Germany's homegrown terrorist organization RAF (Red Army Faction or Baader-Meinhof Group, named after Andreas Baader and Ulrike Meinhof) became the most prominent part of these protests. The protests swept most university campuses and high schools and, once the intellectuals had taken over, they became the expression of an entire generation.

Fassbinder's career began in 1967 at the height of the student rebellion. He became a major spokesperson who hung on to the ideals of the 68-generation (the name given to the members of the protest movement) longer than most of the members of the 68-generation themselves. Fassbinder's films are the most pronounced expression of the feeling of the violent seventies. To this day, Fassbinder's films are considered among the most valid social documents produced by New German Cinema; his plays are still among the most performed of any post-war German dramatist. Originally considered too western and too bourgeois for the GDR, Fassbinder's *The Marriage of Maria Braun* was the only Fassbinder movie officially allowed in East Germany, suggesting that the Communists accepted Fassbinder's criticism of West German society as reflecting their own view.

Fassbinder's protest was only partly intellectual, triggered by the inadequacy of West German responses to the Nazi mentality. It was more emotional than political; it was more artistic than documentary. In a documentary about the responses to the events in the fall of 1977, he produced a short film about his own life, which included an argument with his mother where he accused her of being a Nazi. Fassbinder saw himself as part of the political struggle, not above it, as so many intellectuals did. In an interview he conceded that his work was about "building utopias." He admitted if it came to the point where his fears were greater than his "longing for creating something beautiful" he would quit working, and living as well.

Fassbinder took very seriously Hannah Arendt's accusation that the Second World War had incapacitated the Germans emotionally. In order to keep the memory of Germany's guilt alive he was always interested in movies that could engage viewers to the point where they might become politically active. Relying heavily on the ideas and techniques of dramatist Bertolt Brecht, Fassbinder created movies that distanced viewers from the emotional content of his films in order that they might contemplate their social and political content. Brecht had argued that theater should not mainly be entertainment, but should unsettle the spectator. Brecht's intellectual concept of drama highly influenced the new German movies of the 1960s, the New German Cinema, as it had influenced French Nouvelle Vague movies, the films of Jean-Luc Godard, for example. Although the concept of Brechtian alienation has long been part of American theater, it has never influenced Hollywood, thus American viewers of a film like *The Marriage of Maria Braun* may find its coldness off-putting. But Brecht has influenced some filmmakers. In his paean to thirties America, *Cradle Will Rock* (1999), American actor and filmmaker Tim Robbins borrowed heavily from Brecht to sing the praises of the American working class.

At the bottom of all of this is Fassbinder's own state of being unhappy with the political system he was living in. Unlike the United States, which favors the private market forces of capitalism to drive the economy, West Germany from the beginning of its creation in 1949 had tried to combine capitalism with socialism. In the fifties Ludwig Erhard, the founding father of West German capitalism, wrote *Wohlstand für alle* (prosperity for all), which became the republic's bible: capitalism would serve as the motor to generate social equality. Fassbinder disagreed with this concept, as did most of his literary and cinema contemporaries, who displayed a profound antipathy towards the German system, largely because of its real and perceived ties to old Nazis. "I live in a state whose structure I reject," Fassbinder confessed. This rejection of their own country became the trademark of an entire generation, which was only softened by an idealization of Willy Brandt. Brandt, West Germany's first Social Democratic chancellor, had emigrated to Norway during the Second World War, which put him above any criticism from the left, as we notice in the ending of *The Marriage of Maria Braun*.

EVALUATION

The Marriage of Maria Braun allows several readings. The first would be that Maria's obsession with her marriage is a thinly disguised allegory of postwar Germany's relationship to its past. This interpretation is more prominent among America's critics who often see the movie as critical of West German politics; as film critic Tom Noonan wrote: "*Maria Braun* tells the story of post-war Germany: success at a price—a loss of emotions, a coldness now considered to be characteristic of Germans.... His characters are casualties of the economic rationalism that pervades our thinking:...we spiritually prostitute ourselves in the pursuit of a private materialism."

Of course, given Germany's rapid economic recovery, which is depicted in this film, it is not surprising to find critics emphasizing the person Maria Braun as a metaphor that equates German economic success with loss of soul. And once this equation is made, it is easy to conclude that the film's apocalyptic end uncovers the fatal flaw in this concept of "too much too fast." In this interpretation the destructive explosion becomes a warning to viewers that they ought to reexamine their own priorities in life.

A second reading of the movie would be to regard the film as the personal story of a successful business woman, who is engaged in a role reversal, a woman who is in charge of her own life, who takes on masculine traits in her pursuit of career goals, and who considers those interests superior to those of being a loving partner or of being the standard feminine role model. This feminist reading of the movie sees Maria Braun, who follows masculine rules, as a symbol of her times, that is, as a woman who always takes the initiative in her relationships with men. Maria Braun is an icon for the independent woman who has become liberated after the war, both sexually and politically.

These two readings can also be combined, juxtaposing Maria's and Germany's behavior. As Maria's unpredictable behavior determines the structure of the movie, she apparently wants to forget the past when she throws Hermann's picture under the train wheels. However, Hermann comes back repeatedly to gain power over her, not physically but mentally, the same way that Nazi memories keep recurring and haunting the lives of Germans. Maria's marriage becomes a metaphor for Germany's past. Upon Hermann's second return, his indifference to her during their reunion, which should be like a honeymoon, is so disturbing that she decides to kill herself and Hermann.

With Fassbinder's Brechtian technique we are constantly reminded that Maria is not a real person in the traditional sense. To distance viewers from the emotions of the situation Fassbinder uses stilted movements or affected speech that point out the phony emotions, the false choices, and the artificiality of the society that Germans were creating with social capitalism. The movie's story line is also melodramatic and artificial, which allows reflection on history. With its melodrama, *The Marriage of Maria Braun* undercuts the convention of a love story since the marriage does not end the movie, but starts it.

In order to bring some kind of Brechtian element to the end, Fassbinder changed the ending in two ways: The original script showed Maria driving Hermann and herself off a cliff with the exploding car as the final sound. Fassbinder's eventual ending is both more ambiguous and more melodramatic, and as critics claim, shows Maria's despair over her fate. Essentially Hermann had agreed to sell Maria to Oswald in his contract, and when she realizes that she was never in control of her own destiny she kills herself and Hermann.

The film also linked the world of 1954, the time of the economic miracle, to the time of the Third Reich. The explosion reminds viewers of the opening of the film when a poster of Hitler was shown amid exploding bombs. 1954 is also linked with the future through a series of portraits of the German chancellors Adenauer (1949-63), Erhard (1963-66), Kiesinger (1966-69) and Schmidt (1974-).

This ambiguous ending also seems testimony of Fassbinder's own admission that if there were no hope of permanently changing Germany's political system, he would give up trying. The movie, produced three years before his death, could therefore be seen as an anticipation of the fatal outcome of his own life. That is, as with Maria's death, there has been speculation about whether Fassbinder's own death from a drug overdose was an accident or not.

Fassbinder shot this film in a highly visual manner. Objects are used as instruments to focus the viewer's attention, with close-ups of keys, cigarettes, or pictures. In many scenes people are lined up from front to back, starting with an object to set the scene, such as the clicking keys in the prison scene. This line-up indicates an artificial order in the scene, although it is always stilted and makes the viewer feel uncomfortable. These Fassbinder tableaux, as they have been called, are an important part of his alienating device.

Fassbinder experiments with sound throughout the film, making it an important element of the story being told. There is often a radio blaring in the foreground while the characters speak in muted tones in the background. The authentic news reports on the radio are central for the development of the plot, as in the scene towards the beginning where Maria is waiting for her husband's return while the radio voice can be heard reciting an endless list of missing persons. The final scene uses Herbert Zimmermann's famous radio report of the German 1954 World Cup victory as a background to Maria's self-destructive antics. Equally as important is Fassbinder's use of sound effects such as machinery and jackhammers whose rhythmic din simulate the sound of machine-guns that permeate the film as an ever-present background noise. These background sounds remind us of the rebuilding going on throughout Germany during the economic miracle of the fifties.

Since the sound is not very clear and the radio broadcasts and industrial noises often drown out the dialogue, the subtitles on versions meant for non-German speaking audiences are essential. But the radio announcements remain mostly without subtitles, leaving non-German viewers confused as to the significance of the layered sound track. In showings within Germany, since Fassbinder had not intended to subtitle the film for purposes of comprehending the plot, viewers might be equally confused. For, although German speakers understand the radio announcements, they often do not hear the dialog. Thus the multi leveled narrative remains a mystery to viewers. While the visual text is universally understood, the aural level leads to incomplete interpretation. This dependency on the visual often leads to a flawed interpretation since the auditory is undermined by the visual level.

The music soundtrack contains the hits of the forties and fifties, mixing Nazi songs with German reconstruction songs. "The Horst Wessel Lied," a Nazi Party song, alludes to the Nazi past, as does the Sarah Leander thirties classic "Nur nicht aus Liebe weinen" ("Don't cry for love alone"). Glenn Miller's "Moonlight Serenade" and his popular hit "In the Mood" illustrate the American military occupation culture, whereas the German fifties pop classics "La Paloma," "Capri Fischer," and Catharina Valente's "Ganz Paris träumt von der Liebe" ("All of Paris is dreaming of love") are signs of the new German economic miracle which points to vacation travel to European destinations. Vivaldi's music is used for scenes in an expensive restaurant towards the end of the movie. (RZ)

QUESTIONS

1. Describe scenes where the camera focuses on objects.

2. Give examples of Fassbinder's sound technique. How do the movie characters respond to the sound or do they ignore it? What does the sound element do in the particular scenes?

3. Explain Hermann Braun's motivation for going to jail in Maria's place.

4. What is the significance of the radio reporting Germany's World Cup victory in the final scene? How does the radio report comment on the final tragic scene?

RELATED FILMS

Lili Marleen. Also starring Hanna Schygulla, Lili Marleen tells the story of Lale Andersen, a singer who became famous because of one song, "Lili Marleen," a ballad that for a while was played to the German Armed Forces every evening at the same time.

Lola (1981). Part of Fassbinder's fifties trilogy of women and politics in postwar Germany. Whereas *The Marriage of Maria Braun* focuses on 1954, and *Veronika Voss* on 1955, *Lola* plays in 1957.

Die Sehnsucht der Veronika Voss (*Veronika Voss* 1982). One of the films together with *Lola* and *The Marriage of Maria Braun* that make up Fassbinder's triology of fifties movies. It covers the year 1955 with allusions to Nazi Germany.

Wir Wunderkinder (*Aren't We Wonderful?*, Kurt Hoffmann 1958). This comedy makes connections between the Third Reich and the economic miracle of the fifties.

Deutschland bleiche Mutter (*Germany Pale Mother*, Helma Sanders-Brahms 1980). Sander-Brahms's story about her mother tells of the difficulties women had during the war years, but also of the difficulties they had once the war was over in keeping the independence they had gained.

INFORMATION

The Marriage of Maria Braun (1979). In *Fassbinder's BRD Trilogy* (The *Marriage of Maria Braun, Veronika Voss, Lola*), DVD, in German with English subtitles, color, 120 minutes, Criterion Collection, released 2003.

Haralovich, Mary-Beth. "The Sexual Politics of *The Marriage of Maria Braun*." *Wide Angle* 12.1 (Jan. 1990): 6-16.

Kaes, Anton. "History, fiction, memory: Fassbinder's *The Marriage of Maria Braun*." In *German Film and Literature: Adaptations and Transformations*, edited by Eric Rentschler, 276-288. New York and London: Methuen, 1986.

—. "The Presence of the Past: Rainer Werner Fassbinder's *The Marriage of Maria Braun*." In *From Hitler to Heimat: The Return of History as Film*, 73-103. Cambridge: Harvard UP, 1989.

Reimer, Robert C. "Memories from the Past: A Study of Rainer Werner Fassbinder's *The Marriage of Maria Braun.*" *Journal of Popular Film and Television.* 9.3 (Fall 1981): 138-143.

Reimer, Robert C. and Carol J. Reimer. *Nazi-Retro Film: How German Narrative Cinema Remembers the Past.* New York: Twayne Publishers, 1992.

Rheuban, Joyce. "*The Marriage of Maria Braun*: History, Melodrama, Ideology." In *Gender and German Cinema: Feminist Interventions.* Vol. II: *German Film History/German History on Film,* edited by Sandra Frieden, 207-226. Providence: Berg, 1993.

Rheuban, Joyce, ed. *The Marriage of Maria Braun,* Rainer Werner Fassbinder, director. New Brunswick: Rutgers UP, 1986.

CHAPTER 18

Die Blechtrommel

(*The Tin Drum*, **Volker Schlöndorff 1979**)

Oskar has climbed a tower and is screaming to interrupt the tryst between his mother and Uncle Jan in the hotel across the street. His scream will shatter glass throughout the area, signaling the start of the "Night of Broken Glass," November 9, 1938.

CREDITS

Director	Volker Schlöndorff
Screenplay	Jean-Claude Carrière, Günter Grass, Volker Schlöndorff, and Franz Seitz
Director of Photography	Igor Luther
Music	Maurice Jarre
Producers	Anatole Dauman, Franz Seitz
Production Companies	Argos Films, Artémis Productions, Bioskop Film, Film Polski Film Agency, Franz Seitz Filmproduktion GGB-14, Hallelujah Films, Jadran
Length	142 minutes; color

Principal Cast

Mario Adorf (Alfred Matzerath), Angela Winkler (Agnes Matzerath), David Bennent (Oskar Matzerath), Katharina Thalbach (Maria Matzerath), Daniel Olbrychski (Jan Bronski), Tina Engel (young Anna Koljaiczek), Berta Drews (old Anna Koljaiczek), Heinz Bennent (Greff), Werner Rehm (Scheffler), Fritz Hakl (Bebra), Charles Aznavour (Sigismund Markus), Mariella Oliveri (Roswitha)

THE STORY

Oskar Matzerath, a young man who stops growing at the age of three, narrates the story of his life, beginning twenty years before his birth at the moment his mother was conceived by a Kashubian (an ethnic minority within Poland) peasant woman and an escaped political prisoner. In picaresque style, Oskar takes us through the highlights of his life from birth to adulthood, years that span the period from the early years of the Nazi party (1924) to the Nazis' defeat in 1945. At the age of three Oskar receives a tin drum at his birthday party. Witnessing the difficulties and hypocrisy of adults in their relationship to each other, Oscar throws his drum down the cellar stairs of his home and tumbles after it. This willful act of injury stops his growth. Thereafter he takes solace in his tin drum, which never leaves his hands. When others try to take it away, his screams are so terrible they shatter glass.

As a young child Oskar is an outsider, teased by the other children. He is forced to eat a witch's brew they concoct, but he also has moments of glory, as for example when he interrupts a Nazi rally in his hometown by playing his drum. At the age of twelve Oskar meets the midget Bebra, who like Oskar had decided to stop growing as a child, but who unlike Oskar is actively taking a part in political life. Oskar at first prefers to sit on the sidelines but later also joins Bebra as an entertainer for the Nazis. Highly successful for his gift of being able to shatter glass, Oskar falls in love with one of the performers, and even though there is a war going on, he lives a few idyllic months as a performer for the troops. Oskar's lover is killed as the war ends and he returns home.

As Soviet troops march into his town and discover the family hiding in a cellar, Oskar gives his father a Nazi pin, which the elder Matzerath tries to swallow but on which he chokes instead, and is subsequently shot by a Soviet soldier who mistakes the choking as belligerence. At his father's funeral, Oskar, after having lost most of his family, decides to start growing again.

Within this story of a boy's coming of age, we are introduced to a bizarre cast of characters representing the German middle class under Nazism, as seen through the eyes of a child, Oskar. Through Oskar's eyes we also witness the important events of the Third Reich from the Night of Broken Glass (the evening when German gangs smashed the windows of Jewish-owned shops and burned synagogues) through the start of the Second World War and finally to Germany's defeat by the Allies.

BACKGROUND

It is hardly surprising that the years 1914-55 (the years of Günter Grass's novel *Die Blechtrommel* (*The Tin Drum*) are the subject of hundreds of German feature films which use the Third Reich as a lens to examine mid-century German history. From 1914 to 1955 Germany underwent a succession of cataclysmic events, including the First and Second World Wars, a first try at a democratic government (the volatile Weimar Republic), a tragic dictatorship (the Third Reich), a division of the country (West and East Germany), a geographical and psychological location as the middle point of the Cold War, and an unprecedented economic revival (the economic miracle of West Germany). As one of the most expansive of these films, *The Tin Drum* (1979) covers the years 1924 to 1945 (unlike the novel, the film stops with the end of war) from the viewpoint of the lower middle class, giving us a panoramic view of history as it affects everyday life rather than as it contributes to great historical moments. In spite of the turmoil present in the country—constantly changing governments, clashes between extremist political parties, unemployment, shifting political allegiances, annexations, restriction of freedoms, war, and the tragedy of the Holocaust—ordinary citizens continued to live ordinary lives in extraordinary times.

The Tin Drum plays in that period between the wars which saw Germany grow in power, lusting after the lands it felt were illegally taken from it after the First World War. It is set in Danzig, once a part of Germany but at the time of the film an independent state under the supervision of the League of Nations, and since the Second World War, the city of Gdansk, Poland. As a city that historically had been a part of Germany, Poland, and also an independent state, Danzig housed Germans, Poles, and Kashubians (a distinct Slavic tribe). The city thus serves to accentuate the growing restlessness of the German middle class to be considered a part of German history. Given the intermarriage between Germans, Poles, and Kashubians in the city, the setting also exposes the absurdity of Nazi racial policies, as the Kashubians were too Polish for the Germans, and not Polish enough for the Poles. Yet as the film ends where it began, in a Kashubian potato field, the setting also reminds viewers that conquerors come and go, while the land and the indigenous people remain.

Günter Grass's novel *The Tin Drum* became a cause célèbre when it was published in 1958. Grass's novel was not the first to try to come to terms with the past, but it was the most outrageous and daring, some might even have said irreligious and disrespectful. Beyond bizarre and startling sexual imagery (eels crawling in and out of every orifice in a dead horse's head is one such example), Grass included enough parody of the Catholic Church to insure complaints of sacrilegious behavior. Grass became the *enfant terrible* of German letters. In spite of or maybe because of the notoriety, the book became an international bestseller.

By contrast with the novel, no public outcry greeted the release of Schlöndorff's film in 1979. One reason for this is that the years of the Third Reich were now thirty-five years in the past, allowing for a more distanced relationship to the historical material being lampooned. Another reason the film created no political backlash is that its irreverent treatment of the past was no longer unique. Italian film directors such as Federico Fellini and Lina Wertmueller had broken ground with their films about the role of the common man in the rise of Italian fascism. The use of carnival-like spectacle with a bizarre cast of characters to show the people as willingly manipulated participants in the events of the day was no longer shocking. Nor was the relationship between sexual perversion and fascist power. Indeed the film won a number of German film awards, an Oscar for best foreign film and a Golden Palm at Cannes, tying with Francis Ford Coppola's *Apocalypse Now*. By 1979 the political and moral climate had changed significantly to allow audiences to enjoy seeing the past parodied.

Yet, even though the film had been available for exhibiting for almost twenty years in America without any controversy, in 1997, a case was brought against Blockbuster Video in Oklahoma City for distributing *The Tin Drum*, which the suit alleged violated child obscenity laws that made it illegal to even suggest sexual activity between an adult and a minor. At issue were three scenes in the film, comprising a total of two minutes, fifty-five seconds. Two of the scenes suggest, without actually showing, that Oskar and Maria, playing 16-year-old adolescents, engage in sex. The third scene suggests that Oskar is present as his father is having sex with Maria. The main problem of the scenes is that the actor playing Oskar was only 11 and the actress playing Maria was 24 at the time of the shooting. Thus the suit maintained that the film violated Oklahoma's child obscenity laws. Initially, the police confiscated Blockbuster Video's tapes as well as raided a few private homes that had rented the tape. On appeal, the state's Attorney General lost the case and the movie was ruled not in violation of the obscenity statute.

EVALUATION

Volker Schlöndorff's *The Tin Drum*, which won an Academy Award for best foreign film of 1979, offers viewers a Rabelaisian world view of the Third Reich. A carnival atmosphere prevails throughout the film, which turns the usual presentation of the horrors of the Third Reich on its head, forcing viewers to laugh at the tragic and thereby gain insight into the origins of that tragedy, namely the populace's willingness, even eagerness, to participate in the spectacle. Schlöndorff allows us to see characters outside and inside the spectacle by adopting the double perspective of Grass's novel, which sometimes shows the world through Oskar's eyes and at other times shows Oskar as participant. This doubling of perspective allows viewers to participate in Oskar's exploits and yet to remain distanced from them and thus able to judge them. Moreover, the paradox of seeing Oskar in the middle of events as well as on the outside looking at those events is mirrored in the actions of characters, as they are both being acted upon and acting, both on the outside of events and participating in them.

Schlöndorff's triumph in *The Tin Drum* was capturing the grotesque nature of Günter Grass's characters. For years conventional wisdom held that Grass's novel could not be made into a movie primarily because of the character of Oskar, a child who stops growing physically (but not emotionally nor sexually) at the age of three.

Interpreted by many readers to be a dwarf, an interpretation Grass rejected, Oskar represented a challenge of casting to any director, who had to find an actor who could play a man in a boy's body. For the entire story, Oskar resembles a three-year old in physical stature whose mind must grow from that of a three-year old through adolescent to adulthood. Schlöndorff found the solution to this dilemma in actor David Bennent, a twelve-year old in a diminutive body.

As should be clear from the introduction to the film's characters, *The Tin Drum* revolves around Oskar. As the film opens, we hear Oskar's voice relating his story, beginning before the conception of his mother. In the double perspective that will continue throughout the movie, we see Joseph Koljaiczek, his grandfather, through the eyes of his grandmother, Anna, but then we also see Anna and Joseph together from a neutral or directorial viewpoint. In addition we see the sequence through the eyes of the yet unborn Oskar, giving him participatory status (it is his story), as well as authorial status (Oskar is narrating the story). Since he has not yet been born he cannot really see the event. Schlöndorff thus makes suspect from the

Bebra (Fritz Hakl) on accordion and Oskar (David Bennent) on his drum perform with other members of the troupe for the Nazi military. Bebra has convinced Oskar that they must join the Nazi cause or be destroyed.

beginning Oskar's first person narration. Yet since we see the scenes also through a neutral lens, we are willing to believe the tale.

The Tin Drum presents Oskar's life in a series of vignettes that often close with a memorable tableau. A number of these sequences early in the movie revolve around Oskar's ability to break glass with his screams, which he does whenever his drumming is threatened. For example, at school, after a lengthy set up during which the camera cuts back and forth between Oskar and the teacher, Oskar begins screaming when the teacher grabs his drum. The camera then focuses on the teacher from Oskar's perspective as her glasses shatter and blood spatters on her face. A similar scene occurs in the doctor's office, but here the final shot shows the broken glass jars holding medical specimens, focusing on a fetus. In another of these episodes, the camera shows us Oskar climbing to the top of a tower to get closer to a window behind which his mother is having an affair with Jan Bronski. The camera shows the entire scene, tower, Oskar, windows of hotel, then focuses on the hotel from Oskar's perspective, as he screams and the window glass shatters to the street. In each of these vignettes which become tableaux — and they are just a few of many similar scenes in the movie — Schlöndorff parodies German institutions and human foibles. More importantly they show how the participants are both perpetrator and cause of the action, by threatening the drum, and victim and effect, by experiencing the consequence of the broken glass.

Is the movie a criticism of fascism or an artistic description of it, as has been argued? Oskar represents both witness to and participant in the rise of Nazism. As witness, his child-like status allows the distorted logic of the Third Reich to seem like the aberrations of a child's mind. Thus his father can be both a reluctant and an enthusiastic participant in Party events. In Oskar's eyes, his mother can be attracted to both the irrational, sensitive Jan Bronski and the sensible, loutish Matzerath. More importantly, Oskar's father could be either of these two men. Oskar's status as child also allows him to feel responsible for events that occur, in particular the death of his uncle Jan, his father and his mother. His status as man in a child's body allows for showing the complicity of the German artist class in supporting Hitler and the Nazis.

Schlöndorff adapted the absurdity of Grass's other characters equally well. Alfred Matzerath, Oskar's father, played by noted actor Mario Adorf, represents the German middle class that goes along to get along. Although he exhibits no strong inclination to join the Nazi Party, he eventually does so presumably at the prodding of his wife. Matzerath is the petty bourgeois who wants most to be left alone, a state that historical circumstances will not allow, and who then makes a disastrous choice to join in. Seen through Oskar's eyes, he is a bumbling cuckold, who later becomes Oskar's rival for the young housemaid Maria.

Jan Bronski, Oskar's uncle (who might be Oskar's actual father), offers contrast to Matzerath's middle-class German values of hard work and political patriotism. He represents the Kashubians who want to stay out of the fight for Danzig. Neither German nor fully Polish, he is forced by circumstances to fight for the Polish cause, thereby bringing about the death he had hoped to prevent by remaining neutral.

Agnes Matzerath, Oskar's mother, played by Angela Winkler, helps viewers understand the two men. She exists mostly as cliché, the woman torn between wanting a sensitive man for her bed (Jan Bronski) and a strong man for financial support (Alfred Matzerath). Blaming her husband Alfred for Oskar's physical size, she eventually succumbs to feelings of guilt for being unable to choose between her lover Jan and her husband. That guilt reaches its high point in a sequence of sexual gratification and food consumption. After refusing to eat eels that her husband has prepared, she is sexually gratified by Bronski, as Oskar watches, and then she returns to the kitchen and greedily consumes her husband's eels. Shortly thereafter she dies. Schlöndorff's adaptation of this sequence from the book again reveals his expertise in capturing the supposedly unfilmable on film.

Oskar's parents and uncle reflect the dual perspective of the film as described earlier. For we see them as Oskar sees them, at the same time that we see Oskar as they do. This is true of other characters in the film as well. Anna Koljaiczek, Oskar's grandmother, is Oskar's protector and refuge. She is also the only true survivor of the war. While others in Danzig are forced to flee the coming Russians, she remains tied to the land. The opening and closing tableaux of Anna in the fields roasting potatoes at an open fire suggest the eternal truth of history: events and leaders come and go, the people suffer but remain in place.

Oskar's neighborhood is populated by grotesque stereotypes, at least as we see them through Oskar's eyes, representing various aspects of the German petty bourgeois under the Third Reich. One neighbor for example plays the Communist hymn, the *Internationale*, leaning out his bedroom window, but later as the Nazis gain power, he switches allegiances. The greengrocer (played by Heinz Bennent, David Bennent's real life father) who owns a store near Alfred's fish shop rhapsodizes about the organic principles of the potato, bizarrely imitating the Nazis blood and soil philosophy. Sigismund Markus, a Jewish shopkeeper in the city (played by Charles Aznavour, a well-known French *chansonier* of Armenien descent) refuses to believe the Nazis are dangerous and once he recognizes that he should leave, it is too late to escape. His German first name and last-minute baptism cannot help him. But through the eyes of these three, we also recognize the child in Oskar.

Seen through a child's eyes, the characters and events are exaggerated, sometimes bigger than life, and seem more a reflection through a fun house mirror than a glimpse through a window. Schlöndorff makes effective use of the child's perspective to parody Nazi iconography in the film. He integrates Nazi emblems, speeches, and personalities into Oskar's perception at the same time that he offers them for the viewers' contemplation. Of the many references to Nazi ideology within the film, two in particular underscore Oskar's role as participant and bystander. In the first of these, Oskar has accompanied his father, who has finally decided to join the Nazi party, to a rally in front of the Polish post office. Oskar sneaks under the stands in front of the parade ground, the camera again showing Oskar as he hides under the bleachers, and also showing the scene of the parade grounds as seen from under the stands where he is hiding. When the officials arrive and march toward the podium, a band plays in 4/4 rhythm the opening of a march. Under the stands Oskar is drumming away at random in 3/4 rhythm. We see him drumming and then from his perspective we see the feet of the band members and marchers slipping into a 3/4 rhythm, until all are dancing to the "Blue Danube Waltz." On the one hand, Schlöndorff may be referencing the annexation of Austria (as the scene takes place around the time Austria was annexed into Germany, early 1938) and many viewers would associate the melody with Austria, not Germany. On the other hand, he may be showing how easily people can be manipulated (made to march to a different drummer). In either case, one has to ask if it would really have been that easy to thwart the Nazi propaganda apparatus.

In the second and more frightening sequence, Oskar tells a fairy tale that has Santa Claus turning into the *gas man*. At the mention of the word *gas man*, fires cover most of the screen area. The fairy tale style then continues as Oskar narrates that "once upon a time there was a toy merchant named Sigismund Markus. Once upon a time there was a drummer named Oskar." Eventually the screen reveals the dead body of Sigismund Markus who has committed suicide on the day after the Night of Broken Glass. This scene, like many in the film, plays on multiple levels. On the one hand the reference is literal, as the Nazi apparatus did indeed turn into a machine of destruction, killing millions in concentration camps, many through asphyxiation by gas. On the other hand, the reference is also to the positive mood that reigned in the early years of the Third Reich, when for much of the German population (non-Jews and non-Communists) Hitler and the Nazis brought the country out of economic depression only to destroy the country with a disastrous war.

In addition to camera perspective and historical iconography, Schlöndorff shows culpability through characterization. Nowhere is this clearer than in the figures of Bebra and his circus midgets. Oskar meets Bebra early in the Third Reich, a time at which Oskar proclaims he is only an onlooker. Bebra warns him. "We must not be onlookers, but run the show so others don't run us. And the others will come." When Bebra's prophecy proves correct, and the Nazis do achieve power, Oskar joins their group as they work for the Nazi Ministry of Propaganda entertaining the troops. Schlöndorff, true to Grass's book, here parodies the artists who worked for the Ministry of Propaganda, proclaiming after the war they only did so to be able to work or to have at least some control over what happened to them and others. Using midgets to represent artists is of course a self-explanatory metaphor of powerlessness. But at the same time, it also reflects the lack of moral conviction in the artists as fellow travelers. It also suggests that one could have refused.

The Tin Drum is an expansive epic that examines the question of moral responsibility of ordinary people concerning historical events. It looks at the role that ordinary citizens played in the rise of Nazism, their culpability in keeping the Nazis in power, and the choices that could have, perhaps should have, been made to prevent tragedy. The film, following the novel, conflates physical stature, emotional selfishness, and intellectual immaturity as it points an accusatory finger at everyone for what occurred under Hitler and the Nazis. The film's stance toward its subjects, though, is ambivalent. On the one hand it shows the church, artists, but most of all the ordinary citizens as victims of circumstances. On the other hand, it suggests these groups abdicated their responsibility for making moral choices, allowing the Nazis to come to power and carry out their murderous agenda. (RCR)

QUESTIONS

1. Describe in detail any extensive sequence of shots comprising one of the film's many vignettes. Be sure to include camera perspective, camera movement, musical accompaniment, number of shots, placement of characters and objects within the shots, and overall content of the sequence.

2. Although we are asked at times to identify with Oskar, at other times it is clear he is simply not a likable character. How does Schlöndorff get us to identify with the figure and how does he distance us from him? Give as many specific examples as you can.

3. Discuss the sequence with Bebra, Oskar, and Rostwitha from the aspect of political opportunism.

4. Identify and place into context the film's many references to history.

RELATED FILMS

The following four films all focus on the theme of opportunism during the Third Reich.

Mephisto (Istvan Szabo 1981). Based on the Klaus Mann novel of the same name, the film follows the career of an actor who had the chance to leave Germany during the Nazi period but chose to stay to advance his career. The movie is loosely based on the career of Gustav Gründgens, who successfully sued to keep the novel from being published in Germany.

Hanussen (Istvan Szabo 1988). The middle of Szabo's triology of films, *Hanussen* tells the story of a fortune teller who rises to fame by predicting Hitler will come to power. Based on an historical figure.

Lili Marleen (R. W. Fassbinder, 1981). Fassbinder deconstructs Lale Andersen's assertion that she was not an opportunist, she simply sang a hit song.

Invincible (Werner Herzog 2001) follows a Jewish blacksmith as he makes a career as an Aryan Strongman in the theater of Hanussen, the fortune teller showcased in Istvan Szabo's *Hanussen* (1988).

Die Mitläufer (Eberhard Itzenplitz and Erwin Leiser 1985). This documentary examines the role of Germans who said they were not Nazis but did nothing to prevent the atrocities committed during the Third Reich

The following three films, like *The Tin Drum*, use humor to look at a very serious subject.

Katz und Maus (*Cat and Mouse*, Hans Jürgen Pohland 1967). The movie is based on another of the works of Günter Grass, *Katz und Maus* (*Cat and Mouse*), a novella in which the character of a dwarf who plays a tin drum also appears.

Europa Europa(Agnieszka Holland 1991). Known in Germany by the title *Hitlerjunge Salomon*, Holland's film follows the escapades of a young Jewish man who passes for Aryan German during the Third Reich. The film created quite a controversy when the German film industry refused to nominate it for the foreign film category of the Academy Awards on the grounds that it was not truly a German film.

Wir Wunderkinder (*Aren't We Wonderful*, Kurt Hoffmann 1958). Hoffmann, who began his career under the Nazis, created one of the first humorous portraits of Germans during the Third Reich. Even though successful with the public, the film is criticized for trivializing a serious subject.

INFORMATION

The Tin Drum (1979), DVD, in German w/subtitles, color, 142 minutes, Criterion Collection, released 2004.

Schlöndorff, Volker and Günter Grass. *Die Blechtrommel als Film*. Frankfurt a/ M: Zweitausendeins, 1979.

Franklin, James. *New German Cinema: From Oberhausen to Hamburg*. Boston: Twayne Publishers, 1983.

Moeller, Hans-Bernhard and George Lellis. *Volker Schlöndorff's Cinema: Adaptation, Politics, and the "Movie-Appropriate."* Carbondale and Edwardsville: Southern Illinois UP, 2002.

Reimer, Robert C. and Carol Reimer. *Nazi-Retro Film: How German Narrative Cinema Remembers the Past*. New York: Twayne Publishers, 1992.

CHAPTER 19

Die bleierne Zeit

(*Marianne and Juliane*, US, *The German Sisters*, UK, Margarethe von Trotta 1981)

Marianne (Barbara Sukowa) pounds her fist on the table as she berates her sister Juliane (Jutte Lampe) for her non-militancy. Eventually Juliane will come to understand her sister's point of view.

CREDITS

Director ....Margarethe von Trotta
Screenplay ....Margarethe von Trotta
Director of Photography ....Franz Rath
Music...Nicolas Economou
Producer ....Eberhard Junkersdorf
Production Companies........................... Bioskop Film, Sender Freies Berlin
Length...106 minutes; color

Principal Cast

Jutta Lampe (Juliane), Barbara Sukowa (Marianne), Rüdiger Vogler (Wolfgang), Doris Schade (the mother), Franz Rudnick (the father), Vérénice Rudolph (Sabine), Luc Bondy (Werner).

THE STORY

Die bleierne Zeit (*Marianne and Juliane* 1981) opens with Juliane Klein in her study in the late seventies, its bookcases filled with binders labeled with each year from 1968 through 1980. Presumably, these binders contain media accounts and documents about the West German terrorism wave, the role her sister Marianne played in terrorism, and the after effects of 1977, the year in which three terrorists, including her sister Marianne, died during the same night in an urban prison—deaths interpreted by the government as suicides but by many others as cold-blooded murders perpetrated by the state. Pensively pacing back and forth in her study, Juliane does not seem to have her own definitive version of the recent events. When she opens one of the binders, the flashbacks characterizing most of the film begin.

Unlike Juliane, who champions societal change by working within the West German system, her sister Marianne performs acts of terrorism, which the film shows as arson, bank robberies, and bombings, to jolt German society into effecting sorely needed humanitarian changes. The film shows two episodes with Marianne during the time she hides in the underground—one a clandestine meeting with Juliane in the garden of a sculpture museum and another as Marianne, accompanied by two males from her terrorist group, causes havoc and emotional turbulence when she turns up in the middle of the night in the apartment of Juliane and Wolfgang, Juliane's partner for ten years.

Not long after her visit to Juliane's apartment Marianne is arrested and placed into isolation in a countryside prison. She is later transferred to an urban prison. Juliane regularly visits Marianne in both facilities. These sequences are shown as flashbacks and represent Juliane's attempts to understand Marianne and thus herself as well.

Juliane's obsession with Marianne, arguably Marianne being her other self, escalates after Marianne's death. Soon she has no goal left in life other than to prove that Marianne could not possibly have committed suicide. Sacrificing her relationship with Wolfgang, she moves out of their apartment; she abandons her work at the women's journal. But, when she finally has the proof she needs, no one is interested in publishing her findings, for terrorism and the puzzling prison deaths of the terrorists are no longer relevant news items.

BACKGROUND

The film's title is borrowed from a Friedrich Hölderlin (1770-1843) poem, "die bleierne Zeit, " which translates as "leaden times." As does the phrase in Hölderlin's poem, the title of Margarethe von Trotta's film refers to two different time periods, drawing parallels between the "leaden" present and the restrictive, "leaden" times of a period in the past. For the film the present refers to the 1970s and the past to the 1950s in the Federal Republic of Germany. Summed up best by West German Chancellor Konrad Adenauer's official 1957 campaign slogan "No Experiments," the fifties came to designate a dull, stagnant period, an era of retreat into the authoritarian structures of the German past that affected politics, education, business, and family life. Measures to denazify the German population had been largely halted. In the Cold War atmosphere of the fifties leading to German rearmament and to West German membership in NATO, silence about the Nazi years prevailed in family life, as well as in schools and universities.

By the time of the student revolts in the late sixties, the silence regarding the Nazi period and the attendant lack of mourning for the victims of the Third Reich had become oppressive. While students in West Germany, as many students worldwide, protested the U.S. involvement in Vietnam, giving rise to a strong peace movement, they also railed against the authoritarian stratification of German life. They believed that the Nazi period still influenced public and private discourse and prevented Germans from applying lessons of the past to the present and the future. Without such a confrontation with the past, many felt, there could be no formation of a plausible German national identity.

Despite their strong protests against German institutions, a large number of activists eventually opted to change the system from within. In their so-called "march through institutions", they advocated reform through a politics of "small steps." Impatient at slow progress, others turned to more radical behavior—for example, to the terrorism concluding the last years of the sixties and dominant during several years in the seventies. The most feared terrorist organization became the RAF (Rote Armee Fraktion or Red Army Faction). Beginning with bank robberies, bombings, and kidnappings the RAF tried to provoke authoritarian reactions from the government and its police, thinking that repressive responses from the state would outrage the majority of Germans and would cause them to dismantle their stifling, authoritarian institutions. The organs of the state did respond repressively, eliminating many civil liberties and embarking on a search to find all who sympathized with the terrorists as well as the terrorists themselves. But there was no widespread revolt against the tactics of the state. Instead, as polls indicated, many approved of the steps taken to ensure the security of the population, giving rise to the conviction that the seventies too were confining, reactionary, "leaden" times.

The RAF was also known as the Baader-Meinhof Group ("gang" was the term used by rightists). Because the leftist journalist Ulrike Meinhof was involved in freeing the terrorist Andreas Baader from prison in May 1970, she became associated with Baader as the female leader of the group, although in reality, her friend Gudrun Ensslin (Baader's girlfriend)—if anyone—functioned as the group's female leader. Baader, Ensslin, and Meinhof (along with two other terrorists) were captured in 1972. Meinhof supposedly committed suicide in 1976. According to the official government version, Baader, Ensslin, and a third terrorist committed suicide on Oct. 18, 1977 in Stuttgart's Stammheim prison in response to government commandos seizing a Lufthansa plane in Mogadishu, Somalia. The plane had been hijacked by RAF terrorists in order to force the release of the terrorists imprisoned in Stammheim. Up to today, the suicide explanation remains in doubt, with skeptics believing that the state killed the terrorists, a view that *Marianne and Juliane* endorses. In the fall of 1977 businessman Hanns-Martin Schleyer was also kidnapped and subsequently murdered. The three events — plane hijacking, suicides, and Schleyer's kidnapping – precipitated rancorous debate between the left and right and was the subject of New German Cinema's *Deutschland im Herbst* (*Germany in Autumn* 1978), an attempt by Germany's filmmakers to come to terms with rising terrorism in Germany and the curtailment of political freedoms that it engendered.

Von Trotta has repeatedly emphasized that she did not intend to produce a documentary about terrorism or about the lives of Gudrun and Sigrid Ensslin. Since insufficient time had passed since the terrorist acts and the Stammheim deaths, von Trotta was convinced that an objective, factual film of this controversial chapter in postwar German history was impossible at the beginning of the eighties. Thus she produced a fictional film that merely drew on the relationship of the two sisters.

Unfortunately, von Trotta's fear of still being judged according to documentary criteria—according to the veracity of each filmic episode—was justified. When the film appeared in German movie theaters in 1981—only four years after the Stammheim deaths—the terrorism topic was still relatively present in public memory. Many objected to what was *not* included in the film. Others wished a clear stance on terrorism from the filmmaker or an unambiguous position on the limitations placed on women in the political arena. Von Trotta, on the other hand, continued to stress the fictional nature of the film and its underlying concerns: questions of remembrance and forgetting, of adequate mourning for the victims of the past, of directions taken in life and their repercussions on those who chose opposite directions, of the past in the formation of memory and, in turn, of memory in the formation of national identity. Accordingly, von Trotta neither provides nor wishes to provide an objective depiction of reality but includes many experiences of her generation. She explores how the times are reflected in individuals—in their emotions, thoughts, and behavior. How the personal reflects the political, how the personal *is* the political—this summarizes the essence of the film, a theme in most of her films, including *Das Versprechen* (*The Promise* 1995), discussed in another chapter, and *Rosa Luxemburg* (1986).

EVALUATION

In spite of the American translation of the title, Juliane and not Marianne is the main character of the film. Appearing in almost every sequence of the film, Juliane reacts—mainly emotionally—to everything that occurs, much in keeping with von Trotta's preference for showing the significance of events through their subjective repercussions on those experiencing rather than causing them. In the course of the film, flashbacks mostly to the 1970s but also to the fifties and even the years immediately after the war, reveal how Juliane increasingly assumes the rigorous, non-compromising nature of the adult Marianne, suggesting that Marianne represents her own repressed self, in part the solitary non-conformist she was as a teenager.

Though the time frame of the film is the beginning of the eighties (its establishing and final shots occur then), the flashbacks constituting most of the film focus on the seventies, but within these there are flashbacks to the fifties and also to immediately after the Second World War. In the first flashback, at an unspecified time at the beginning of the seventies, Marianne's husband Werner brings Jan, their child, to Juliane, requesting that she assume responsibility for him. But Juliane refuses to change her life for either Marianne's or Jan's sake, stressing the importance of her work and her time-consuming commitment to it. Why did Marianne have to abandon family life, asks Juliane, at exactly the point where she (Juliane) was beginning to settle comfortably into something approximating a bourgeois kind of life? Her presumption that Marianne was acting this way merely to spite her introduces the sibling rivalry and resentment that will surface in other flashbacks throughout the course of the movie.

Juliane's (Jutta Lampe) distance from her sister's radical politics is underscored by the barrier between the two sisters.

Marianne's deprecatory attitude toward Juliane's work and life style compounds Juliane's resentment. Sarcastically, Marianne says that thoughts—Juliane's arsenal in her essays and lectures—do not alter anything, implying that only her kind of revolutionary deeds will succeed in changing the world. During the second flashback, Marianne's nocturnal visit to her apartment, Juliane watches with helpless anger as her sister disparages her clothes, disgustedly throwing some of them on the floor. When Marianne, before departing with her terrorist companions, sarcastically tells Juliane to go on sleeping, Juliane senses that Marianne is contemptuously referring to the way she conducts her life. Though there were two flashbacks up to this point in the film that suggest a common bond between Juliane and Marianne, they do not dispel the impression that Juliane seethes with a resentment toward Marianne that leaves no room for either understanding or affection.

In the sequence immediately following the nighttime disruption, Juliane tries to visit Marianne in prison. As she looks at the prison walls from her waiting room, she recalls a similar wall in front of her family's house and a childhood race with Marianne from the wall to the house entrance, a race neither of them won. Another flashback in the wake of this one also accentuates the sisters' similarity: in unison, both slow down their walk through the family house as they approach the Grünewald painting of the Crucifixion in the hallway. Quite likely more favorably disposed to Marianne due to these memories of experiences uniting them, Juliane is particularly jolted when she finds out that Marianne refuses to see her. At this point, she starts the questioning that is to characterize her throughout many of the remaining filmic episodes.

To change Marianne's mind about seeing her, Juliane writes her a letter that recalls their childhood and teenage times together. Later Marianne comments that Juliane neglected to mention only the nightshirts they had always buttoned for each other, regardless of how ill-disposed the one was toward the other. By highlighting the nightshirts at least four times, the film stresses this childhood bond of sisterly love as the one that irrevocably unites them (certainly it is the only concrete memory from their mutual past that Marianne recalls with pleasure). After mailing the letter that had prompted Juliane to remember many aspects of their mutual past, the film presents the third and fourth flashbacks from the seventies into a remote past, the fourth consisting of four episodes from the fifties.

Occurring in 1955, at the midpoint of the "leaden" fifties, the flashbacks emphasize Juliane's rebellious teenage attitudes and Marianne's considerate, helping nature—that is, for the first time the fundamental personality differences between the two sisters appear, rather than their similarities. Juliane mocks Marianne's wish to be needed in life, dismissing it as voluntary enslavement. Juliane belligerently defends her habit of going to school in black jeans rather than in the dresses girls were expected to wear. When her father is on the verge of hitting her for irreverent comments, she dares him to lay a hand on her if he can reconcile beating his daughter with his Sunday sermons as the pastor of their church. Later Juliane disparages Marianne's intercession with their father on her behalf. At the dance held at the end of the school year, Juliane wins a wager made with Marianne: Juliane waltzes by herself over the entire dance floor, contemptuous of the consternation she causes all around her.

The flashbacks to 1955 mark a turning point in the film, as it is here that the film reveals Juliane's growing understanding of and identification with Marianne, and suggests that she recognizes her own repressed self in Marianne. Juliane is not yet prepared at this point to write the article on Marianne her co-workers on the women's journal wish from her, stubbornly resisting to embrace the credo that the personal is the political.

So that Juliane learns to dilate her personal experiences into the experiences of her generation—that is, to make her personal identity serviceable for the formation of a national identity—von Trotta provides her with other sets of flashbacks that clearly link the personal and the national. These flashbacks proceed backward, first touching on the fifties and then on the last war months in 1945. In one way or another, all involve the war and German reactions to it. In 1945, the two sisters, as young children, are shown as victimized by the war, its air raids, and the atmosphere of terror extending even into the air raid shelters. In an episode that takes place in school, Juliane tries in vain to induce a class discussion on Paul Celan's *The Death Fugue* in place of Rainer Maria Rilke's *Autumn Day*, the former a poem stressing victimization and recalling suppressed German deeds in the Second World War, the latter a so-called timeless poem of little relevance to the actual times, at least not to any efforts to forge a national identity predicated on confrontation with Germany's recent past. In another episode, Juliane and Marianne watch Alain Resnais' newly released film *Nuit et brouillard* (*Night and Fog* 1955) on the concentration camps. Both sisters feel ill after watching emaciated victims being piled into mass graves. While these flashbacks unite the personal and national political aspects of German life, they also identify wartime and postwar memories as generational experiences shared by many Germans.

The episode following the viewing of the Resnais film centers on Marianne recounting to her sister the terrors of imprisonment in an isolated cell, ostensibly drawing parallels between the wartime Nazi tortures and fascist-type state control in the seventies. Once the national turns into the personal for Juliane, as occurs in this episode, she is finally ready to write the article about Marianne for the women's journal. Almost as an afterthought, when she is already writing, another flashback (in a sense the missing link) materializes: In 1968, after viewing a film about Vietnam with Juliane and Wofgang that shows emaciated victims reminiscent of those in Resnais's film, Juliane recalls Marianne pronouncing that she will never come to terms with political activity in the face of such horrors. Though not specified, it is implied that Juliane interprets Marianne's turn to terrorism as the result of the Resnais film (when she could not do anything against an event that had already transpired) and the Vietnam film showing horrors committed in the present and demanding political engagement. Juliane's article on Marianne focuses therefore on the personal and national biographical incidents that shaped Marianne's militancy. For her part, Marianne rejects Juliane's thesis that the personal has led to the political. By considering people solely as products of their societies, Marianne emphasizes, Juliane justifies remaining among the guilty, of finding a rationale for her inaction.

Juliane's obsession with Marianne increases after Marianne's transfer to the modern prison, as does Marianne's dependency on Juliane and her visits. At the end of the last prison scene, Juliane's face is briefly superimposed on Marianne's, indicating that Marianne is no longer the Other but now decisively a part of Juliane. Though Marianne's face, a singular face, is obliterated after her death, one could also argue that Marianne's disappearance provokes the disappearance of Juliane as a separate personality. After Marianne's funeral, Juliane's fainting and subsequent illness echo Marianne's death. To Wolfgang's consternation, Marianne's belongings, transferred to his and Juliane's apartment, seem to be taking over the apartment. Julianne's single-mindedness in attempting to prove that Marianne could not possibly have committed suicide—implicitly also an assault on the state—mirrors Marianne's single-mindedness in attacking the state. When she in addition relinquishes her job at the women's journal and leaves Wolfgang, Juliane seems to be imitating Marianne's rejection of her accustomed environment and accustomed mate. Finally, Juliane in a sense becomes just as isolated as Marianne had been.

No one is interested in publishing Juliane's findings when she can prove, after three years of research, that Marianne's death was not the result of suicide. Much as the repressed Nazi past, Germany's terrorist past had become a history to be repressed. Having explored the repressed parts of her own personal and national self through her obsession with Marianne and having accepted them through imitating Marianne, Juliane is no longer prone to repressing the past. Acting independently of Marianne, she now willingly does what Marianne did not do: Juliane rejoins society by taking custody of Marianne's son Jan. (MS)

QUESTIONS

1. The film does not satisfactorily explain Marianne's conversion from an obedient, dutiful daughter to an enraged combative militant. On the basis of what the film does show, however, what do you think is the basis for this change?

2. Draw a timeline for the events in the film starting with the film's opening in the 1980s.

3. Von Trotta clearly intends us to understand Marianne's death as murder at the hands of prison guards and not suicide. What suggests that she did not commit suicide? Is there evidence to the contrary?

4. Von Trotta includes scenes that work well to further the story but also have meaning beyond what is being told. Analyze the scenes in which the girls button each other's nightshirts and the one in which they stand in front of the Grünewald painting "The Crucifixion." What might these scenes be saying about the girls' relationship to each other, and to German history?

5. What role does the father's religious vocation play in the film?

RELATED FILMS

Das zweite Erwachen der Christa Klages (*The Second Awakening of Christa Klages* 1978). One of many films that were part of the rebellious wave of German movies in the seventies. The film tells about a group of women that rob a bank to help a day care center.

Deutschland im Herbst (*Germany in Autumn*, Consortium of directors 1978). A group of German directors, among them R. W. Fassbinder, Volker Schlöndorff, and von Trotta, produced the film as an answer to Germany's rise in terrorism and the country's increasingly restrictive political policies.

Rosa Luxemburg (1986). Von Trotta creates an ode to Germany's most famous female revolutionary, active during the First World War.

Die Stille nach dem Schuß (*The Legend of Rita* 2000). Volker Schlöndorff revisits the turbulent times when the Red Army Faction was still active.

INFORMATION

Marianne and Juliane (1981), VHS, in German w/subtitles, color, 106 minutes, New Yorker Films, released 2001.

Hehr, Renate. *Margarethe von Trotta: Filmmaking as Liberation*. London: Edition Axel Menges, 2000.

Knight, Julia. *Women and the New German Cinema*. London and New York: Verso, 1992.

Linville, Susan E. *Feminism, Film, Fascism*. Austin: U of Texas P, 1998.

Weber, Hans Jürgen and Ingeborg Weber, eds. *Die bleierne Zeit. Ein Film von Margarethe von Trotta*. Frankfurt a/M: Fischer-Taschenbuch Verlag, 1990.

CHAPTER 20

Das Boot

(*The Boat*, **Wolfgang Petersen 1981**)

Johann (Erwin Leder) tries to keep engines running during an attack.

CREDITS

Director ....Wolfgang Petersen
Screenplay ....Lothar G. Buchheim, Wolfgang Petersen
Director of Photography .... Jost Vacano
Music...Klaus Doldinger
Producers ....Michael Bittins, Mark Damon, Ortwin Freyermuth,
John W. Hyde, Edward R. Pressman, Günter Rohrbach
Production Companies......Bavarian Film, Radiant Film, Süddeutscher Rundfunk,
Twin Bros. Productions, Westdeutscher Rundfunk
Length................149 minutes (original release); 216 minutes (director's cut); color

Principal Cast

Jürgen Prochnow (Captain), Herbert Grönemeyer   (Correspondent), Klaus Wennemann (Chief Engineer), Hubertus Bengsch (1st Lieutenant), Martin Semmelrogge (2nd Lieutenant), Bernd Tauber (Chief Quartermaster), Erwin Leder (Johann)

THE STORY

Germany's submarine fleet was a feared enemy at the start of the Second World War, but by 1941, U-boat assignments were becoming more and more dangerous as the Allies improved detection through reconnaissance flights and sonar. The opening credits tell the fate of German submarine crews, announcing that of 40,000 men on submarines, only 10,000 survived the war. Wolfgang Petersen's *Das Boot* (*The Boat* 1981) tells the story of one of the boats.

Under command of Captain-Lt. Heinrich Lehmann-Willenbrock, the German submarine sets out with a mix of seasoned and fresh crewmembers. Included among the crew are: a reporter for the Ministry of Propaganda who is to document the boat's exploits, a gung-ho lieutenant, the Captain (Lt. Heinrich, also known as *Der Alte*), the chief engineer, and Johann, the veteran crew chief. As in most submarine epics, in order to test the readiness of the crew, the beginning of the voyage includes a mandatory drill, during which the boat dives to depths beyond the limits specified by the boat's technical specs. Later, when the boat is under actual attack, the film reprises the diving sequence, complete with shots of gauges, the scared looks of the men's faces, and the sound of creaking seams and popping bolts. In addition to diving sequences, the film contains skirmishes with destroyers and a narrow escape through the Straits of Gibraltar. On the whole though, the story takes second place to characterization of life aboard a submarine, which we see as confined, tedious, tense, and scary. We might not need an elaborate story as the credits and history itself have already told us that the outcome of the boat's battles will turn out badly.

What story there is follows the convention of most war films, especially those set at sea. There is a simulated attack to test the vessel, a genuine first attack to test the mettle of the men, calm after the storm to give viewers respite from the tension of a battle film, a second more harrowing attack which endangers the ship and individuals, and victory. These sequences are framed as in most war films by a prologue that introduces the characters before setting off and an epilogue that shows them arriving home. It is in the framing (prologue and epilogue) that Petersen includes any critical commentary that the film might contain of war in general and of the Nazis in particular.

The movie is based on the best selling novel, *Das Boot* (*The Boat*), by German author Lothar G. Buchheim. Petersen follows Buchheim's plot closely, eliminating only the book's brief references to the Captain's backstory and that of some of the minor characters.

BACKGROUND

An article in *Der Spiegel* magazine traces the fascination with the submarine as a German secret weapon to gain military superiority back to the First World War. Early in the war, German submarine attacks gained early successes, as for example when the U-9 sank three British destroyers in 30 minutes. Such success led to use of submarines in questionable situations, leading to the policies after 1916 that allowed the boats to break a blockade around England by sinking all commercial vessels, even if the ships were from neutral nations. The sinking of one of these neutral ships under this policy, the *Lusitania*, led to America's eventually entering the war, and perhaps hastened Germany's defeat. According to the *Spiegel* article, the German military's belief in the superior fighting power of its submarine fleet led to over-reliance on the *U-Boots* in the Second World War, which from a National Socialist perspective was an ill-advised strategy. The degree to which the strategy was ill-advised can be seen in the mortality rate of the submarines: from 1939 when nine boats were lost, the number escalated until by 1944, 251 German submarines were destroyed. The month of May, 1943, was particularly disastrous for the U-boats. Forty-one boats were destroyed, 25 percent of the fleet, with a loss of 1,785 men. 183 men survived.

The Boat reprises a trend of German films of the fifties, examining the fate of ordinary servicemen during the Third Reich. While most of the films from that earlier era focused on the Army, Petersen's film looks at men in the German submarine fleet. Moreover, whereas films such as *Hunde wollt ihr ewig leben?* (Frank Wisbar, *Dogs, Do You Want to Live Forever?* 1958) and *08/15* (Paul May 1954/55), to name but two, stress the division between enlisted men and their officers, *The Boat* focuses on the unity of the boat's crew, even within their ideological differences. The crew's enemies are first and foremost the British destroyers hunting them and second the German High Command, whose orders run contrary to the realities of submarine combat.

Nonetheless, *The Boat* reflects the same values of patriotism, camaraderie, and sacrifice of the earlier films which has led some critics to dismiss the movie as an apology for Germany's armed forces. To be sure, the film presents war in all its ugliness of death and destruction, but, as critical reviews in America and Germany at the time of the film's initial release point out, it also presents the values of war as independent of the cause. Rather than engaging the reality of submarine combat critically, the film involves viewers in the fate of men who are dying bravely, one character even exhibiting superhuman endurance after earlier suffering a crisis of courage that had led to a nervous breakdown. To be sure, his act of heroism is realized only after a humiliating breakdown and knowledge of certain court martial once back home. In this respect Petersen follows the convention of many war films, where acts of courage are often exhibited by characters who earlier had displayed fear when confronted by enemy fire.

Petersen's *The Boat* remains unique in the history of German film. Not only was the film a success in Germany, but it also attracted large numbers of viewers and fans in England and America, even out-earning Tom Tykwer's phenomenal success twenty years later with *Lola rennt* (*Run Lola Run* 1998). Moreover the film was released as a five-hour mini-series version for television in 1985, four years after its theatrical run, again scoring well with viewers and critics in Germany and England. In Germany, the extended television version received a 50 rating, meaning half of the country's television sets were tuned in to *Das Boot*. To commemorate its twenty-fifth anniversary, the film was recut and released as a 216-minute movie, as opposed to the original 149 minutes. Petersen's intent in re-releasing the film at this time was to take advantage of innovations in sound production. The creaking boat, popping bolts, and depth charge explosions, already impressive in the original cut, become another actor in the reedited version, as each pop or explosion ratchets up the fear factor of the movie.

The film's popularity also made Petersen's career. Shortly thereafter, he was invited to Hollywood, where he has scored success with films such as *Enemy Mine* (1985), *Air Force One* (1997), *In the Line of Fire* (1993), *Outbreak* (1995), *The Perfect Storm* (2000), and *Troy* (2004). Knowing Petersen's origin as a German director adds an historical chill to films such as *Outbreak* and *Enemy Mine*, which both use concentration camps to confine those different from the population. Petersen's movie has also influenced the reception of other films. For example there is hardly a review for Joseph Vilsmaier's *Stalingrad* (1993) which does not pay homage to *The Boat* and compare the later film with its predecessor. In addition the trailers and adverts for the American submarine epic *U 571* (Jonathan Mostow 2000) trade on the fame of Petersen's film.

EVALUATION

That viewers identify with the men of the submarine is not surprising as Wolfgang Petersen has structured his film along the lines of both classic Hollywood war films and also classic Hollywood disaster epics. As already mentioned, Vilsmaier also had success later with the Hollywood formula for war films in his epic *Stalingrad*, again a war film told from the perspective of Germans in the Third Reich. In this film, as in *The Boat*, the director asks viewers to identify with men fighting for a regime that public and popular opinion are grateful lost the war. But whereas Vilsmaier melds Hollywood with the German war films of the fifties, Petersen's film is pure Hollywood, concerned first with entertaining the audience with a taut, suspenseful drama, sympathetic characters, and special effects. Only secondarily does the film offer critical commentary on the futility of war, and only for viewers familiar with history does the film serve as a reminder of the Nazi terror. If one removed the prologue and epilogue that frame the sub's adventure, these characters could just as easily be on an American submarine attacking the Japanese in the Pacific.

The opening scene captures the men of two *U-boot* crews, one just returning and one shipping out the next day, celebrating at a club. Petersen's mise-en-scène and camera work evoke both the idealism and the cynicism of various members of the crew, who vomit, pass out, chase a female singer, and make disparaging but also laudatory remarks about their leadership. On the one hand, one could read the scenes as critical of the war effort, since the men drink themselves into oblivion. On the other hand, the scenes reflect the film cliché of men on leave. As veterans the men know what is in store for them. Moreover, the opening corresponds to the war film formula by introducing the (stereo)types familiar to us from other films: a hardened but kind captain, a seasoned veteran, a member of the military press, a young kid with a pregnant girl friend, and a gung-ho second in command. The introductory scenes give a preview of things to come.

As the submarine's voyage gets underway Petersen both exploits and parodies his genre. He transforms Hollywood clichés of life on a submarine into horrific scenes of tedium, heroism, and death. The boat puts out to sea amid waving from shore and a martial arrangement of the German folk song "Muss i

Petersen emphasizes the cramped quarters on U-Boat 96 by shooting from entirely within the space rather than from outside. An analogy would be being on stage where the action is taking place instead of viewing the action from the audience.

denn." The captain gives a short motivating speech, and we see the men settling down in the ship. But the motivating speech is nothing more than four words, "Well men, everything OK?" And from the beginning the camera shows the boat to be nothing more than a long tube crammed full with provisions and men. Even one of the toilets has to be used for storage. The cramped quarters that one expects to find on a submarine here are made more claustrophobic through shots down the middle of the boat that block our vision as we try to see through to the end. In similar fashion, a long tracking shot that introduces the various compartments follows the journalist as he moves forward, doubles back, circles around, and dodges people and objects in a tour de force of choreographed motion.

Petersen also uses a conventional war film arc: simulation, first attack, calm after the storm, second more harrowing attack, and victory. Again, however, his camera work, audio track, and plotting raise the film above conventional war movies. Petersen's shots are always close in, even more than is necessary for the cramped quarters of the set, an effect he achieved by filming from within the action rather than from outside of it. Individuals are isolated, their faces emerging from shadows as if subjects of a Carravagio or Goya portrait, two Spanish artists who specialized in chiaroscuro, a style that emphasized light and shadow. The tempo of the editing builds suspense during the four submerge sequences, the first a drill, the second when the sub is on the attack, the third when the sub is being attacked, and the final when the sub is trying to resurface. The visual and audio tracks during the scenes of submerging under attack alternate close-up scenes of the crew's faces with shots of the dial of the depth gauge, and the voice of a crew member announcing the depth of the boat with sounds of bolts popping. The intensity of the visuals and sounds builds through the first three scenes of submerging until during the third ordeal, when gloom hits its deepest point as the men admit to each other they believe the captain knew the mission had to fail. Then, as in a Hollywood movie, the scene is reprised one last time, as depth gauge and the worried look on men's faces alternate rapidly until the screen goes black, followed by a shot of the gauge needle as it rises. Here again though, even with the apparent happy ending, Petersen challenges the genre and acknowledges historical reality, turning victory into defeat as planes destroy the boat in its safe harbor.

Petersen may follow the war genre, but he also follows the genre of the disaster movie, so popular at the time *The Boat* was being filmed. Films such as *The Poseidon Adventure* (Michael Neame, Irwin Allen 1972), *Airplane* (James Abrahams, David Zucker 1980) or *Jaws* (Steven Spielberg 1975) rely on mystery, physical confinement, and disbelief in the possibility of the disaster to create suspense and draw viewers into the impending doom facing the characters (Douglas Fowler in *Studies in Popular Culture 4* 1981). Petersen structures *The Boat* along similar lines. Thus the enemy ships and planes remain, for the most part, an unseen threat. The first time the destroyer attacks, the periscope view shows nothing until the ship is on top of the sub. Likewise the planes that dive toward it are spotted at the last moment, and the disaster that befalls the sub going through the straits occurs after it seems the boat just might pull off its escape. In all these situations Petersen hides the danger until the last possible minute. And similar to films such as *Jaws*, at such heightened danger he imposes a threatening melodic line in the background. Physical confinement is of course a must on a submarine, but as mentioned earlier, Petersen makes the confinement more claustrophobic than most boat movies. Here, taking a cue from *The Poseidon Adventure*, Petersen does not allow outside shots once the ultimate disaster occurs. And even before the disaster, shots outside the ship only remind viewers of the trapped nature of the men on the sub. Finally, Petersen even employs the strategy of disbelief in the disaster. The boat's mission is doomed from the start. The captain knows this and tries to get two of his men off the submarine before leaving port, but the German High Command denies his request, signaling to viewers that something bad has to befall the mission.

Perhaps the most difficult aspect of the movie is that it is told from the German crew's point of view. Just how problematic this point of view could be is revealed by a video game based on the film and released in 1990 with the tag line "stalk and destroy Allied warships during winter of 1941 in the midst of World War II." In brief, players are being encouraged to have fun destroying Nazi Germany's enemies. For the intended purchaser, an adolescent in America or England, this meant of course destroying the boats that their ancestors could have been on. To be sure Petersen's film is not that crass. Moreover he attempts to mitigate the situation for viewers who may have sympathized and maybe even empathized with the enemy by shocking them through the conflagration that ends the film into a realization of who the men on the boat represent. His coda or epilogue to the film is not a triumphal return to homeport. Rather as the U-boat docks and the men disembark, Allied planes attack, killing most of the men and sinking the submarine. In this way, the film references Germany's defeat and cancels out the jubilation at their victory in the Straits of Gibraltar. (RCR)

QUESTIONS

1. Wolfgang Petersen's *The Boat* has been called one of the best antiwar films ever and yet has also been criticized for turning a blind eye to the cause for which the German submarine crew was fighting.

    A. Support the view that the film is antiwar, giving examples from the film.

    B. Support the critics who say that the film is not critical enough of the historical facts; again cite examples from the film.

2. Petersen's film follows classical film structure with earlier scenes being reprised later in the film for dramatic or ironic effect. Locate the instances where the following scenes take place and explain how they function within the movie.

    The captain tells the crew: "Well men, everything OK?" ("Na Männer, alles klar?")

    The men listen to "It's a Long Way to Tipparary."

3. Identify the songs used in *The Boat* and describe their function.

4. Compare this film to the story, perspective, and structure of other war films you have seen.

RELATED FILMS

08/15 (Paul May 1954/55). May introduced the formula for German war films in which the focus is on the trouble enlisted men have with their superior officers rather than with the historical enemy.

Haie und kleine Fische (*Sharks and Small Fish*, Frank Wisbar 1957). An early submarine epic extolling the bravery of the men in Germany's navy.

Stalingrad (Joseph Vilsmaier 1993). This war epic is often compared favorable to Petersen's *The Boat*.

Hunde wollt ihr ewig leben? (*Dogs, Do You Want to Live Forever?* Frank Wisbar 1958). An early movie about the Second World War on which Vilmaier based *Stalingrad*.

Die Brücke (*The Bridge*, (Bernhard Wicki 1959). Like Petersen, Wicki crafted a film with a strong pacifist message about the horrors of war.

U 571 (Jonathan Mostow, USA 2000)). Mostow's film trades on the popularity of *The Boat*. It also miffed the British as the film changes the successful mission that the film is based on from a British operation to an American one.

INFORMATION

Das Boot: The Director's Cut. (1982), DVD, in German with English subtitles, color, 209 minutes, Columbia/Tristar Studios released 2001.

Buchheim, Lothar-Günther. *Der Film "Das Boot": Ein Journal.* Munich: Goldman, 1981.

Petersen, Wolfgang and Ulrich Greiwe. *Ich liebe die großen Geschichten: vom "Tatort" bis nach Hollywood.* Cologne: Kiepenheuer und Witsch, 1997.

Prager, Brad. "Beleaguered under the Sea: Wolfgang Petersen's *Das Boot* [1981] as a German Hollywood Film." In *Light Motives*: *German Popular Film in Perspective*, edited by Randall Halle and Margaret McCarthy, 237–258. Detroit: Wayne State UP, 2003.

Reimer, Robert C. and Carol J. Reimer. *Nazi-Retro Film: How German Narrative Cinema Remembers the Past*. New York: Twayne Publishers, 1992.

CHAPTER 21

Der Himmel über Berlin

(*Wings of Desire*, **Wim Wenders 1987**)

Damiel (Bruno Ganz) looking down from his position high above the streets of Berlin, wearing a black trench coat. At the time of the film's release, Berlin was still a divided city. Damiel's position high above the city unites East and West Berlin, at least from the point of view of the angels, who make no distinction in the geography of division.

CREDITS

Director	Wim Wenders
Screenplay	Wim Wenders and Peter Handke
Director of Photography	Henri Alekan
Music	Jürgen Knieper
Producers	Anatole Dauman, Wim Wenders
Production Companies	Argos Films, Road Movies Filmproduktion, Westdeutscher Rundfunk
Length	128 minutes; color and b/w

Principal Cast

Damiel (Bruno Ganz), Marion (Solveig Dommartin), Cassiel (Otto Sander), Homer (Curt Bois), Himself as an angel turned human (Peter Falk).

THE STORY

The theme of *Der Himmel über Berlin* (*Wings of Desire* 1987) is established in the opening sequences as the camera glides through the sky above Berlin, as it picks up scenes of life below with conversations and thoughts. It is 1986 and the city is still divided by the Wall. The camera adopts the view of an angel, as Damiel's (Bruno Ganz) eye opens the film. Damiel is then introduced wearing a black trench coat atop Berlin's Gedächtniskirche. His wings are the only indicators of his existence as an angel, while the rest of his outfit contradicts our image of angels. Damiel is invisible to adults, but visible to children. We continue to follow Damiel as the camera wanders through the city, moves through apartments and enters Berlin's central library, where more angels are introduced.

During their first meeting, Damiel and his companion-angel Cassiel (Otto Sanders) exchange observations, which testify to their ability to survey and record, and also their inability to shape the events in the human world: Cassiel fails in an attempt to save a young man from committing suicide. Other scenes show individuals suffering physically or emotionally as the angels observe, unable to intervene. Their helplessness is a source for Damiel's motivation to seek fulfillment as a human being. When he meets Marion (Solveig Dommartin), a circus trapeze artist with angel wings affixed to her costume, his desire to join the world of mortals becomes overwhelming. The face-to-face encounter between Damiel and Marion climaxes in Marion's long monologue as an appeal for the necessity of human relationships, and, above all, love.

BACKGROUND

Wim Wenders is one of the most prominent German directors. Born August 14, 1945 in Düsseldorf, he studied philosophy and medicine and moved to Paris. After enrolling in the Graduate School of Film and Television in Munich, Wenders began his professional career as a filmmaker in 1971 and quickly became a leading figure of New German Cinema. Francis Ford Coppola invited him to the United States in 1978. Wenders spent four years living and working in the United States during which time he directed *Der amerikanische Freund* (*The American Friend* 1977) and *Der Stand der Dinge* (*The State of Things* 1982). In 1982 Wenders moved back to Germany. Other films of Wenders include: *Paris, Texas* (1984), *Bis ans Ende der Welt* (*Until the End of the World* 1991) and *Buena Vista Social Club* (1999). Many of Wenders' films are classified as road movies and tell the story of a journey or search.

The setting of *Wings of Desire* is decisive to the meaning of the film. For Wenders Berlin was the cultural and historical heart of Germany, a city that still bears the wounds of the Second World War and its consequences. He felt that "Berlin is divided like our world, like our time, like men and women, young and old, rich and poor, like all our experience .... My story isn't about Berlin because it's set there, but because it couldn't be set anywhere else. ... The sky is ... the only thing that unites these two cities, apart from their past of course."

During the Second World War Berlin was the most heavily bombed city in Germany, enduring air raids nearly every day. After the end of the war, the

Although he cannot see him, Peter Falk (right), playing himself but also a fallen angel, tells Damiel (Bruno Ganz) that he knows he's there.

city was divided into four sectors, one for each of the allied forces. Three of these sectors formed West Berlin; the fourth became the Soviet sector and remained separate during the Cold War. West Berlin was referred to as the Island Berlin, because it was surrounded by Communist East Germany and was accessible only by air, land and sea corridors. On the evening of August 13, 1961, East Germany began the "Wall of China" operation. This operation called for the closing of all borders. At 1:00 AM, sixty-three of the eighty-one check points were closed. By dawn, roads connecting the two cities were dug up and barbed wire barricades set up. Soon the first wall was built; it was rebuilt four times over the next twenty-eight years. The final Berlin Wall, built around 1979, consisted of concrete slabs with steel rods. With the construction of the Wall, West Berlin lost more than three hundred thousand commuters from East Berlin. Potsdamer Platz, once a bustling square in the middle of Berlin, became no-man's land. On November 9, 1989, after the East German government was overthrown, the wall was torn down and German reunification began the following year. Berlin is quickly becoming a modern capital city of united Germany.

EVALUATION

Wim Wenders is a director who works outside of Hollywood's commercial bastion, and as such takes great liberty in the crafting of his films. He is known for inventing the story as he goes along, a practice that often brings him to the brink of despair, but has proven effective. Wenders believes that no text can "approximate the feeling you get while you're making a film, the feeling for the style, the look, the idiom of a film." The only available text at the outset of *Wings of Desire* were several dialogues that Austrian writer Peter Handke had written upon Wender's request. Handke had worked with Wenders on a previous film, *Die Angst des Tormanns beim Elfmeter* (*The Goalie's Anxiety of the Penalty Kick* 1972), based on Handke's book with the same title, and *Falsche Bewegung* (*False Movement* 1975), but he declined to write the script for *Wings of Desire*. Wenders did not consider this to be a problem, and started filming. Wenders describes Handke's dialogues as "lighthouses" he had to maneuver around. Most of the scenes were drafted either the night before the shooting or were devised during the actual shoot.

The absence of a conventional story and the film's loose structure led critics such as Alexander Graf to describe the film as "a fragmentary collection of impressions [that] is linked only by the figure of Damiel." Although Damiel is the central figure in the film, he is not its protagonist. Wenders wanted to have three characters in the film, each experiencing the world differently. The trio of Damiel, Marion, and Cassiel should be seen as a unity who, with their opposing characteristics, represent the complexity of the human mind. Through their eyes Wenders wants the viewer to understand the relationship between opposites such as angel/human, man/woman, loneliness/partnership, and how they complement rather than contrast with one another. Wenders and Handke regard these opposites as a platform from which the full spectrum of life develops.

Damiel plays a key role, since he takes the viewer on a journey through both worlds and transcends the opposites. He distances himself from the world of the angels and moves towards the world of mortals, the world of Marion, a trapeze artist with whom he has fallen in love. Damiel is a character without a history of his own. He is an observer. In his conversation with Cassiel, Damiel expresses a desire to "feel a weight grow in him to end the infinity and to tie him to earth." Damiel longs to unite with the human world and become a participant who connects with humans and has his own history. His journey is the ultimate transformation from an immortal to a mortal, a sort of anti-transition, in that transcendence has traditionally meant passing from the mortal to the immortal world. In becoming human Damiel does the opposite, yet for him it is the ultimate transcendence. It is this anti-transition that brings together the opposing elements in Damiel and unites him with his human counterpart Marion.

After his transformation, Damiel's desires and fascinations with the mortal world are validated and his suspicions about the benefits of becoming a participant are true. Until this point, he had been the observer of many people's thoughts and lives, a great diversity of people who had in common only their solitude and their existential or spiritual questions, and perhaps their dreams of the "world behind the world," the spiritual world. These people are a mirror for Damiel, showing him what he is by making him aware of what he is not. What they have are real senses and experiences, something Damiel lacks, while he has wings and eternal life, something that real people dream of. People, however, can directly change their lives and the world around them; Damiel cannot. What sets them most apart from Damiel is that the answer to their questions is exploratory rather than absolute. In contrast to Damiel, there are no black and white answers in their world. That is, experience rather than distanced observation shapes human beings.

Marion is the perfect balance for Damiel, except that she is fixed to the trapeze rather than suspended in the sky. She is a human angel, which explains Damiel's fascination. As part of a traveling circus, she has no roots. Also as part of the circus, her life is filled with sensual experiences, something Damiel is missing. Yet she longs for what he hopes to shed, the permanence of the spiritual world.

The closing of Circus Alekan makes Marion wonder about her future. The feeling of emptiness scares her. In an inner monologue, she reflects on her childhood's desire for solitude. But now the loneliness makes her unhappy. Instead of wanting to be alone, she now finds herself longing and searching for something real that she can call her own. She longs for transcendent experience, although she is deeply grounded in this world. Marion and Damiel both hope to find the missing side of existence they cannot access but to which they feel a deep connection. Their search is one and the same.

Despite his yearnings, Damiel has doubts about whether becoming human is right. His angel companion, Cassiel, does not make this choice an easy one for him. Cassiel is more observant of the darker side of human nature than Damiel. Cassiel follows Homer (Curt Bois) around, a storyteller in search of listeners. Homer is "the representative and bearer of collective memory, the spirit of history … the spirit of Berlin." In his reflections on devastation and death as the consequences of the Second World War, he opens up the window to the past for Cassiel. Cassiel is then reminded of recurring human tendencies to harm one another, to destroy, and to kill. Humans have a conscience; they suffer and witness horrors that are impossible to forget. Homer embodies this conscience. He hopes to restore peace through his stories, but ironically, his age will not allow it, and he has lost his listeners. In this light, Cassiel's skepticism is justified, and so is his influence on Damiel's decision.

It is Peter Falk (playing himself), an angel turned human, who lends validity to Damiel's desire to join the world of mortals. Falk is actually the only human who senses Damiel's presence, aside from children. Falk is grounded; in a humble, down-to-earth location (a snack stand), he talks to Damiel about the simple joys of being human: how good it feels to drink coffee, smoke cigarettes, and rub one's hands together when it is cold. Most importantly, however, Falk mentions the importance of having friends and of being able to look people in the eyes. He wishes that Damiel could be his friend and then shakes his imaginary hand.

After he makes the "leap into humanity," Damiel sets out to search for Marion, whom he aptly finds at a concert where anonymity and group feeling blend into a strange synergy. The music at the concert also has a fateful element to it. Nick Cave screams his ethereal, eerie, and hypnotizing blues in "From Her to Eternity" (1984) as they meet. Damiel feels that his fate is the same as that in the song when he finally meets Marion. In the final scene at the bar, Marion delivers a long, cryptic monologue about the unification of opposites: "There is no greater story than ours, of man and woman. It will be a story of giants, invisible, transferable, a story of new ancestors. Look, my eyes! They are the image of necessity, of the future of everyone..." It is fitting that Marion, who longs for the spiritual, gives such an esoteric commentary.

The monologue is revealed visually in the next scene where Damiel reflects on his choice to become human while Marion is spinning in a circle on a suspended rope that Damiel is holding. They are now an entity, and this is symbolized by Marion's circular motion and their dependence on each other for this acrobatic maneuver. To complete the picture, Cassiel is shown sitting on the stairs in the background in his role as an eternal observer. This shot represents the only blend of the two earthly angels in color while Cassiel's figure is inserted in black and white, a visually arresting combination of the two worlds. Damiel now knows what no angel knows, the beauty of the mortal and the immortal, opposites that give meaning to one another. (AH/ ADz/ AD)

QUESTIONS

1. Describe the relationship between the two angels. Refer to the contrast between their personalities and desires.

2. Describe the different ways in which the storyteller bridges the German past with the present of divided Berlin.

3. Discuss the central role that the lyrical narration "Als das Kind, Kind war" ("when the child was a child"), which begins the film, plays in creating meaning in the movie.

4. What role does Peter Falk have in the film besides being a former angel?

RELATED FILMS

Bis ans Ende der Welt (*Until the End of the World* 1991). Wenders' films are often described as metaphorical journeys to the self. In this film, an actual journey by a son to help his mother see before she dies also brings him insight into his life. The film's musical score was a particular hit with younger art cinema fans.

In weiter Ferne, so nah (*Faraway, So Close* 1993). Wenders' sequel to *Wings of Desire* covered some of the same territory as the first film, but now the Berlin Wall was gone and the two German states were united.

Das Leben ist eine Baustelle (Wolfgang Becker, *Life Is All You Get* 1997). Becker's film was one of many made after the fall of the Berlin Wall to treat the historic period on film.

Goodbye Lenin (Wolfgang Becker 2003). Becker's film, highly successful in Germany and art cinemas in America and England, tells of a son who after the fall of the Berlin Wall recreates a German Democrat Republic that never existed in order to help his mother recover from a heart attack. The film is treated elsewhere in this book.

INFORMATION

Wings of Desire (1987), DVD, in German with subtitles and English, color and b/w, 128 minutes, MGM/UA Video, released 2003.

Cook, Roger, ed. *The Cinema of Wim Wenders: Image Narrative and the Postmodern Condition*. Detroit: Wayne State UP, 1997.

Graf, Alexander. *The Cinema of Wim Wenders*. London: Wallflower Press, 2002.

Kolker, Robert Phillip and Peter Beicken. *The Films of Wim Wenders: Cinema as Vision and Desire*. Cambridge: Cambridge UP, 1993.

Wenders, Wim and Peter Handke. *Himmel über Berlin* (original screenplay). Frankfurt a/M: Suhrkamp, 1987.

Wenders, Wim. *Wim Wenders: On Film: Essays and Conversations*. London: Faber and Faber, 2001.

Wim Wenders' official web site: www.wim-wenders.com

Information on Berlin and the Berlin Wall from: www.wall-berlin.org

CHAPTER 22

Das schreckliche Mädchen

(*The Nasty Girl*, **Michael Verhoeven 1990**)

Sonja (Lena Stolze) and Martin (Robert Giggenbach) reveal aprehension on their wedding day. They are looking through the rear window of a car smashed by hooligans objecting to Sonja's research into her town's past.

CREDITS

Director ....Michael Verhoeven
Screenplay ....Michael Verhoeven
Music........................Mike Hertung, Elmar Schloter, Billy Gorlt and Lydie Aubray
Director of Photography ....Axel de Roche
Producers ....Helmut Rasp, Michael Senftleben
Production Companies.............. Filmverlag der Autoren, Sentana Filmproduction,
Zweites Deutsches Fernsehen
Length...94 minutes; color and b/w

Principal Cast

Lena Stolze (Sonja Wegmus), Hans-Reinhard Müller (Juckenack), Monika Baumgartner (Sonja's mother), Elisabeth Bertram (Sonja's grandma), Michael Gahr (Paul Rosenberger), Robert Giggenbach (Martin), Udo Thomer (Archivist Schulz), Richard Suessmeier (The mayor), Rudolf Klaffenböck (The judge), Willie Schultes (Father Brummel).

THE STORY

The story of Michael Verhoeven's *Das schreckliche Mädchen* (*The Nasty Girl* 1990) is based on the experience of Anna Rosmus, "Sonja Wegmus" in the movie, whose naiveté in growing up in the Bavarian town of Passau (Pfilzing in the movie) turns to aggression against her fellow citizens once she finds out how Jews were treated in Passau during the Nazi period. Sonja has won a European essay competition and is awarded the town's "Silver Medal" by the mayor. Now she wants to take part in another essay competition, "My Home Town during the Third Reich." But when she begins to research the topic, she encounters unforeseen problems. The city archives are reluctant to release the desired documents. What she finds to her surprise and dismay is that the Catholic clergy and businessmen, whom she was raised to respect and admire, and whom she fervently believed defied the Nazis, did just the opposite. After deciding to write a book on the subject, the more she digs, the more she is thwarted. Eventually she is even threatened physically by rock throwing and bombs.

After marrying her teacher, Sonja settles down with her own family in the community and pursues her research into the town's past. Sonja turns up at the municipal archives again and again demanding access to the documents. She is no longer a child now and can no longer be stopped in her determination to find out the truth about her town.

BACKGROUND

Rosmus states in her memoir *Against the Stream: Growing up Where Hitler Used to Live* (2002) that she had never heard that Hitler had lived in Passau, that Eichmann had grown up there and that Eichmann's father had been a teacher at Rosmus's *Gymnasium* (German academic high school), and that other Nazi celebrities had lived or visited the city frequently – in short, that Passau had been a hotspot for Nazi activities in Germany. That history had been deliberately erased from official memory and Rosmus's teachers never talked to her about it. Rosmus single-handedly showed through her investigation that her hometown had covered up the city's past with the help of most of the people she had grown up with, her teachers, neighbors and friends. When she interviewed her fellow citizens in the mid 1980s they still were not interested in discussing the Nazi past, but continued to cover up everything as if nothing bad had ever happened, and they continued to delay her investigation by limiting her access to the city archives. Rosmus's investigative zeal derives from this experience and embarrassment, which Verhoeven shows in his movie.

In 1996, Rosmus was awarded the highest honor by the German Jewish community, the Galinski Prize. During the 1990s, with Rosmus's activities and popularity increasing, she decided to move to the United States after divorcing her husband. Anna Rosmus now lives in Maryland just outside of Washington, DC where she continues to work as an independent scholar and researcher for the

Sonja (Lena Stolze) kisses her teacher and future husband Martin (Robert Giggenbach) in front of the Gnadenbaum, a tree with symbolic meaning for the characters.

United States Holocaust Archive. She has been awarded the American Society of Journalists and Authors' Conscience in Media Award, the Sarnat Prize and the Myrtle Wreath Award from the Washington DC Hadassah, and the Holocaust Survivors and Friends' Holocaust Memorial Award. Her recent work is the subject of a documentary, *Passau-Washington: The Nasty Girl in America*. She has also been profiled on *60 Minutes*. Her many publications are available over the internet and at bookstores.

The movie shows only a short part of Anna Rosmus's life, with her first steps into Nazi research. It also reflects in a way the process of coming to terms with an important phase of Germany's Nazi past. It is but the first phase in this process. The movie is a document to Rosmus's courage and determination. She is one of the first young Germans to systematically uncover the past. To be sure, there had been trials about Auschwitz and the other concentration camps in the 1960s. These originated largely because a clause in Germany's legal system required these trials to be conducted within twenty-five years after the events took place. Otherwise they would have been *verjährt* (voided by a statute of limitations clause). But the trials do not mean that the public was ready to deal with the atrocities on a broader basis. "Auschwitz" became a code word for any Nazi atrocity. Indeed one could see the trials as displacing the guilt of many to the guilt of an aberrant few.

It was not until the American TV series *Holocaust* played on West German TV in 1979 that the code word "Auschwitz" was changed permanently to "Holocaust." The series generated the most intensive and emotional public discussion of the Nazi Holocaust persecution and extermination of the Jews since the end of the Second World War. At least twenty million West Germans, more than half the adult population, watched the program. More importantly, the show created public awareness that precipitated a new historical discourse at all levels of German society.

Did this interest mean that by the late 1970s, Germans were prepared to abandon the comforting insulation from feelings of guilt and responsibility that the narrative of their own "victimization" by Hitler had supplied? Indeed, the confrontation with the Holocaust set free new energy in the West German state, and once the accusations of the 68-generation (the term often given to the members of the protest movements in the late sixties in Germany and France) were overcome, a meaningful dialogue about the Nazi past began. The public discourse began to develop a more liberal viewpoint, not only towards the Jews but also to the incoming flood of foreigners from south and southeastern European countries.

The Nazi atrocities now had a name, and in the mid-eighties, forty years after the fact, school boards decided that Holocaust instruction needed to become part of the school curricula. Rosmus's example shows how reluctantly the teachers in her hometown faced this task. The main reason was that some of these teachers at that time had served in the military, most likely on the eastern front, some might have been part of the Waffen SS and were now history teachers in German schools. The student revolts of the sixties had not changed very much as they had approached the question of the Nazi period too academically and thus had very little impact on the general public.

Rosmus's one-woman vendetta soon became popular and resulted in numerous citizens' initiatives to uncover the past of German cities. Several of them founded Jewish memory centers and memorials, the largest resulting in the construction of the Berlin Holocaust Memorial and the Berlin Jüdisches Museum. Both projects had started as *Bürgerinitiativen* (citizen initiatives), going back as far as the 1980s.

With this background Rosmus's work became an important part of Holocaust education. Michael Verhoeven recognized her role in bringing Germany to confront the past when he approached Rosmus for permission to base the film on her life as an example of an outspoken German Holocaust researcher.

EVALUATION

The Nasty Girl is a fictionalized account of Anna Rosmus's life and work as an investigator of Nazi crimes in her Bavarian hometown of Passau. When developing the idea for the movie Michael Verhoeven was faced with the task of portraying the work of a twenty-four year old woman. It was clear to him that she had just begun her investigations. And thus *The Nasty Girl* looks very much like a work in progress as Rosmus's life did at that time, 1989. The direction her work was taking, her dynamic energy, and her character made it appealing to make a autobiographical movie about such a young historian who had just published one book, *Exodus: Im Schatten der Gnade* (1988). In turn, Verhoeven helped popularize Anna Rosmus' life; she then became one of the best-known Nazi hunters in Germany. By casting Lena Stolze as Anna, Verhoeven gave his film added depth. For Stolze had portrayed Sophie Scholl, a young Nazi resister who was executed, in *Die weiße Rose* (*The White Rose* 1982) and also played Sophie Scholl in Percy Adlon's biography of the young woman, *Fünf letzte Tage* (*The Five Last Days* 1982).

Although depicting real events and real people, Michael Verhoeven created a very stylized film, changing names and places. His use of Brechtian alienation and distancing, a technique meant to keep people out of the story and focus instead on its political meaning, was not met well by many American critics. Roger Ebert, for example, objected to the film's style, preferring a more realistic depiction of the events instead of the experimental approach Verhoeven used. Hollywood, even in its political films, is primarily a medium that entertains, that moves through emotions and not the intellect. Thus when Wegmus talks directly into the camera and explains what is happening, viewers who want a more conventional approach to drama may be confused as to how to respond to the film.

Since Verhoeven was using Rosmus as an example to educate his audience about the importance of Holocaust research on a local level, something that had been done only on a very limited scale until the 1980s, he has her talk directly to the audience, as if wanting to engage them in the film's discourse. Verhoeven's film has clearly been influenced by Bertolt Brecht, a German theorist and dramatist who employed various symbols in his parables or medieval morality tales. Like Brecht, Verhoeven uses symbolic figures, such as the figure of Justice sleeping in court, to illustrate and satirize the political situation in Germany. Verhoeven adopts other Brechtian techniques as well. The most notable Brechtian distancing device occurs when Rosmus's family listens to anonymous threatening telephone calls in their living room while the town moves past them in the background. The effect is that of an open living room moving through the city streets, as if they were on a carnival float. However, unlike a carnival parade, the scene is not meant to be funny or elicit laughter.

The story is beautifully framed by introducing a *Gnadenbaum* in the first scene, a symbolic Catholic tree of wishes and repentance, and by closing with Wegmus, in the final scene, at the tree in despair, thus leaving an open end for the viewer. The movie changes between color and black and white, a technique used in other German movies of the time such as Margarethe von Trotta's *Rosa Luxemburg* (1986) and *Das Versprechen* (*The Promise* 1995) or Wim Wender's *Himmel über Berlin* (*Wings of Desire* 1987). Verhoeven introduces scenes of Wegmus's past in black and white, notably when she is with her grandmother, her most important mentor, who is also the only person to share information about the Nazi period. The plot surrounding the Zumtobel family and Professor Juckenack's exposure is filmed in color. Here Brechtian theater influence is the strongest in the open stage setting, where sets are simply images projected by slides. Illusionary film is completely destroyed in this fashion and viewers must focus on the information that is presented rather than the emotion. Sonja's final discovery of the files and her unapproved copying of them, accompanied by her yodeling, is the climactic scene of her investigation.

The movie admittedly does not follow Anna's research, but rather the screenplay reduces everything to the the Juckenack-Zumtobel story. Most importantly, this change reduces the host of characters opposing Sonja's research to one major character, Professor Juckenack, who when exposed by Sonja as a Nazi is dropped by the Passau media, a *persona non grata*. Instead, almost as in a Western movie, Anna is instated as the new Pfilzing heroine in a celebration where her statue is presented to the public. When she discovers that this is a ploy to silence her and to grant her iconic status in Pfilzing, she begins to scream. Her withdrawal to the *Gnadenbaum* at the end of the movie is not really a withdrawal from the public but—as the story shows—just a phase when she will emerge as a much stronger and more aggressive investigator, one who refuses the closure of silence. (RZ)

QUESTIONS

1. Why did Verhoeven choose this theatrical style of telling Sonja's story?

2. Show how the relationship between Sonja and her husband changes in the movie.

3. Why did Verhoeven focus this movie at the beginning of Sonja's story when her investigation had just begun?

RELATED FILMS

Die weiße Rose (*The White Rose* 1982). Also starring Lena Stolze, Sonja in *The Nasty Girl*, this Michael Verhoeven film crafts a thriller around the story of Germany's best known resistance movement, The White Rose.

Fünf letzte Tage (*The Five Last Days*, Percy Adlon 1982). Whereas Michael Verhoeven focuses on the entire group in the resistance movement The White Rose in his film of the same name, Adlon tells Sophie Scholl's story from the time of her capture until her execution.

Die Mörder sind unter uns (*The Murderers Are among Us*, Wolfgang Staudte 1946). Staudte tells the story of an army officer who after the war hunts down his superior officer for having ordered the execution of a village during the Second World War.

The Stranger (Orson Welles 1946). This is one of the first films to deal with the topic of hunting down those responsible for the Holocaust.

INFORMATION

The Nasty Girl (1990), VHS, in German with English subtitles, color and b/w, 94 minutes, HBO Studios, released 1992.

Reimer, Robert C. and Carol J. Reimer. *Nazi-Retro Film: How German Narrative Cinema Remembers the Past*. New York: Twayne Publishers, 1992.

Rosmus, Anna: *Against the Stream: Growing Up Where Hitler Used to Live*. translated from the German *Was ich denke* (2000) by Imogen von Tannenberg. Columbia, SC: U of South Carolina P, 2002.

CHAPTER 23

Keiner liebt mich

(*Nobody Loves Me*, **Doris Dörrie 1995**)

Fanny Fink (Maria Schrader) does an African ritual dance with Orfeo (Pierre Sanoussi-Bliss) as he helps her come out of her shell in order to find love.

CREDITS

Director	Doris Dörrie
Screenplay	Doris Dörrie
Director of Photography	Helge Weindler
Music	Niki Reiser
Producers	Christoph Holch, Gerd Huber, Renate Seefeldt
Production Companies	Cobra Film GmbH, Zweites Deutsches Fernsehen
Length	104 minutes; color

Principal Cast

Maria Schrader (Fanny Fink), Pierre Sanoussi-Bliss (Orfeo de Altamar), Michael von Au (Lothar Sricker), Elisabeth Trissenaar (Madeleine, Fanny's mother), Inge Naujoks (Lasse Laengsfeld), Joachim Król (Anton), Peggy Parnass (Fanny's friend).

THE STORY

This black comedy opens as Fanny Fink sits in front of a video camera and tapes an introduction to herself for a dating service, an introduction which also serves to characterize Fanny for the film audience and also to introduce one of the film's major themes, finding love in a seemingly fast, impersonal world. After reciting her virtues and faults in front of the camera, she concludes that she would not want to go out with herself either. The opening scene of Doris Dörrie's *Keiner liebt mich* (*Nobody Loves Me* 1995) sets the melancholic tone of the movie. As Fanny tapes, the soundtrack plays Edith Piaf's signature song, "Je ne regrette rien" (I regret nothing), providing a perfect complement to Fanny's low self-esteem.

Fanny's search for love occurs against a background of carnival in Cologne, a celebratory time of partying and sexual pairings. There is however little occasion for partying in Fanny's life. Her apartment building is being modernized and gentrified. Although the new owner apparently takes an interest in her, his attentions are selfish and lead to increased unhappiness. Moreover, Fanny is obsessed with death. A seminar in dying that she attends provides a unifying arc through the film. A coffin she constructs provides a two-sided leitmotif, first as a metaphor of the emptiness she feels because of her missing love life and then as a sign that she has been cured of her self-created depression.

Orfeo, a gay black man, advises Fanny on pseudo-spiritual methods for attracting love. He himself, however, also has difficulty finding love, and in addition is dying from an undisclosed illness, perhaps AIDS. The two help each other through their difficulties, allowing each to find what the other wants, proving that a German film can be warm and fuzzy even in the face of death.

BACKGROUND

American popular culture, particularly as represented by Hollywood, influences popular culture worldwide. German music and film display Hollywood's influence in preferred styles and thematic content. Considering that Doris Dörrie spent part of her years studying film in America, it is not surprising that in style and often in content her films are easily accessible to an American audience. They are generally light and focus on attractive, usually professional, thirtysomethings working their way through puzzling relationships. Yet in spite of the antecedents found in the romantic and screwball comedies of Hollywood directors such as Billy Wilder or Preston Sturges, her stories stay rooted in contemporary German culture. In *Nobody Loves Me* Dörrie tells a conventional Hollywood love story about a young woman looking for romance, but she sets the film in a real location, rather than Hollywood's land of fantasy: Cologne during Carnival season, allowing her characters to play dress-up as they explore questions of personal identity.

Dörrie's characters often disguise themselves in an attempt to assume new personalities, hide from others, or find out who they are. In four of her films, *Mitten ins Herz* (*Straight to the Heart* 1983), *Männer* (*Men* 1985), *Paradies* (*Paradise* 1986), and

Geld (*Money* 1989) all based on her novellas of the same name, characters undergo physical makeovers by dying their hair, donning wigs, or wearing a different style of clothes than usual. All are struggling to discover who they are or trying to change who they are in order to improve their chances for a successful relationship. This is also true in *Nobody Loves Me*, but sometimes the disguise is harder to locate culturally. Fanny Fink's friend Orfeo, for example, dresses as a skeleton, Bessie Smith, and Nana Mouskouri.

Orfeo's skeletal costume refers of course to his name, a derivative of Orpheus, the singer in the Greek myth about a man (Orpheus) who escorted his wife (Eurydice) back from Hell. Orfeo too sings to charm his friend Fanny back, from the spiritual death she has succumbed to since turning thirty. Unlike Orpheus, who does not succeed in rescuing Eurydice, Orfeo succeeds in bringing Fanny out of her spiritual death, symbolized by her depression and attendance in a seminar on dying. Dressed as a skeleton, Orfeo dances with Fanny to Edith Piaf's song "Non, je ne regrette rien," freeing her from her hypercritical analysis of herself that is the primary cause of her death fixation. The words of Piaf's song speak of having no regrets about the pain and sorrows of her life because her life begins anew from the day she meets a new love.

There is a double connection between the lyrics of "Non, je ne regrette rien" and the love life of both Fanny and Orfeo, as the words not only speak of sorrow of past loves and the joy of finding a new love, but in a sense mirror Piaf's difficult life, in particular her persona of suffering lover. The four times the song is heard, the last with the entire cast singing during the credits, thus reflects a European view of love: sometimes temporary but worth the pain and suffering because of the passion when a new love begins.

Fanny has yet to find love's passion but Orfeo has achieved it with his latest lover who is now telling him goodbye. In the same way, Bessie Smith, a black American blues singer whose music would be well known to many Germans, reflects Orfeo's pain at the hands of a cruel lover. Conversely, his pantomimed rendition of "Ein Schiff wird kommen" (A Ship Will Come"), dressed as Nana Mouskouri, a near-sighted Greek singer very popular in Germany among older Germans, reflects the happy outcome of Fanny's story.

EVALUATION

Doris Dörrie's black comedy *Nobody Loves Me* focuses on the novelist and filmmaker's favorite topic, thirtysomethings, particularly women, struggling to find and also make sense of themselves and their relationships. Introspective to a fault, Dörrie's characters brood and obsess about getting older, being alone, and death. Moreover her women tend to suffer from low self-esteem, seeking refuge in ill-fated romances. They wish they were someone other than who they are, donning disguises that temporarily give them a new identity, and, in her non-comedic works, sometimes abuse their bodies, overeating or undereating in order to achieve change. As a black comedy, *Nobody Loves Me* tells a story of *eros* and *thanatos* (love and death) through its eccentric characters, carnival setting, and expressive music track.

The main character, Fanny Fink (Maria Schrader), is an attractive, but not glamorous, thirty-year-old woman with low self-esteem. Obsessed with death and the thought that she has a better a chance of dying in a nuclear disaster than finding a husband, Fanny represents a parody of Western Europe's single woman, as reflected in film. On the one hand she is emancipated, independent, and attractive.

On the other hand she is neurotic, dependent on others, and not sure how best to show her attractiveness. In spite of the qualities that would place Fanny at home in any western European film, she is part of a trend in German film heroines in films of the nineties, best represented by the actor Katja Riemann in such films as *Abgeschminkt* (*Making Up*, Katja von Garnier 1993), *Der bewegte Mann* (*Maybe, Maybe Not*, Sönke Wortmann 1994), *Bandits* (Katja von Garnier 1997) and *Die Apothekerin* (*The Pharmacist*, Rainer Kaufmann 1997). The women in these films seem doomed both because of their pessimism and their bad choices and yet, at least in Riemann's persona, embody a degree of feminism that bespeaks change. Fanny is more complicated than her cinematic sisters, though. She is undeniably a quintessential Dörrie heroine. She is unsure of who she is and seeks her identity through a number of different (dis)guises. She longs for love and happiness but is certain that she will never find either. Yet she is sufficiently vulnerable to elicit the viewers' love.

Fanny's companion and mentor in her search for identity and love, Orfeo de Altamar (Pierre Sanoussi-Bliss) is in many ways as confused as she. He is an African-German born in East Germany to a German mother and African father, claims to be from another planet, awaiting the day when his alien friends will come to take him back, and is dying of an apparently incurable illness, perhaps AIDS. To support his eccentricities, Dörrie films him as he performs ritual dances on the roof of his apartment building, begs for money in Colgone's downtown, and appears as a cross-dresser in a gay bar, impersonating such divas as Bessie Smith and Nana Mouskouri. Yet, since Orfeo also earns money by reading palms, one is never sure if even in his friendship to Fanny he is not also trying to con her out of her money. Besides giving Fanny the self-confidence to first meet and then forget her lover, Orfeo is also dependent on Fanny. She nurses him through illness, humors his claims of being rescued by extraterrestrials, and provides him with a coffin for his death/departure from earth.

As mentioned earlier, death provides an arc that gives the film its macabre humor. More importantly death gives the story its cohesion, relating Fanny's figurative dying to Orfeo's physical disappearance, which we can interrupt as actual death, physical transcendence, or sham. Furthermore, the arc provides the film its resolution, which, when coupled with an ending reprise of Piaf's song, has viewers leaving the theater smiling, a rare occurrence for a German film.

If Orfeo helps Fanny overcome her feeling of low self-esteem, the film's minor characters contribute to her hypercritical approach to self-analysis, the primary cause of her death fixation. Fanny's mother, landlord, friends, and co-workers expose Fanny's weaknesses from character judgment to a penchant for self-pity, and in the case of her mother offer reasons why Fanny may be so afraid of life. As played by the noted German actor Elisabeth Trissenaar, Fanny's mother, Madeleine, writes erotic novels that are seemingly well-received by the public but attacked by the critics. She exudes the flashiness and sexuality that Fanny lacks and reacts hypercritically to Fanny's boyfriends. Each characteristic alone might explain Fanny's low esteem.

The owner of Fanny's apartment building acts as a catalyst for many of Fanny's foolish actions. Played by Michael von Au, even his name, Lothar, suggests his Lothario-like personality, a major cause of Fanny's deepening depression. Lothar also serves as the focus for many of the film's sight gags, from uncontrolled crying to holding a stuffed elephant to watching as Fanny smashes into his car. Fanny's co-worker and girlfriend likewise functions as a catalyst for the plot, but in addition, her outgoing personality and selfishness help put Fanny's personality in

Fanny (Maria Schrader) comforts her mentor and friend Orfeo (Pierre Sanoussi-Bliss), who appears to have an incurable illness and has moreover just been rejected by his lover.

relief. Finally Lasse (Ingo Naujoks), a friend from Fanny's death experience class, lends credence to Orfeo's fortune telling and allows for the film's happy end.

Featured prominently in the film is carnival season in Cologne. The festive masquerade of carnival allows for characters to dress in disguise, to act other than as they are, and lends a note of believability to an otherwise outlandish story. As already mentioned, masquerade or wearing disguise, whether in carnival season or not, plays a role in much of Doris Dörrie's writing and in most of her movies. On the one hand, disguise reflects the confusion of identity confronting individuals in postmodern, multicultural society. It addresses questions of what it means to be German, historically and culturally, what it means to be male or female, gay or straight, married, divorced, or single. On the other hand, by masquerading as others, characters get to play-act without commitment, sometimes learning and sometimes being hurt by the experience. In disguise, characters can function with a new personality, expressing emotions not otherwise freely expressed. Thus, Fanny plays the fool wearing fishnet stockings and lingerie as she tries to captivate Lothar. Orfeo dresses as Bessie Smith and Nana Mouskouri to express his love to the friend who will later jilt him. Fanny's friend dresses as Pippi Longstocking to express innocence not noticeable in her act of stealing Fanny's lover.

Finally, music functions as another character in the film, an outside narrator commenting on Fanny's life. Doris Dörrie has made the film score of *Nobody Loves Me* an integral part of the film's story. Songs which are generally diegetic, that is, part of the screen world, comment on characters' moods, motivations and feelings. When Orfeo mimes Bessie Smith's "Lover Man" in a gay night club, the number not only establishes his relationship to his lover, who is at the end of the bar, but it also comments on Fanny's search for a relationship. As Orfeo continues singing, Dörrie cuts in quick succession to a number of scenes: a dog running through the hall of the apartment house where Fanny and Orfeo live, clouds moving in front of the moon, lit-up apartment windows, Fanny lying in bed, a woman of the apartment house dancing alone in the hallway, the outside door of Orfeo's apartment, and the club where Orfeo is singing. The seemingly disparate images relate to each other through their theme of loneliness and the music thus underscores a motivating factor in Fanny's and Orfeo's relationship as the images take that relationship to a deeper level. A similar intensification occurs as Orfeo, dressed as Nana Mouskouri, a popular singer of sentimental songs, sings "Ein Schiff wird kommen" (The singer on the soundtrack, though, is not Mouskouri but Lale Andersen, a songstress who became famous during the Third Reich). The lyrics, which tell of finally achieving one's desires, comment on the relationships both characters are hoping to have but also ironically signal the end of Orfeo's affair as the camera shows his lover with another man.

The strongest relationship between song and narrative is found in the Edith Piaf number "Non, je ne regrette rien." Used for both the beginning and end credits, the song also appears midway through at a pivotal point in the friendship between Fanny and Orfeo and again at the end as an echo of Orfeo's continuing influence. During the opening credits, which also include Fanny's self-deprecating videotape for the dating service, the song adds a strong counterpoint to Fanny's whining. She is clearly a woman who regrets everything, as the first half of the movie will show. Piaf's voice is heard again a little over half way into the movie, after Fanny has been betrayed by her friend Charlotte and after her mock burial. Seemingly at a low point in her life, Fanny comes home to Orfeo, who is dressed as a skeleton and holds a birthday cake lit with thirty candles. Fanny has reached her dreaded milestone, but rather than mark the end of her happiness, the scene marks the beginning. For as the song ends, Orfeo's health worsens and Fanny finds a purpose in nursing her friend. She truly has nothing to regret when Orfeo dies (leaves her) as she has connected with another when it was important. Finally as the film ends, Fanny puts on Piaf's song at a spontaneous coffee hour, and dances with Lasse, a man from her class in dying. Not only does he have the number 23 on his jersey (a seemingly magical number in the movie), which he reveals while dancing with Fanny, but as Fanny had said during her tape for the dating service, a relationship always begins with a cup of coffee.

Equally as significant as Piaf's "Non, je ne regrette rien," is the film's background music, which consists of a simple melody that repeats in several variations, and although it is often soft, almost imperceptible, the music plays an active role in delineating character and establishing mood. As a slow mournful tune, the six notes of the melody are heard in church, during romantic interludes, and when referencing Orfeo's illness. As a bouncy bosa nova rhythm, the same notes accompany Fanny's makeover, her flirtations with Lothar, and her preparations for a surprise tryst. In most of the situations the melody seldom plays beyond a few measures, after which it abruptly stops, calling our attention to its sudden absence and also to the visuals on the screen when it stops. These moments include Orfeo touching the face on a TV screen of the lover who is leaving him, or Lothar confessing to Fanny that the tears she has been kissing away were caused by an allergy, not some great loss. Sometimes the music segues from one rhythm to the next as the visuals change. For example, a tango melody plays as Fanny gets into her car. This changes to a slow melody as Fanny removes a dead bird from her windshield. It returns to the tango rhythm as Lothar gets into his car, this rhythm slows down as the camera zooms in on the car's license plate number 2323 (as noted, 23 is a special number for Fanny) and then speeds up to a frantic rhythm as she crashes her car into Lothar's.

Finally, a mournful version of the melody is heard over an extended period during two critical moments in the film, when Orfeo tells Fanny his life story and again when he tells her his life philosophy. In the first instance, Orfeo relates his abduction by aliens, his refusal to fly off with them in hopes of experiencing love one last time, and his extraction from them of a promise to return and take him to their home planet. The sequence is followed by Piaf's "Non, je ne regrette rien," contrasting with the melancholy mood of the moment which suggests perhaps there is something to regret. At the same time the sequence foreshadows the next extended use of the melody. After Fanny has prepared for Orfeo's death (departure) – she has bought a gold bar to place in his coffin and dressed him in an Armani suit -- he tells her it is time. But before he lies down in the coffin Fanny has built, Orfeo tells her she must live for the moment. In the background during this sequence , we hear the mournful melody. It has been so slowed down and is played so quietly that at first it is not recognizable. At the same time, the music's softness and tempo call attention to it. (RCR)

QUESTIONS

1. Describe in as much detail as possible the death symbolism in *Nobody Loves Me*. How does such emphasis on death relate to a film about love and people barely thirty years old?

2. At one point in the movie Orfeo tells Fanny: "Your past is a skeleton that walks behind you, your future is the skeleton in front of you. They'll both never leave you, but sometimes they want to talk to you. ... don't listen to them. ... They'll remind you what time it is. It's always the same time. It's always now." How does this extended speech reflect the themes of the movie?

3. Describe each of the minor characters in detail and explain their role in the movie either in relationship to Fanny or to Orfeo.

4. What importance does Carnival have for the film?

5. Look up the myth of Orpheus and Eurydice. What significance does the myth have, if any, for the film?

6. What clues in the way the story is told reveal that the director of the film is a woman? Or conversely, how might the film's story have been told if a man had directed the movie?

RELATED FILMS

Männer (*Men* 1985). *Men* was Dörrie's first hit movie in Germany and in art cinemas in America. As with almost all of her films, she treats relationships with serio-comic irony.

Erleuchtung garantiert (*Enlightenment Guaranteed* 2000). Dörrie's fascination with contemplation, which is hinted at in *Nobody Loves Me*, is given full treatment in *Enghtenment Guaranteed*, a film which follows two German brothers to a Japanese Buddhist monastery.

INFORMATION

Nobody Loves Me (1995), VHS, in German with subtitles, color, 101 minutes, CFP Video, released 1996. Sometimes available through eBay.

Keiner liebt mich (1995), DVD, in German, region 2 (requires a multi-region DVD player), color, 101 minutes, released 2001.

Dörrie, Doris: *Bin ich schön?*: Erzählungen. - Zürich: Diogenes, 1994.

Angier, Carole. "Monitoring Conformity: The Career of Doris Dörrie." In *Women and Film: a Sight and Sound Reader*, edited by Pam Cook and Philip Dodd, 204-209. London: Scarlet Press, 1993.

Birgel, Franz A. and Klaus Phillips, editors. *Straight through the Heart: Doris Dörrie, German Filmmaker and Author*. Lanham, MD and Oxford: The Scarecrow Press, Inc., 2004.

Quart, Barbara Koenig. *Women Directors: The Emergence of a New Cinema*. Westport, CT: Praeger Publishers, 1989.

CHAPTER 24

Das Versprechen

(*The Promise*, **Margarethe von Trotta 1994**)

Sophie (Meret Becker) and Konrad (Anian Zollner) in Prague with Konrad's Doktorvater (dissertation advisor) Professor Lorenz (Otto Sander).

CREDITS

Director...Margarethe von Trotta
Screenplay ....Felice Laudadio, Peter Schneider, Margarethe von Trotta
Director of Photography ....Franz Rath
Music...Jürgen Knieper
Producer ....Eberhard Junkersdorf
Production Companies......................Consortium including Bioskop, Studio Canal
and Westdeutscher Rundfunk
Length..115 minutes; color

Principal Cast

Meret Becker (Sophie as young woman); Corinna Harfouch (Sophie as a middle-aged woman); Anian Zollner (Konrad as a young man); August Zirner (Konrad as a middle-aged man); Otto Sander (Professor Lorenz).

THE STORY

Das Versprechen (*The Promise* 1994) is the story of life under difficult circumstances. The setting as the film opens is the Berlin Wall in the fall of 1961, a few weeks after the Wall was built, when a group of high school students escapes to the West through the underground sewer system. Sophie makes it to the West while her boyfriend Konrad stays behind in the East. For the next twenty-eight years they lead separate and different lives but keep their love going. They see each other only three times, in Prague in 1968, then in East Berlin and in West Berlin in the early 1980s. They have a child, Alexander, who grows up with his mother in West Berlin, and finally, when the Berlin Wall comes down, they can begin their life together, at the age of 46 and with a 20-year old son. The film asks whether being together after over twenty-eight years of separation is possible.

The central story is surrounded by several other stories. Konrad's sister Barbara, a protestant minister, and her husband, Harald, offer the church as a sanctuary to protesters against the Communists and in return, are harassed by the *Staatssicherheit* or *Stasi*, East Germany's security police. Konrad's and Barbara's parents offer both anxious support to the East German state and reprimands to their children. Konrad and Sophie each has a relationship with another partner that results in a child; Konrad with his former assistant Elisabeth and Sophie with the French journalist Gerard, who interviews Konrad when he visits Sophie in West Berlin during a scientific convention. Konrad's professor Lorenz plays a major role in creating a strategy for Konrad's and his own existence as academics in a controlled Communist society.

BACKGROUND

The Promise is obviously a symbol-laden story that combines private life with German history; it was one of the first films about the fall of the Wall and was Germany's contribution to the Berlin Film Festival of 1995. The movie drew a lot of attention but remained almost unknown in Germany, where it was criticized for having a foreign view on German history. Since its initial release, it has claimed an increasing following among American high school and college teachers precisely because it offers a window onto recent German history.

Margarethe von Trotta, the director of *The Promise*, is known as a filmmaker of feminist movies, *Rosa Luxemburg* (1986) and *Die bleierne Zeit* (*Marianne and Juliane* 1981), among others. As one of only a few female directors of the New German Cinema she superbly captures situations from a female perspective. Von Trotta had been married to and had worked closely with the filmmaker Volker Schlöndorff, whom she later divorced. *The Promise* was her first independent film without Schlöndorff and the result is an emotional, almost Hollywood-like movie that was Germany's Oscar nomination for 1995. Von Trotta calls *The Promise* a German *Gone with the Wind*, an aspect not appreciated in a post–Brechtian atmosphere, where drama should not aim at "emotional impact," as a critic wrote, but should have analytical qualities.

Margarethe von Trotta was born in Berlin in 1942. In the 1960s she moved to Paris where she worked for film collectives, collaborating on scripts and co-directing short films. She also pursued an acclaimed acting career, starring in films by well known German directors such as R. W. Fassbinder. With her third film, *Marianne and Juliane*, von Trotta's position as New German Cinema's most prominent and successful female filmmaker was fully secured. Her films feature strong female protagonists, and are usually set against an important political background. Themes in her work include the effect of the political on the personal, and vice versa, as well as the relationships between female characters, often sisters.

Having lived and worked in Italy for six years in the 1980s, von Trotta returned to Germany to make the major film about German unification. The incentive for von Trotta's and Schneider's script came from an Italian filmmaker, Felice Laudadio, who had thought that after the Wall came down German filmmakers would have rushed to make a film about it and its history. But in the 1990s most Germans were not ready to make films about German unification.

With its linking of personal and political stories *The Promise* is an immensely political movie. To understand these connections we have to look at the film's many allusions to German history.

After the Wall went up in Berlin on August 13, 1961, many East Germans tried to escape to the West, but most failed. Eventually Easterners came to agree with their country's prescribed ideology, socialism, but not with its repressive form as practiced in the GDR. When in 1968 the Czechoslovakian Communist Party leader Alexander Dubçek tried to liberalize the country's Communist regime by introducing free speech and freedom of assembly, most East Germans felt elated by the prospect of combining socialism with free speech. The period that came to be known as the Prague Spring ended when Warsaw Pact troops invaded on the night of August 20, 1968. "Our people will never accept this occupation" Czech leaders insisted. More than a hundred people were killed, and the Communist leaders, including Alexander Dubçek, were arrested and taken to Moscow. Despite fierce resistance, a protocol was issued within days of the invasion that banned all parties and organizations which "violated socialist principles."

Socialist ideology was back to square one, where it had been in the 1950s during Stalin's regime. The years following the Prague uprising became a period with increasing supervision by the *Staatsicherheit* or *Stasi*, the security police of the German Democratic Republic (East Germany) from 1950 until German unification in 1990. Increasingly the *Stasi* became the de facto ruler of East Germany. As Müller, one of the organization's men, tells Konrad, "The truth, my dear professor, is always with us."

The security police apparatus was established by German Communists with Soviet help in the latter's zone of occupied Germany soon after World War II, and in 1950 this became the new Ministry for State Security. Under the direction of Erich Mielke from 1957, the *Stasi* was responsible for both domestic political surveillance and foreign espionage, the latter mainly directed against West Germany and its allies within NATO. Over the course of four decades the East German security police built up a formidable reputation for effectiveness; under its longtime chief of foreign operations, Markus Wolf, brother of East German filmmaker Konrad Wolf, the *Stasi* extensively penetrated West Germany's governing circles and military and intelligence services. The discovery in April 1974 that Günter Guillaume, a top aide to West German chancellor Willy Brandt , was in fact an East German spy led to Brandt's resignation two weeks later.

According to information gleaned from the agency's own internal records after the Communist regime in East Germany collapsed in 1989–90, the *Stasi* at its peak employed about 85,000 full-time officers in its thirty-nine departments. It kept files on 5,000,000 East German citizens (one-third of the entire population), and it relied on several hundred thousand informers to monitor the East German citizenry.

Besides maintaining many undercover agents in West Germany, the security police ran a highly sophisticated effort to electronically eavesdrop on West German governmental and military communications. The *Stasi* fed some of its information to the KGB in the Soviet Union, with whom it maintained close relations. The organization also had links to various terrorist groups, notably the Red Army Faction in West Germany. Following the unification of East with West Germany in 1990, the *Stasi* was disbanded by the German government.

By late October 1989 crowds numbering more than 300,000 rose up in Leipzig and Dresden to demand the ouster of the Communist regime. On November 1 the East German cabinet bowed before the unrelenting, nonviolent pressure of its people by reopening its border with Czechoslovakia. On November 4, a reported 1,000,000 demonstrators jammed the streets of East Berlin's *Alexanderplatz* (East Berlin's main square) to demand democracy, prompting the resignations of the rest of the cabinet.

After 50,000 more people had fled the country in the ensuing week, the East German government capitulated. On November 9 it was announced on East German TV that exit visas would be granted to all citizens wishing to visit the West and that all border points were open. At first, citizens did not dare believe— hundreds of East Germans had lost their lives trying to escape after the Berlin Wall went up in August 1961—but once some accepted the opening as real and crossed the border, the news flowed like electricity that the Berlin Wall had fallen. A week later the dreaded *Stasi*, or state security police, were disbanded. By December 1 the East German *Volkskammer* (parliament) renounced the Communist Socialist Unity Party's "leading role" in society and began to expose the corruption and brutality that had characterized the Honecker regime. A new coalition government took control and planned free national elections for May 1990.

EVALUATION

With von Trotta's feminist background it comes as no surprise that Sophie is the prominent character in the movie – the story is told from her perspective. Sophie is the one who arranges the escape, she has a wealthy aunt in West Berlin, and she also tries to help Konrad escape a second time. Sophie decides to live with Konrad in Prague and she decides to break off the relationship later because it is not possible to keep their relationship going. Sophie is the strong one, the active partner; Konrad is the reacting element in this relationship. Since there are no West Berliners or West Germans in the movie, other than Sophie's aunt, Sophie represents the West Berliner, resourceful, impulsive, independent, dynamic, in charge. As a Westerner she cannot understand Konrad's eastern passivity: "Do not be ridiculous. You cannot blame twenty missed years on a pair of open shoelaces, on the Wall, the *Stasi*, on whatever...". Unlike a typical Westerner she carries the psychological baggage of a refugee: "I left, that is true, but I don't know if I arrived anywhere. I always missed somebody, you, my mother." Sophie's fragile mind is representative of the situation immediately after unification.

Sophie (Meret Becker) and Konrad (Anian Zollner) dance at a party in East Berlin on the eve of their planned escape to the West.

In spite of its focus on German history from 1961 to 1989 *The Promise* does not try to analyze East German history, it simply wants to present a symbolic rendition. Nonetheless von Trotta gives part of the movie the feeling of a documentary. The film's opening newsreel footage reinforces its documentary feel. Historical footage of the Wall going up, as we see people crying and also people escaping, recalls the events for older viewers and informs the young about what occurred. Later the movie reprises the emotionalism of the opening shots by inserting documentary footage of the Soviet invasion of Prague which Konrad and Sophie watch on TV. Von Trotta juxtaposes the footage of the invasion with fictional scenes in a restaurant showing customers running as the camera follows them, as if it were a scared customer as well.

Prague provides the heart of the movie. It is here where the two lovers meet for the first time after Konrad's botched escape. Von Trotta's filming of the meeting is reminiscent of old Hollywood films in which lovers fail at first to connect at an agreed-upon meeting place, as in *An Affair to Remember* (1957). But von Trotta allows Sophie and Konrad to finally come together after a suspenseful few minutes. Their subsequent love-making begins with an argument over coffee, followed by a breathtaking run up a circular staircase in a Prague hotel as they stop repeatedly to kiss and embrace, the camera encircling them, adding to the romantic moment. The interlude ends with them making love and conceiving their son. In an otherwise tragic film, the sequence stands out in its beauty and exuberance.

Prague also provides the film with a feeling of failed possibilities. Later, when Konrad gives a presentation on sun protuberances at the Prague astronomers' convention, his reason for the trip to the city, he sees a great future ahead of himself as a privileged scientist. He hopes to be delegated to the Czech academy of science, since both he and Sophie believe in "socialism with a human face," a third way between socialism and capitalism. Lorenz, Konrad's professor, who accompanies him to Prague, helps him get an appointment at the Czech academy of sciences where he and Sophie will be able to live and work. Of course things turn out differently for the fictional characters and for history.

The events in Prague present a very believable personal story, as Sophie and Konrad attempt to overcome the seemingly indefinite division of the world into two ideological camps. Subsequently millions and millions of people in East and West tried to arrange their lives accordingly, although not always as dramatically as Sophie and Konrad. The sadness expressed in the film stems from the fact that even in hard times, life must go on, and people must cope in their daily lives, whether they agree with the political conditions or not. Sophie and Konrad believed that Prague was the answer to the Cold War. For them, as well as for much of the West at the time, hopes were high that Dubček's "socialism with a human face" could not be ended by military force. When the Russian tanks advance therefore, they not only destroy Sophie's and Konrad's dream (and that of von Trotta and Peter Schneider, the screenwriter, as well), they also destroyed the hope for western liberals and socialists that capitalism and socialism could be united.

Professor Lorenz's reaction to the Prague events is important, since as a representative of the older generation he gives insight into the survival tactics of that generation. Lorenz is a tragic figure who finally realizes he has been used by the government. Since his original enthusiasm for socialism has run out, he finally gives in to the *Stasi* demands and signs a letter in support of the Soviet invasion with a cynical comment: "Anger is something quantitative that gets used up. It will get used up in you as well. I no longer have the strength. I have talent and not much time. I must protect my talent."

After Prague, Lorenz realizes there is no hope left, and the film turns melancholy, if not tragic. Sophie visits Konrad only once in East Berlin, closely monitored by the security police. Konrad, too, visits Sophie in the West during another convention of the International Astronomical Association being held in West Berlin. Alexander is able to visit his father several times in East Berlin, but each visit puts more strain on Konrad's marriage to his assistant Elisabeth. They finally separate, as does Sophie from a French journalist, Gérard, the man with whom she has had a long affair in the West.

Konrad is the weaker of the two main characters, reflecting von Trotta's intention of using both as characters with a symbolic political dimension. As the GDR became more prominent as a partner for West Germany, so does Konrad's presence dominate the movie's second part. Konrad's character shows clearly the misery of East Germans, their lack of power, and how what power and initiative they had was slowly stripped away by the Wall and the law prohibiting them from traveling abroad. Although the *Stasi* control Konrad with their demands and supervision, Konrad still displays some enthusiasm for socialism, as expressed in a conversation with his son Alexander: "To stay here was a dare, an adventure. We wanted to build something radically new." However, as his visitation privileges are traded for obligations, and the request to spy on colleagues, he finally falls apart and hits the representative of the security police. With that act—a courageous act to a western viewer—Konrad loses everything, his wife and his prestigious job as an astronomer, and he is forced to lead the existence of an impoverished janitor. Konrad's final downfall shows the misery of most GDR citizens during the 1980s.

With Konrad's sister Barbara, the movie introduces an interesting subplot dealing with the role of the church under socialism. Barbara is a protestant minister who preaches tolerance and peace and is harassed by the security police. When Konrad witnesses the impertinent behavior of the *Stasi* he is ready to fight them, but he is stopped by Barbara's friends. "That is all the government needs," she tells Konrad, "to malign the peace movement as violent." Barbara's husband Harald is the movie's most tragic figure, perhaps portrayed a little too heroically and symbolically as a Christ-figure. Harald protests against the East German government and is finally expelled to West Berlin against his will. After arriving in the West he cannot bear being separated from his wife, and rather than killing himself, walks right into the border fence where he is killed. "How long will the existing socialism vegetate until it dies? Too long for a human life."

As the movie begins with a documentary of the building of the Berlin Wall, it also ends with a semi-documentary, using scenes von Trotta recreates from well-known documentary footage. The movie shows the party atmosphere of the opening of the Wall on Glienecke Bridge with Konrad and Sophie staring at each other with blank faces. The viewer is left to speculate on how their lives and how Germany's future will develop, whether they will get together or whether the statement of one of the pedestrians interviewed in this scene is true, that "forty years is too long a period" to get back together.

The Promise lives through its characters, and offers no surprises, no flashbacks, but a traditionally told story. As in a play the focus is on the characters, who are symbolic representatives of historical forces. It is a very upsetting movie to watch and leaves the viewer with numerous options to consider for Germany's future. (RZ)

QUESTIONS

1. What are the differences in the way Sophie views life vs. the way Konrad views life?

2. What is the history of the Berlin Wall and why Germany was separated?

3. Are there reasons for Konrad's and Sophie's separation beyond the Cold War?

4. What role does the professor play in the film?

RELATED FILMS

Die verlorene Ehre der Katharina Blum (*The Lost Honor of Katharina Blum* 1975). Made with her husband of the time, Volker Schlöndorff, the film stands as one of New German Cinema's most political and yet accessible films.

Rosa Luxemburg (1986). Von Trotta creates an ode to one of Germany's greatest revolutionaries.

Die bleierne Zeit (*Marianne and Juliane* 1981). The film, although fictional, reflects the lives of two of Germany's female radicals, Gudrun and Sigrid Ensslin.

INFORMATION

The Promise (1994), VHS, in German w/subtitles, color, 115 minutes, New Line Studios, released 1998.

Hehr, Renate. *Margarethe von Trotta: Filmmaking as Liberation*. London: Edition Axel Menges, 2000.

Schneider, Peter and Margarethe von Trotta. *Das Versprechen: oder Der lange Atem der Liebe; Filmszenarium*. Berlin: Volk und Welt, 1995.

Moeller, Jack, et al, eds. *Kaleidoskop: Kultur, Literatur und Grammatik*. 6th edition. Geneva, IL: Houghton Mifflin Company.

Naughton, Leonie. *That Was the Wild East: Film Culture, Unification, and the "New" Germany*. Ann Arbor: U of Michigan P, 2002.

CHAPTER 25

Rossini,
oder die mörderische Frage,
wer mit wem schlief

(*Rossini or the Fatal Question, Who Slept with Whom***,**
Helmut Dietl 1996)

Schneewittchen (Veronica Ferres) preparing her next move at the Rossini, with Bodo Kriegnitz (Jan Josef Liefers) and Charlotte Sanders (Hannelore Hoger).

CREDITS

Director	Helmut Dietl
Screenplay	Helmut Dietl and Patrick Süskind
Director of Photography	Gernot Roll
Music	Dario Farina (Music)
Producers	Helmut Dietl, Norbert Preuss
Production Companies	Bavaria Film, Diana-Film
Length	110 minutes; color

Principal Cast

Götz George (Uhu Zigeuner), Mario Adorf (Paolo Rossini), Heiner Lauterbach (Oskar Reiter), Gudrun Landgrebe (Valerie), Veronica Ferres (Schneewittchen), Joachim Król (Jakob Windisch), Hannelore Hoger (Charlotte Sanders), Armin Rohde (Dr. Sigi Gelber), Jan Josef Liefers (Bodo Kriegnitz), Martina Gedeck (Serafina), Meret Becker (Zillie Watussnik), Hilde Van Mieghem (Fanny Zigeuner), Burghart Klaußner (Tabatier), Edgar Selge (Meik), Erich Hallhuber (Hopf).

THE STORY

Munich's Italian restaurant Rossini serves as a "home away from home" each evening for a number of single celebrities. They use the restaurant as a living room and office, both for their private and their public show, where they portray themselves to the public, and we get to look into their erotic eccentricities. We witness a busy cosmetic surgeon (Gelber), a man-devouring journalist (Sanders), a loud and jovial film producer with three bankers waiting to stop his credit (Reiter), an unconventional poet (Kriegnitz), a beautiful woman who cannot choose between two lovers (Valerie), another stunning beauty who wants to be a film star (Schneewittchen), a nervous film director (Zigeuner), a misanthropic bestselling author who only eats in the private room (Windisch), and the restaurant owner (Rossini). The story shows how all of them are somehow connected in their eccentric life style.

BACKGROUND

Rossini, oder die mörderische Frage, wer mit wem schlief (*Rossini* 1996) is not a biopic about nineteenth century opera composer Giacomo Rossini, but the name of a fictitious restaurant in Munich, which serves as a stage for one of Germany's most bizarre films. The model for the restaurant Rossini is Munich's upscale restaurant Romagna Antica, where such film celebrities as the director of *Rossini*, Helmut Dietl himself, hang out.

Similarities with existing people are intentional: director Dietl, his co-author Patrick Süskind (Windisch in the movie) and his producer Bernd Eichinger, the owner of Constantin Film (Reiter in the movie), are the real-life models for the film's Vanity Fair. The background for the main story, however, is quirky Patrick Süskind's much-publicized reluctance to sell the film rights for his 1986 bestseller *Das Parfüm* (*The Perfume*), Germany's biggest international bestselling novel ever, and which in spite of Süskind's reluctance has since been announced as a project in production by Tom Tykwer and Bernd Eichinger. Another commingling of reality and fiction occurs in the character Schneewittchen (Snow White), played by Veronica Ferres, who in real life is Dietl's girl friend and whose character in the movie sleeps with the fictive director Uhu Zigeuner (Götz George) – an intriguing mix of fiction and reality.

The director Helmut Dietl managed to enlist many important German film actors for this movie: Mario Adorf, Götz George, Gudrun Landgrebe, Veronica Ferres, Heiner Lauterbach, for example, a who's who of Munich's *schickeria* (societal A-list) and of German Film at the time. He knew them all from his evenings spent at Romagna Antica where Dietl himself had become a player in the Munich jet set. The movie not only feels like a documentary, it is a movie about Dietl's life and the interaction between himself and his celebrity friends, especially with its focus

Bodo Kriegnitz (Jan Josef Liefers) and Oskar Reiter (Heiner Lauterbach) fighting over Valerie (Gudrun Landgrebe).

on Ferres as Schneewittchen, Dietls' girlfriend. The actors seem to have lots of fun being in this movie, since they are playing their own lives.

EVALUATION

Viewers enter the film as they would a restaurant, as the camera passes tables of people on the way to being seated themselves. As in a documentary, the movie pulls the viewer into the noisy restaurant, as a guest would enter, while the characters are waiting. Although viewers see them only briefly, they know that they will get better acquainted with them later, and with their problems and their intricate relationships, which all center around the main story: how to produce yet another movie. Since the film the patrons want to produce cannot be realized, the ambitious plan ends in failure.

The movie is a satire, although Dietl prefers the term *comedie dramatique* to distinguish it from the flood of relationship comedies that swamped German theaters in the 1990s such as *Der bewegte Mann* (*Maybe, Maybe Not*, Sönke Wortmann 1994), or *Abgeschminkt!* (*Making Up!*, Katja von Garnier 1993). Dietl also calls his film a modern parable. However, this *danse macabre* seems to reveal more truth about the state of German society in the 1990s than any social study could. It is a sad film about the new Germany, a rare glimpse at the *zeitgeist* and the decadence of Germany's *Schicki Micki* (the in crowd) society at the end of the millennium, with its endgame feeling, a rather consistent topic in Teutonic culture and perhaps an homage to the same decadence prevalent in society one hundred years earlier as depicted in the works of Arthur Schnitzler.

With its stunning opening sequence, very much reminiscent of Robert Altman's style in *Nashville (1975)* or *Gosford Park* (2001), the film announces its high gloss at the outset with a roving camera and overlapping conversations that allow viewers to eavesdrop on the restaurant's patrons. But according to film critic Peter Culley what really puts the story over are the art direction, design and cinematography. Blonde actresses seem to emerge from candle flames, while depths of field will shift unnoticed, drawing our attention to yet another subplot. This film has an old-style glow which directors rarely attempt these days.

Rossini cost 11 million Marks, a rather extravagant amount of money for Germany's impoverished film industry. But it was not just the money that produced a stylish film, rather it was also the director's talent as a satirist. Dietl is the satirical talent in current German film –his biting satire *Schtonk* (1990) about a journalistic scandal involving forged Hitler diaries was nominated for an Academy Award, and his *Rossini* won the German Film Prize. It took Dietl two years to complete the script with Süskind, and another two years to produce the film since he had trouble combining the schedules of all the film stars that appear in this movie.

Dietl's images are arrangements of casual elegance, with a canny sense for the rhythm of a film. Dietl knows exactly when the full potential of a scene has been reached and when it is time to cut; each scene leaves us waiting for more. We enter Dietl's restaurant as a guest, and observe the various tables and conversations, which lends the film a semi-documentary quality. As in Altman's films, the dramatic structure opens after a few minutes and draws the viewer into the elegance of the movie. Once the initial chaos of the crowded scenes is overcome, and the viewer finds a comfortable reference point, the movie's themes are established rather quickly. They are foremost love, or the absence thereof, then passion, which is presented in an over-dramatic manner in keeping with the satirical nature of the film. At the core of the movie is a sense of power and money, with the *danse macabre* around the contract for the movie.

The rich textures of the movie with its intertwining stories allow for multiple variations on the themes of love, lust, power and money. Each character finds its own interpretation of these themes: The sad Charlotte with her seeming nonchalance has the most urgent basic sexual needs, requiring a man in order to cure her headaches. In contrast the more tragic Valerie dedicates her entire life to men and perishes from her unfulfilled longing. Windisch's romantic withdrawal from life is brought back to a manageable level by Serafina while Schneewittchen as the richest character is able to turn the artificial setup in *Rossini* to her favor. Although a cliché, she epitomizes the sadness of the Rossini clientele.

There are those scenes of sad beauty when we realize that the characters' language reaches its own limitations, as in a tender moment between Schneewittchen and her friend Zillie Watussnik. "Watussnik liebhaben" ("Watussnik love"), says Ferres, and for a second we glimpse her loss before she is again devoured by her hectic lifestyle. *Rossini* is a beautiful and well-balanced film that pulls the viewer into the scene and lets him participate in the life of seemingly real, if confused and shallow, people.

An example of Dietl's stylish and kitschy over-the-top satire is the first appearance of Schneewittchen at Rossini. It demonstrates Dietl's technique of fusing various styles and genres. The scene opens with a shot of Schneewittchen's back moving with the camera towards the front of the restaurant. The dialogue shows Dietl's melodramatic style of fusing two languages, Italian and German, with two dramatic styles, Italian opera and Brechtian theater. The dialogue between Rossini (Mario Adorf) and Schneewittchen (Veronika Ferres) is pure Brecht with quotes from Brecht's theater, for example the famous line "die im Dunkeln sieht man nicht" (We don't see those in the dark) from the song "Mack the Knife" in *Die Dreigroschenoper* (*The Three Penny Opera*). The scene is framed by Verdi music and melodramatic elements of Italian opera, with shots of the hundreds of candles burning in the restaurant and the rainstorm at the end. The scene has the feel of an Italian opera transported to a German setting, Italy in Munich, a multicultural experience such as the Munich elite loved in the nineties, and which borders on kitsch.

As in other German restaurant movies, such as *Bella Martha* (*Mostly Martha* 2001), discussed elsewhere in the book, Italy represents the desired culture with its language and music. Germany and it mythology ("Schneewittchen" and "Lorelei") represent the other extreme. This contrast between German romantic seriousness and Italian superficiality, its *bellezza* or beauty, turns out to be the movie's constituting theme. Since the restaurant Rossini dominates the movie, in its pragmatic ways, Windisch's romantic German Lorelei story does not materialize because Windisch knows that Romantic concepts are elusive. True love does not happen either, as even Serafina's and Windisch's tender relationship falls apart. Italy and Germany cannot merge, dramatic pragmatism and deeply felt romanticism, art and love, can never come together, as Windisch proclaims. (RZ)

QUESTIONS

1. Choose a scene to illustrate Dietl's casual documentary style of using the camera.

2. Why is the movie's central character called Schneewittchen (Snow White), and why is the movie within the movie called "Lorelei", after the famous mountain on the Rhine River?

3. Although Dietl calls his movie a satire there are tragic elements in the story. Name a few and describe the tragic parts in them.

RELATED FILMS

Schtonk (Helmut Dietl 1992). Dietl satirizes the scandal that arose over the forged Hitler diaries.

Stadtgespräch (*Talk of the Town*, Rainer Kaufmann 1995). This was one of the many comedies of the nineties in Germany.

Bandits (Katja von Garnier 1997). This film not only starred Riemann, who was a favorite in German comedies of the nineties, but was directed by Garnier, who started the comedy boom with *Abgeschminkt!* (*Making Up!* 1992).

INFORMATION

Rossini, oder die mörderische Frage, wer mit wem schlief (1996), VHS, in German w/English subtitles, color, 110 minutes, available from Goethe Institute, Germany.

Dietl, Helmut and Patrick Süskind. *Rossini. Oder die mörderische Frage, wer mit wem schlief*. Zürich: Diogenes, 2000.

Pflaum, Hans Günther. "Rossini or the Fatal Question, Who Slept with Whom," at http://www.goethe.de/uk/mon/archiv/german/gh98/erossini.htm

CHAPTER 26

Sonnenallee

(Sun Alley, **Leander Haußmann 1999)**

Miriam (Teresa Weißbach) gives a speech at the young Communist Party organization. During the same speech the fingers raised, an oath of loyalty to the Communist ideal, will be crossed behind her back, indicating her youthful disdain of the system.

CREDITS

Director .... Leander Haußmann
Screenplay .... Thomas Brussig, Leander Haußmann
Director of Photography .... Peter Joachim Krause
Music..Stefan Keusch, Paul Lemp,
Einstürzende Neubauten and others
Producers ....Claus Boje, Detlev W. Buck
Production Company .... Boje Buck Produktion GmbH
Length...101 minutes; color

Principal Cast

Alexander Scheer (Micha Ehrenreich), Alexander Beyer (Mario), Katharina Thalbach (Mother), Henry Hübchen (Father), Detlev Buck (ABV), Teresa Weißbach (Miriam), Elena Meißner (Sabrina), Robert Stadlober (Wuschel), David Müller (Brötchen), Martin Moeller (Kosscke), Margit Carstensen (Principal).

THE STORY

Wanting to portray life in the GDR when they were growing up in the seventies, Thomas Brussig and Leander Haußmann tell a story of how a family of four (father, mother, 20-year-old daughter, and 18-year-old son) cope with the irritations of living in East Germany. Shortages of material goods, the inconvenience of inferior products, and restrictions on personal freedoms form a background for stories about finding a first love, rekindling a marriage that's gone cold, and being thrust into the adult world.

Brussig and Haußmann's story portrays the fun they had growing up in the GDR when young people in love imagined what their Western counterparts were experiencing. *Sonnenallee* shows the GDR as a light-hearted hippie republic. Micha, the narrator and main character, is Brussig's alter ego. *Sonnenallee* (*Sun Alley* 1999) offers a collage of short, mostly exaggeratedly funny episodes that center around Micha's coming of age.

The times are the late seventies, when Micha is a senior in his GDR high school and his family and acquaintances undergo what might be considered stereotypical GDR experiences. Micha has an older sister, Sabrina, who to the consternation of her parents and brother comes home with a new boyfriend every week, each representing a different political or life philosophy. Micha meanwhile craves both pop-stardom and the love of beautiful Miriam, a neighbor who attends his school. He hangs out with Wuschel, with whom he plays air guitar and who longs for Rolling Stones albums. In this Communist world, records are bought secretively from street sellers, who try to satisfy their clients' whispered pleas for "something psychedelic." Meanwhile, Micha's father secures a telephone, a convenience for which there is a long waiting list, by obtaining a doctor's certificate falsely testifying that he has epilepsy. Micha's best friend, Mario, throws an improvised party at which an herbal remedy for asthma is the drug of choice. Other bizarre episodes include the story of Micha's uncle, who smuggles everything from tights to lychees from West Berlin into the East, and whose body is smuggled back into the East in a coffee jar after he dies and is cremated during one of his sojourns in the West.

In a secondary story of sorts, a police chief turns up in most of the episodes, a constant reminder of East German officialdom. Played with superb comic timing by Detlev Buck (himself a director and one half of the Boje/Buck team which produced *Sun Alley*), the police chief weaves in and out of the action, eventually falling from grace himself with his superiors, for playing the forbidden rock song "Moscow." Eventually the small vignettes of East German life culminate in the main character's coming of age, as he eventually gets the girl of his dreams to sleep with him, and as he realizes the world is not ideal when he falls out with his best friend Mario because he (Mario) has joined the *Stasi* to support his young wife and their child. The group of friends had been united throughout in their opposition to official Germany. Meanwhile, overlooking the action in the East, a group of western observers, standing on a walkway and serving as a condescending Greek chorus, make snide comments about the *Ossies* (the degrading nickname given to East Germans by West Germans after the Wall fell).

BACKGROUND

Sun Alley proved so popular in Germany, especially the former East Germany, that Thomas Brussig, East Germany's most popular author of the 1990s, wrote a novelization of the film, *Am kürzeren Ende der Sonnenallee* (*At the Shorter End of Sun Alley*) shortly after the film's release. The novel fleshes out the world of the film. Brussig includes material, characters and ideas that could not be used in the movie. He also changes the timetable of some of the events and modifies characters' names. However the basic plotlines remain identical: Micha is madly in love with Miriam. He pursues her throughout the novel as he had in the film, and manages to get into a fair amount of trouble along the way. While the novel still uses music titles as chapter titles, there is less dominance of English music, French *chansons* taking their place and giving the book a more thoughtful and introspective atmosphere. For example, Edith Piaf's "Je ne regrette rien" relocates the sentiment from the slapstick of the film to the comic remembrances of a wistful memoir. Jane Birkin's popular seventies sexual *chanson* "Je t'aime" gives the novel a European flavor.

The movie presents less a story than a series of episodes typical for East German society, superbly timed and portrayed by the various actors. Micha and his gang are all played by fresh actors who had never stood in front of a camera, including Alexander Scheer (Micha), Alexander Beyer (Mario), Teresa Weißbach (Miriam) and Robert Stadlober (Wuschel). Stadlober later became the star in another movie about adolescence in a boarding school, *Crazy* (Hans-Christian Schmid 2000), based on the book by Benjamin Lebert. The senior members of the *Sun Alley* cast are all well known Berlin stage actors who had worked with Haußmann in various theater productions, Katharina Thalbach as Micha's mother, Henry Hübchen as his father, and above all, Detlev Buck as the ABV.

In 1961, after having lost thousands of their citizens to West Germany who were leaving the country through West Berlin, East German authorities built a wall closing off travel between the two halves of the divided city. After the construction of the Berlin Wall the Communists no longer worried about western ideas and products corrupting their citizens since the access of escaping to the West had been cut off. At the same time, censorship was increased for critics of the social system in order to support a new literature that the GDR could call its own. Then in 1971 Honecker became party secretary of the SED. Confident of the social progress made in the 1960s, Honecker began with further liberalization. He permitted free expression of different opinions, thus allowing Easterners to listen to western rock music, and wear western clothes such as jeans, t-shirts and sneakers. But the western look had a decidedly eastern flavor. As citizens could not afford to buy the original items from the West or in the Intershops, they wore mostly East German copies of western brands. These East German products, such as *Club Cola*, *Rotkäppchen* champagne, and *Cabinet* cigarettes, knockoffs of American or West German products, and the notorious plastic car Trabant, have since acquired cult status in Germany, helped along by the popularity of films like *Sonnenallee* and the later *Good Bye, Lenin!*

EVALUATION

Sun Alley blends buffoonery, pathos, and parody to create a film that seems to be telling the truth about East Berlin. At the same time the movie is a tongue-in-cheek stylization of history, a sophisticated method of playing with historic, personal and artistic elements to show a country swallowed up by history.

Haußmann reproduced the entire set of *Sun Alley*, including the Berlin Wall and the checkpoint, in the Filmstadt Babelsberg (a studio that had been in the eastern part of Germany and since reunification has again become a major film studio in Europe). At a cost of several million German marks, the film above all captures the authenticity and precision of every detail of everyday life in the East, including the notorious Mufuti (multi-function table), seventies clothes and everyday GDR products. These give the film its unique and remarkable realism. As Veronica Rall, in *Frankfurter Rundschau*, writes: "The color composition along the lines of GDR aesthetics and the careful composition of décor and costumes energize the image with an artificiality which follows a special kind of realism."

The theater set gives the movie its stylized atmosphere. Everything seems a touch too chic for East Germany. The movie has the feel of a reality show in an outdoor theater, where the stage setting keeps reminding viewers that they are not watching real life but make believe. On one level the film is like a production of a novel by Karl May, Germany's first author of stories set in America's West. DEFA studios, the film studio in East Germany, made a number of May's books into films over the years, which *Sonnenallee* alludes to by including a scene from the author's *Winnetou*. In one of the surreal moments in the film, Micha, under the influence of drugs at Mario's party, opens a door where the Indian character Winnetou tells him "Take her as your squaw." Coming just before Micha is to meet Miriam, this insert adds a touch of magic realism that was not unheard of in GDR movies, particularly in *Die Legende von Paul und Paula* (*The Legend of Paul and Paula*, Heiner Carow 1974) which *Sun Alley* seems to be consciously referencing. For example, the actor who played Paul in *The Legend of Paul and Paula* makes a cameo appearance in *Sun Alley*, asking "Do you need an axe?" a line that references his character in the central scene in Carow's film.

As with many fresh-looking and youth-oriented movies, *Sun Alley*'s major achievement lies in its music, which gives the film the feel of an MTV-style music video. The film includes songs of classic GDR bands like The Pudys, the GDR's most popular sixties rock band. The group's thoughtful lyrics such as "Geh zu ihr" ("Go to her") are contrasted with socialist songs performed by the Choir of the Young Pioneers, for example "Fröhlich sein und singen" ("Be happy and sing"). The conflict between East and West is thus replicated on the audio track. As the film progresses, western pop music dominates, beginning with Alex Hacke's rendition of Woody Guthrie's "This Land is Your Land", GDR style: "This land is your land, this land is my land, from Karl Marx City, to Rügen Island, from Thuringia Forest to Frankfurt-Oder, this land was made for you and me." In this nostalgic movie America takes the place of anything exotic and unattainable to the GDR citizens locked up behind the wall. They were able to listen to western music on West Berlin TV, as in a scene with two visitors from Dresden, which was derided by East Berliners as the "valley of the innocent" where no western TV reception was possible. The two visitors, although reluctant at first, are completely taken in by western TV and stay up all night watching. This desire to escape to an exotic land as shown on western commercial TV was a powerful force for most

Micha (Alexander Scheer), in the center of his friends, dances at the school disco, hoping to attract the attention of the girls. As in many of the teen movies of the fifties, on which these characters are patterned, boys dance together while the girls watch.

Easterners, which increased as the years went on. Thus American songs add a curious layer to the film, with the feeling of having lost a wonderful country with the vanishing of the GDR. Just as in America's West, discoveries could still be made, with tumbleweed rolling in the wind and Mario and his girlfriend exploring the beautiful countryside in an endless summer (a reference to the 1969 GDR musical film *Heißer Sommer* (*Hot Summer*, Joachim Hasler 1967)). Obviously, the movie does not show the GDR as it really was, but in hindsight as a place of fun.

Adventure comes out in other episodes as well. For example, Wuschel's search for the Rolling Stones album and Micha's and his performance of an American rock song ("The Letter," performed by Dynamo 5 in the movie, originally by the Memphis group Box Tops) suggest everything was possible back in 1973 in East Berlin, and not just if you were young. This feeling of a fun-loving society prevails even to the end of the film when the narrative stops and a musical number anticipates the fall of the Berlin Wall. Everybody, old and young, all of Micha's friends and family, even the ABV, dances to rock tunes towards the Wall while the sun is setting. Haußmann comments: "With the dance scenes I wanted to imitate the cult-like dance scenes in Quentin Tarentino's *Pulp Fiction* (1994)." Yet separated from the narrative as the closing is, the ensemble's choreographed movements make a political statement in hindsight: music, especially western rock music with its rebellious underpinnings and potential for protest, is what got the the GDR out of its misery. Even though the film is taking place in 1973, freedom is near. As if to underscore the anachronism, the border guards react as they would in 1989, unsure, nervous and ready to step aside at any minute.

The dance scene is not the final scene, however. *Sonnenallee* ends with Nina Hagen's seventies song about color film: "Du hast den Farbfilm vergessen mein Michael, nun glaubt uns kein Mensch wie schön's hier war, alles blau und weiß und grün und später nicht mehr wahr." ("You have forgotten the color film,

Michael, now no one will believe how beautiful things were here, everything blue and white and green and later no longer true"). In the movie's context the old song takes on a new meaning: The GDR really had been a colorful experience (as documented in Boje/Buck's movie), but since Micha had forgotten his color film he and everybody else do not remember how beautiful life had been. This motif is repeated in Micha's feat in finally making contact with Miriam: He wants to show her his non-existent diaries to prove how complex a person he is and, since she seems interested in his elaborations, he has to make up these diaries of his childhood in retrospect. The movie *Sun Alley* presents a colorful, rich and exciting GDR in the same way that Micha made up a richer life during the long night he wrote his diaries. As a result, Miriam is so overwhelmed with Micha's interesting life that she sleeps with him.

The movie is a representation of nostalgia for life in East Germany, a warning not to forget the good old times people had in the seventies. But more importantly, it is also a plea for Westerners to understand that the GDR could be fun, as unbelievable as that sounds to a West German (or to an American), and that Westerners need to understand this nostalgia. These contradictory feelings represent the current German-German dilemma. The lukewarm reception the movie had in West Germany attests to the lack of this dialogue. (RZ)

QUESTIONS

1.   Explain why Mario and Micha fight in the *Stasi* office.

2.   What is the role of the Karl May Indian Winnetou whom Micha discovers during the party at Mario's place?

3.   How do the portraits of the actors shown during the credits add to their characters?

4.   Identify two or three of the pop songs and relate their lyrics to the visuals and themes on screen.

RELATED FILMS

Go Trabi Go (Peter Timm 1991). The first of the post-Wall comedies to laugh at residents and life in Eastern Germany, *Go Trabi Go* was highly successful with the public, if not with the critics.

Das Leben ist eine Baustelle (*Life Is All You Get* 1997). This is one of Wolfgang Becker's successful movies taking place in Berlin.

Good Bye, Lenin! (Wolfgang Becker 2003). *Good Bye, Lenin!* is the latest in the series of movies made since 1990 and the fall of the Berlin Wall that look back at life in the GDR.

Die Legende von Paul und Paula (*The Legend of Paul and Paula*, Heiner Carow 1974). Haußmann's *Sun Alley* pays homage to this East German cult film about love under the Communist regime.

INFORMATION

Sonnenallee (1999), VHS (PAL format, requires converter) and DVD (Region 2 format, requires multi-region player), in German, color, 101 minutes, Highlight Communications, 2003.

Cafferty, Helen. "*Sonnenallee*: Taking Comedy Seriously in Unified Germany." In *Textual Responses to German Unification: Processing Historical and Social Change in Literature and Film*, ed. by Carol Anne Costabile-Heming, Rachel J. Halverson and Kristie A. Foell, 253-271. Berlin: Walter de Gruyter, 2001.

Cooke, Paul. "Performing 'Ostalgie': Leander Haußmann's *Sonnenallee*." *German Life and Letters*. 56.2, 156-167.

Haußmann, Leander, ed. *Sonnenallee: das Buch zum Film*. Screenplay and interview with Leander Haußmann und Thomas Brussig. Berlin: Quadriga, 1999. (in German)

Naughton, Leonie. *That Was the Wild East: Film Culture, Unification and the "New" Germany*. Ann Arbor: U of Michigan P, 2002.

http://www.thomasbrussig.de. Thomas Brussig's home page with information about the movie (in German).

http://www.sonnenallee.de. The *Sonnenallee* home page (in German).

CHAPTER 27

Lola rennt

(*Run Lola Run*, **Tom Tykwer 1998**)

Lola (Franka Potente) runs through a group of nuns on the streets of Berlin. In the first two sequences represented in the photo, Lola rushes through the nuns, not noticing that she forces them off the walk. In the third sequence, she steps off the walk and runs around them. In a similar fashion she bumps into the woman with a stroller in the first two runs but not in the third, suggesting non-aggressive behavior leads to better results than aggression.

CREDITS

Director .... Tom Tykwer
Screenplay .... Tom Tykwer
Director of Photography .... Frank Griebe
Music ....Reinhold Heil, Johnny Klimek,
Franka Potente, Tom Tykwer
Producers .... Stefan Arndt, Gebhard Henke,
Maria Köpf, Andreas Schreitmüller
Production Companies......... X-Filme Creative Pool, Westdeutscher Rundfunk, rte
Length ....81 Minutes; color

Principal Cast

Franka Potente (Lola), Moritz Bleibtreu (Manni), Herbert Knaup (Vater), Nina Petri Hansen), Armin Rohde (Herr Schuster), Joachim Król (Norbert von Au), Ludger Pistor (Herr Meier), Suzanne von Borsody (Frau Jäger), Monika Bleibtreu (the blind woman), Hans Pätsch (Narrator).

THE STORY

After announcing that life is a soccer game and that everything else is theory, *Lola rennt* (*Run Lola Run* 1998) begins to tell its story. Unfolding in a mere twenty minutes and then repeated in two additional twenty-minute segments with only slight, though crucial variations, the narrative is surprisingly simple. Receiving a frantic phone call from her boyfriend Manni, located in a phone booth far away from her, Lola promises to come up with 100,000 marks, the amount Manni needs to deliver to racketeers for a successfully executed smuggling deal, the same amount that he had carelessly left on a subway train in a reflex action to escape from policemen checking passengers for tickets. Lola has exactly twenty minutes to not only locate this large sum but also to deliver it to the far-away Manni, whose criminal boss would definitely kill him were he to show up empty-handed.

Lola's impassioned attempt to secure the money from her banker father fails. She ends up helping him during a supermarket holdup and is accidentally killed by a policeman. But, refusing to die, Lola receives a second chance to accomplish the hopeless task of securing 100,000 marks to save Manni. This time she obtains the necessary money by robbing her father's bank, and reaches Manni within the allotted twenty minutes, but this time Manni is killed accidentally, by a speeding ambulance. Since neither ending is satisfactory for a comedy, Lola receives another twenty minutes, which this time concludes with a happy Hollywood ending. Lola wins 100,000 marks in a casino, which can be spent as the couple wishes, as Manni has also succeeded in recouping the lost money from the derelict who had taken it from the subway car.

BACKGROUND

During one week in September 1998, Tom Tykwer's *Run Lola Run*, a low budget film costing slightly more than three million German marks (one and a half million dollars), suddenly transformed a particularly quixotic German dream into reality: a German film, rather than a Hollywood production, garnered the largest number of moviegoers. Just as astonishing as its success in Germany was the film's success outside Germany, particularly America, where *Run Lola Run* continues its success in student film programs. Viewers are undoubtedly responding to the style of the film, which is uncharacteristically hip for a German movie. *Run Lola Run* is incredibly fast-paced and fun to watch. It truly is a film filled with "Chaos, Verwirrung, Liebe, Tod" (chaos, confusion, love, death), as the movie flyer distributed to Berlin audiences in the fall of 1998 proclaimed .

Like the recent *Butterfly Effect* (Eric Bless, J. Mackye Gruber 2004), and Krzysztof Kieslowski's *Przypadek* (*Blind Chance* 1987), whose sequences of a young man running after a train clearly influenced the structure of Tykwer's movie, *Run Lola Run* sets out to demonstrate the chaos theory, but the film's success rested less on perceptions of its conceptual depth than on its immensely successful blend of image, motion, and sound. Responding to Tykwer's accomplished, playful use of a broad array of filming techniques and with unrestrained admiration of his Lola and the film's soundtrack, German cinema critics emphasized that Tykwer had not only created something new but had expanded the possibilities of the filmic medium itself.

As in Germany, many U.S. reviews express astonishment that a German film can be so enjoyable. Generally Americans, especially critics, view German cinema as slow, humorless, dark, and depressing. Indeed, this perception exists outside America too. In Australia, the film's marketing purportedly avoided emphasizing the fact that *Run Lola Run* was a German film. Reviews suggest that with its American style and pace, nothing is foreign about it. Even Tykwer suggested that the film could be set in any large city.

When elaborating on the appeal of *Run Lola Run* for Americans, Tykwer stresses its universal theme (a tiny moment has immense repercussions), its romance aspects, and the emotional identification its main protagonists Manni and Lola generate. For most Americans, however, the film's universal nature is attributable mainly to its innovative, even dazzling recycling of familiar elements of international youth culture (music, video games, interactive links). The emotional identification with the main protagonists is far less pronounced than in Germany, where its male star Moritz Bleibtreu, who plays Manni, has the stature of a youth idol.

In spite of striking universal chords with an international audience, in spite of claims that the film doesn't resemble a German film, and in critics' views that the film could be set anywhere, *Run Lola Run* tells a uniquely German story of the new Germany. The film resonates with some of the most prevalent Berlin discourses at the turn of the millennium. This Berlin connection, even if perceived only on a subconscious level, provides the film with a cultural relevance on its home territory that it cannot possibly have for international audiences.

Tykwer, who as mentioned above emphasizes the universal aspects of *Run Lola Run* to international audiences, highlights its connection to Berlin with German audiences, usually by referring to his second film *Winterschläfer* (*Winter Sleepers* 1997), a beautifully slow-paced film that depicts the personal and societal stagnation suffocating an entire generation of Germans that had experienced no German chancellor other than Helmut Kohl. In contrast, *Run Lola Run* (Tykwer's third film), shot in the spring preceding the fall 1998 elections that removed Kohl from the chancellorship after a sixteen-year tenure, becomes a wake-up call from the lethargy of the Kohl years. It is a clarion call for change, a reflection of a younger German generation's dissatisfactions at conducting business as usual.

In Berlin Lola attained the status of a political icon expressing passionate commitment and movement. The film's multi-option plot helped turn the film into a multi-option icon that could be adopted just as readily by the staid political spectrum as by the progressive one. For example, Berlin's mayor Eberhard Diepgen (CDU), advised by a savvy new marketing agency, appropriated the design of *Run Lola Run* posters for the posters of his reelection campaign. These "Diepgen rennt für Berlin" posters (Diepgen runs for Berlin), six hundred of them plastered all over Berlin by the end of December 1998, were intended to signal a zestful leap into the new year and to depict a physically fit, totally committed Diepgen, already running to ensure advantages for his city, even though the mayoral election was not to take place until October 1999. Because of the threats of lawsuits for appropriating the film's image, the Diepgen posters were removed early.

In contrast to his reaction to the Diepgen appropriation, Tykwer did not protest on June 15, 1999, when the Lola-look was transferred to Michael Naumann (SPD), Germany's first Minister of Culture, in a large digitized photo printed by the *Berliner Morgenpost*. There Naumann appears in Lola's attire with Lola's tattoo, running through Berlin flanked by nuns—exactly as Lola had appeared in one episode during the first round of the plot. Because Naumann had already become a firm advocate of change during his few months in office, Tykwer presumably did not mind this adoption of the Lola icon.

EVALUATION

Run Lola Run is a film about time and process. The opening metaphor of life as a soccer match suggests that life is open to any and all possibilities. It implies that outcomes depend on the speed, force, and trajectory of the ball. Moreover, beyond some simple, unchanging rules, anything goes. There is continuous motion leading to results that may or may not be permanent. Indeed after a limited amount of time the whole game starts over again. While the metaphor applies to Lola, Manni, and those around them, Tykwer's playful use of chaos theory as applied to a soccer match refers also to Berlin, a city which only a decade earlier had been divided and which was now in the process of becoming the metropolis it had once been.

Tykwer accentuates the constructed, changing nature of Berlin in the opening sequence of the film. First, an aerial shot shows a Berlin without the Wall, but still divided into halves. Suddenly, accompanied by an unpleasant, deafeningly loud clank, similar to an explosion, the two parts (separated by the Spree River) are forced into union with each other, as if spoofing Willy Brandt's well known words "Es wächst zusammen, was zusammengehört" (things that belong together will grow into each other), a 1989 pronouncement on the two Germanys, by now legendary because of the myriad of reformulations it has inspired. Much as he commands the fusion of the two opposite parts of Berlin, Tykwer forcibly merges areas scattered throughout Berlin, creating spatial unity where none exists, certainly a prerogative of cinema but in this case purposefully forced in order to suggest the synthetic quality of Berlin (at least to Germans familiar with Berlin's topography). His personal design of Berlin represents a filmic contribution to the architectural designs of a new Berlin that had proliferated in such large numbers during much of the nineties. In keeping with his heroine Lola, whose credo is to create a world pleasing to her, Tykwer fabricates a Berlin pleasing to him.

Large sections of the movie were filmed in Berlin-Mitte, with several other districts such as Charlottenburg, Friedrichshain, Kreuzberg, Schöneberg, Wedding, and Wilmersdorf also involved. Regardless of how well one might know Berlin, it becomes impossible to untangle the filmically fused locations. The synthetic Berlin presented on the screen turns into a unified Berlin, a Berlin where it is difficult to distinguish even between East and West. Indeed, *Run Lola Run* becomes the first German film to present a truly unified Berlin. Likewise Lola, who is as much at home in the Karl-Marx-Allee as in Wedding's Gartenstraße, becomes the first filmic protagonist equally at home in all of Berlin's disparate parts.

Tykwer's location outside the supermarket where Lola is shot in the first sequence, and where Manni is run over by an ambulance in the second, resembles a street in an American western: Lola and Manni need to meet here at 12 noon, the high noon showdown time of American westerns; gun in holster, Manni approaches the Bolle supermarket with the swagger of a self-righteous cowboy, his movement accentuated by the use of slow motion. The entire setting is a spoof

Lola and Manni strike an aggressive pose as they are trapped while fleeing the police after robbing the Bolle supermarket. Not until they resolve their money problems without force does the couple achieve a happy ending.

of the current inorganic nature of Berlin-Mitte. Tykwer is convinced that his film succeeds in being so alive precisely because of the contrast between its absurdly synthetic background and the emotions expressed so honestly and vividly by its main protagonists. To encourage the perception of Lola and Manni as particularly genuine and consequently deserving of viewer identification, the scenes in which they appear are shot with 35mm film rather than with the video footage reserved for the other, less real characters.

An absence of traffic adds to the constructed artificial feel of the film's Berlin. In the midst of the film's many unnaturally empty streets, heightening the recurring impression of Berlin as a set of props, people still act as if the streets belong to them and not to vehicles on the road. They are constantly surprised by the few vehicles that do appear. Lola never counts on vehicles obstructing her way and is surprised when a truck almost hits her in the last twenty-minute sequence, whenever a bicycle materializes next to her, or when businessman Mr. Meier's Citroen appears in front of her. Workers crossing the street with a huge pane of glass are caught unawares by the ambulance that rushes into the pane. Manni too, walking in the middle of the street (toward the end of the second twenty minutes) as if he owned it, certainly does not expect a car to hit him, much less the ambulance. While the ubiquitous ambulance specializes in crashing into people, the only two personal cars driven in the center of the German capital, a Citroen and a BMW, keep crashing into each other. When there are more than two cars on the road in Berlin-Mitte (other than on the Karl-Marx-Allee), they tend to be police cars rapidly materializing in surreal abundance. Rather than naturally belonging to urban life in Berlin, they seem transplanted from the many TV programs now zealously fashioning Berlin into Germany's capital of crime. On her sprint across the Berlin-Mitte section of the German capital, Lola does of course meet at least a small number of people, each a representative of a social class:

the sharp-tongued housewife with the baby buggy, the derelict with his plastic bags (including Manni's bag with the 100,000 marks), the youth with his stolen bicycle, businessman Mr. Meier (her father's associate) in his elegant car, and an old woman with a watch. Yet, other than a group of nuns strangely out of place in Berlin-Mitte, she encounters no crowds and no evidence of teeming life.

Surprisingly, Lola nimbly forges ahead in Berlin-Mitte (despite her heavy Doc Martens boots) and reinvigorates it by her presence. Not once does she pause to ascertain the right direction, for she never experiences spatial dislocation. Her metropolis contains no fragmentary, disassociated spaces. Rather, the most disparate city spaces readily fold into each other. A sea of GDR apartment high-rises, for example, yields to the Neo- Baroque Bodemuseum. Oblivious to contraries, Lola in essence affirms them. In contrast to the angels and Berlin inhabitants in Wenders' *Wings of Desire*, who wander aimlessly about, Lola exudes a sense of belonging.

The fact that Lola is upbeat, forward looking, and tenacious should not imply that Tykwer consciously fashioned Lola according to the traits coupled with the Generation Berlin, defined as self-reliant individualists unbound by convention on whom Germany's tortured past no longer has a hold. It is well-known that images rather than concepts lead to his initiation of film projects, and *Run Lola Run* is also the product of an image that would not release its hold on his imagination: that of a red-haired woman running (rather than jogging) through Berlin. And in the attempt to find possibilities of translating this image into a filmic plot, Tykwer created a film about the possibilities of life and, by extension, about the possibilities of the filmic medium.

Music plays a large role in Tykwer's Berlin construct. The song "Believe," not included in the film but placed at the beginning on the *Lola rennt* CD, meant to supplement the film, provides a long list of what Lola doesn't believe in, such as trouble, silence, panic, fear, history, truth, chance, and destiny. But she does believe in one thing: fantasy. Thus the songs initiating her first and third runs ("Running One" and "Running Three"), as well as the song "Wish" (Komm zu mir), accompanying the closing credits of the film, all express wishes of pure fantasy, none possibly capable of being realized. The following, occurring in varying order from song to song, exemplify the kinds of wishes expressed: "I wish I was a forest of trees that do not hide;" "I wish I was a stranger who wanders down the sky;" "I wish I was a heartbeat that never comes to rest." "Running Two," with its list of "nevers" (for example: "never letting go;" "never saying no;" "never giving up"), consists of similarly unrealistic wishes, but they are placed into the context of Lola's and Manni's love for each other, a love proving that no impossibilities exist in their lives. The concluding song of the film stresses that it commenced with an explosion that shattered all limitations. And at the end of the first sequence we hear "What a Difference a Day Makes," conjuring up time and the possibilities it provides.

That the best possible future has a chance of being realized is conveyed in the film in various ways, but especially at the beginning with the off voice of Germany's consummate fairy tale narrator Hans Paetsch, his audio tapes a household presence in most German children's lives, and with the cartoon Lola (in the opening tunnel sequence and as she spurts down the staircase before turning into the real Lola outside), animation of course signaling that anything, even the most positive outcome, could happen. In Berlin, arguably the iconic millennial city, much is happening. Needed in this setting are individuals like Lola, who respond with various answers to single challenges as not only the repetitions of the twenty-minute plot sequence but also Lola's behavior within each version indicate (e.g., in the second version, when her father refuses to give her the needed money, she snatches the guard's gun, thereby getting her way; in the third version, when her father had departed before her arrival, she decides to obtain the money in a casino). Lola's seemingly cursed twenty minutes turn into lucky twenties at the roulette table, suggestive as well of lucky fortunes in the millennial year 2000.

Lola wins her battle against fate because of her ability to make decisions and her talent to forge ahead, exactly the ability her banker father and many other Berliners lack. Lola generates endless possibilities for the people into whom she crashes on her run, particularly for those whose lives seem the most humdrum and inconsequential. The Polaroid camera flash-forwards, projecting in five-second linear narratives the future lives of these people, vary radically on each of Lola's three rounds. The woman with the baby buggy, for example, may end up as a child kidnapper, a lottery jackpot winner, or a Jehovah's Witness. Only the stationary mother, sipping drinks and talking on the phone all day, remains impervious to and consequently unaffected by Lola as she sees her daughter before the fateful run-in with the dog on the stairs.

In essence *Run Lola Run* accommodates multiple ways of perceiving and responding to images, just as it accommodates diverse perceptions of time and dissimilar means of filling it. While Manni's twenty minutes are constrictive, allowing room for maneuvering only in the last segment, Lola's same twenty minutes expand and contract, fill out or fill up, rush forward and back, and influence outcomes in unforeseen ways. The film thus points to the delights of improvisation in the midst of an uncompleted environment. Surely *Run Lola Run* is the ideal film to impel more participation and thrill at involvement in shaping yet another temporary future of Berlin. (MS)

QUESTIONS

1. *Run Lola Run* tells the same story three times.
   a. Which elements of the story are exactly the same each time, if any?
   b. Which elements change?
   c. Which elements are found in only one or two of the versions?

2. Tykwer's film uses the conceit of being able to relive a day. *Groundhog Day* (1993) and *Butterfly Effect* (2004), two Hollywood films, also ask the question of "what if I could do that again?" If you have seen either of these films or both, describe similarities and differences in the films.

3. Describe the music. When is techno music used in the film? What is the difference in the text of the predominate song that accompanies the three runs? What other styles of music can you identify in the film?

4. Describe the scenes in this film which follow Run One and Run Two, when Lola and Manni are lying in bed. What function do they play in the structure of the film? What function do they play in the story?

5. Why is beginning the film with a soccer match an appropriate way to introduce the film's story?

6. What role do the various cartoon elements play in the film?

7. Does Lola change at all in the course of the three running sequences? Why does Tykwer reward her with success at the end?

8. Does the film treat feminist concerns? If so, in what respect? If not, why not?

RELATED FILMS

Winterschläfer (*Winter Sleepers* 1997). Tykwer's first successful film, *Winter Sleepers* uses the same idea of coincidence and chaos to tell the story of four young people in their late twenties or early thirties who are searching for love.

Der Krieger und die Kaiserin (*The Princess and the Warrior* 2000). Tykwer tries his hand at a German fairy tale in which a bank robber and a nurse escape to a house on a cliff.

Przypadek (*Blind Chance*, Krzysztof Kieslowski 1987). *Blind Chance* provided Tykwer with the bare outline of his idea, a person who by running just a bit differently in three situations changes his life.

Butterfly Effect (Eric Bless, J. Mackye Gruber 2004). The hero of *Butterfly Effect* is able to daydream changes in his reality and that of the people around him.

Groundhog Day (Harold Ramis 1993). The main character is condemned to relive his day over and over, with some changes, until he figures out how to escape from the time loop.

INFORMATION

Run Lola Run (1998), DVD, in German with English subtitles, color, 81 minutes, Columbia/Tristar Studios, released 2001.

Haase, Christine. "You Can Run, but You Can't Hide: Transcultural Filmmaking in *Run Lola Run* [1998]." In *Light Motives: German Popular Film in Perspective*, edited by Randall Halle and Margaret McCarthy, 395-415. Detroit: Wayne State UP, 2003.

Meik, Oliver. *Lola rennt - aber wohin?: Analyse, Interpretation und theologische Kritik eines postmodernen Films über den Menschen und seine Möglichkeiten.* Frankfurt a/M: Lang, 2002.

Sinka, Margit. "Tom Tykwer's *Lola rennt*: A Blueprint of Millennial Berlin. At http://www.dickinson.edu/departments/germn/glossen/heft11/lola.html.

Tykwer, Tom. *Lola rennt: das Buch zum Film.* Reinbek bei Hamburg: Rowohlt, 1998.

CHAPTER 28

Vergiss Amerika

(*Forget America*, **Vanessa Jopp 2000**)

From left, David (Marek Harloff), Anna (Franziska Petri), and Benno (Roman Knižka), three friends struggling with love and life after high school in eastern Germany. Even though Anna at first has an affair with Benno, the mise-en-scène throughout the film indicates she has a closer relationship with David and will end up with him.

CREDITS

Director .... Vanessa Jopp
Screenplay .... Maggie Peren
Director of Photography .... Judith Kaufmann
Music.. Michael Beckmann
Producers .... Alena Rimbach, Herbert Rimbach, Katja de Buck
Production Companies............. Avista Film, Brainpool, Kinowelt Filmproduktion,
Westdeutscher Rundfunk
Length... 90 minutes; color

Principal Cast

Marek Harloff (David), Roman Knižka (Benno), Franziska Petri (Anna), Rita Feldmeier (Frau Ludoff), Andreas Schmidt-Schaller (Herr Ludhoff), Ursula Doll (Doreen), Rainer Gohde (owner of photo shop), Gerd Lohmeyer (Herr Schreyer)

THE STORY

David and Benno have been friends since childhood. After finishing school, Anna, the daughter of a preacher, enters their lives, and the three spend a carefree summer hanging out together. Although both boys have fallen for Anna, and she genuinely likes both, she chooses Benno, the more outgoing of the two friends. As summer ends, Anna goes off to acting school in Berlin. David wants to go to Berlin to study photography but must stay in his small town because of his father's accident. Benno opens a car dealership specializing in American autos.

Vergiss Amerika (*Forget America* 2000) is part coming of age, part youth rebellion, and part love triangle. Told in flashback from David's perspective, the movie follows the pains of three young people as they enter their twenties and try to accommodate their dreams with the realities of entering adulthood in a small town in eastern Germany.

When Anna has no success in Berlin, she returns to Aschleben and becomes Benno's girlfriend. David is forced to take a job at a fish counter in a large supermarket and continues to pine for Anna. Benno does contract work for the Polish Mafia, fixing stolen cars. Eventually Anna cools to Benno because of his temper. When Benno discovers her and David together, he first blows up, then invites David on a business trip to Poland. Driving in separate cars, Benno passes David and crashes his car; the brake linings had been cut, perhaps by the underworld car thieves for whom he was working and perhaps by Benno himself from a desire to commit suicide. The final scene shows Anna and David, each unaware of the other's presence, sitting on a train to Berlin to finally enter the adult world.

BACKGROUND

On November 9, 1989 the Berlin Wall, the barrier separating East and West Berlin, came down. On July 1, 1990, the economies of East and West Germany became one. A few months later, the political divisions that had existed for forty years between the Federal Republic of Germany (West Germany) and the German Democratic Republic (East Germany) vanished as the two German countries were united. In the initial euphoria that greeted the end of the socialist regime in the East, East Germans welcomed the influx of western quality goods, the availability of more foodstuffs, the buying power of the West German mark, and the freedom to travel to the West, including America. For the decade following unification, things Western were valued as good, those Eastern as not desirable.

EVALUATION

Forget America is Vanessa Jopp's first feature film and was directed as her final project for graduation from the Munich Academy of Film and Television. The story itself might seem trite, the music too obvious, the characters too predictable, and the camera work too studied. Yet, there is no denying Jopp's cinematic expertise: she tells her story of coming-of-age perfectly. Indeed her obvious skill at directing actors, her use of camera angles, lighting and mise-en-scène, and her choice of music transform a story of generational conflict, confused youth, and coming-of-age, which we have seen many times before, into a fresh examination and critique of life in contemporary Germany, of the post-unification blues. She is especially adept at filming her characters in situations that through the mise-en-scène reveal relationships being denied by the dialogue. Furthermore she entices performances from her three principal characters that dig beneath the story their words tell us. Finally by including a soundtrack consisting mainly of American pop music, she keeps the attraction of western pop culture in the forefront without ever actually dealing with or criticizing U.S. culture.

The opening shot behind the credits captures an upside down reflection of a country road landscape in a rearview mirror. The scene, whose tragic meaning is not clear until the end of the film, introduces two young men driving separate cars as one pulls up alongside the other. The parallel position of the cars, the sharing of information on which radio station is playing better music, and the eventual driving ahead of one car which then flies over a cliff as the frame freezes, reveals the closeness of the friends and leads directly into the first narrative line. "Benno and I had been friends since I can remember." As the movie now flashes back to tell the story of the friendship and how the film got to the point of the accident, the camera captures the two young men in situations that take the story from the innocence and carefree attitudes of youth to the harsh realities of adulthood.

Jopp structures her film with a number of reprises. Three scenes that occur early are repeated later in the movie, turning the world from one that is fun, void of responsibility, and open to opportunity into one that portends a frightening, perhaps even bleak, future. Thus, an early scene in which the male leads, David and Benno, dive into a wishing well in search of money with which to buy beer is later reprised when they throw money into the same well as David remarks that people aren't worthy of their wishes. In another early scene, the young men pretend to hot-wire and steal a car, which actually belongs to them, in order to impress Anna. When he enters the adult world, Benno begins repairing cars for a Polish car theft ring. Finally, in the third establishing scene, Benno and Anna jump into a river and begin their relationship as David looks on. Later in the film David and Anna jump from the same bridge, beginning their affair, an event that leads to Benno's final breakdown and his possible decision to commit suicide.

These scenes, which capture Anna's movement from being Benno's girlfriend to being David's, are set up and lighted in a way that anticipates the shift that will occur. Thus in the scene when Anna first meets David and Benno as the young men climb out of the wishing well, David receives the majority of the lighting, leaving Benno in shadow. In the third of the scenes mentioned in the preceding paragraph, when the trio is on the bridge, Anna stands closer to David, even though it is Benno with whom she will jump into the water. Jopp establishes the weakness in Anna and Benno's relationship in other ways as well, suggesting that perhaps Anna has chosen the wrong man, long before she realizes this. She and Benno confront each other continually, often about the most trivial of matters. While Anna and David also disagree when they are together, they argue about things that matter in life and relationships. Whereas Anna and Benno will fight over what should be on a pizza, she and David fight over what they are doing with their lives.

Jopp uses the film's major lyrical interlude to underscore that Anna should be David's partner, not Benno's. Long before David and Anna become lovers, the two of them, encouraged by Benno, ride off on a moped, walk along a beach, bird watch and lie next to each other in the grass. In most films, a long interlude of this sort would finalize the romantic liaison between two lovers. Jopp in contrast uses the sequence to suggest what should be. Later in the film, Benno's complicity in bringing his lover and best friend together is reprised as he encourages David to take Anna to her acting engagement, which turns out to be the dubbing of a porno film. The camera captures David's understanding of Anna's acute embarrassment at her predicament, a situation which finally brings the two together.

Forget America is not primarily a love story as the above description might suggest. Rather the film derives from a tradition of youth rebellion and coming-of-age films. Jopp adapts the formula for a film of youthful rebellion to economically depressed eastern Germany. In this way, the film revisits the coming-of-age movie, focusing on the generational dilemma found in that genre, which asks the question: How can young people hold on to youthful ideals as they come face to face with the realities of love, friendship, family, and work in an adult world? The genre is ideal not only for exploring emotions at their most volatile, namely in the young, but also for exposing the generation gap during times of change. In the fifties, American directors Nicholas Ray and László Benedek exposed the soft underbelly of postwar America in their movies of rebellion, *Rebel without a Cause* (1955) and *The Wild One* (1954) respectively. In 1957 East German director Gerhard Klein looked at youth dissatisfaction in the workers' state in *Berlin—Ecke Schönhauser* (*Berlin—Schönhauser Corner*) Meanwhile, in the Federal Republic of the fifties, West German directors Georg Tressor and Josef von Báky explored the theme of father/son conflict in *Die Halbstarken* (*The Hooligans*, also known as *Teenage Wolfpack* 1956) and *Die Frühreifen* (*The Rowdies* 1957) respectively.

Similar to her predecessors, Jopp focuses on the absence of adult behavior that could serve as a model or moral compass as the young people pass into adulthood. The hero's father in *Rebel without a Cause* wears an apron and helps with housework, which in the eyes of the film's youthful rebel of America's 1950s implies ineffectuality. In *Forget America*, the father of the film's hero has an accident and is confined to a wheelchair, requiring that his son take care of him. At a time in their lives when the fathers should be providing guidance they are incapable of giving support, either emotionally as in *Rebel without a Cause* or physically as in *Forget America*. Indeed, all of the adults in Jopp's film represent weaknesses of the present state of affairs in eastern Germany. Benno's mother fails to buy him a present on his birthday and instead sends him a card with a picture of her new child under which she has written, "unser Wunschkind," (the child we wanted). His adult benefactors are part of the Polish Mafia, drawing him into illegal activity. David's two bosses likewise give him no help, both being incapable of living in the reality that is a united Germany. Anna's father, a minister, the traditional teacher of values, appears totally absent from his daughter's life.

As the genre of rebel films would seem to demand, Jopp locates her characters into the contemporary *Zeitgeist*. Youth culture films are ideal for situating the narrative in a contemporary setting. *Rebel without a Cause* and *The Wild One* capture the angst of America's war babies (the generation between those who were adults during the war and those born after it). *The Rowdies* and *The Hooligans* reflect the disillusionment of German youth with their parents, indeed with the entire adult generation that fought the war. *Berlin—Schönhauser Corner*, while paying homage to the East German political system, also exposes that system to criticism, begging the question, however veiled: if this is the workers'

David (Marek Harloff) driving to Poland to help his friend Benno (Roman Knižka). The eastern German landscape provides at the same time a wide open, hopeful vista as well as a lonely, empty space, two themes the director handles in her film.

paradise, why do these problems with our youth exist? On her own work, Jopp stated in an interview she wants viewers to be able to recognize Germany in her films, she wants them to recognize real people. David, Benno, and Anna may thus be modeled after earlier rebels in American and German film, but they represent not the aimless youth of the films of rebellion, but the filled-with-doubt youth of a conflicted economic system. She places her protagonists in post-unification Germany, ten years after the fall of the Berlin Wall, a time span that represents half the lifetime of the protagonists. Their wishes are modest: automobile dealership, photographer, actor, but even these modest desires clash with the reality of 20 percent unemployment. Yet David, Benno, and Anna have to realize their potential in Germany. They have to forget earlier pipedreams about the West, they have to "forget America" and focus on making a life in Germany.

But the ubiquity of American culture makes it difficult to forget the West. As is true for many German films about contemporary Germany, *Forget America* relies on pop songs sung in English. In *Im Lauf der Zeit* (*Kings of the Road*), Wim Wenders' cult road film of 1976, one of the lead characters remarks as he hears a pop tune that America has colonized Germany's subconscious, when he cannot get a popular melody out of his head. The question for *Forget America* is, can the characters and viewers get the songs out of their heads? Jopp helps the viewers by including songs whose English language lyrics provide a double irony. On the one hand, her implied intention that we forget America is made impossible. For even if America is made inconsequential by the title, the music elevates it to importance. Her use of American or American-sounding pop songs keeps the America of the title always in focus, even if the story seldom mentions America. On the other hand, the songs are mostly negative, commenting not only on the imaginary America of the title but also on the action on the screen. Such double negativity reaches its apex at the end of the film as David and Anna, unaware of each other, leave their hometown of Aschleben as the soundtrack plays "This is Babylon," a reference to America and the now ten-year-old united Germany. The song which starts the movie and is reprised later in the film, "Been through the

Desert on a Horse with No Name" plays as the friends drive through the eastern part of Germany near the Polish border, an area that seems empty of any human activity.

Movies of youthful rebellion are generally popular because they embed a private story, generally a love story, within the public story that is examining the alternative and rebellious lifestyles of the young as they struggle to prove themselves to the older generation. The family trinity of *Rebel without a Cause*, the love triangle in *The Rowdies*, the good girl/bad boy romances of *The Wild One* and *The Hooligans*, the pregnancy of the young girl in *Berlin—Schönhauser Corner* exemplify how directors blend social issues and personal issues. That is, in these films issues of love are felt all the more passionately because they have to exist in an environment made unfriendly by the adult world, the world that the young lovers will someday have to join.

At the same time, dealing with the realities and compromises necessary in the adult world are made that much more difficult by being in love. David, Benno, and Anna face ethical and moral issues as they try to make the transition from adolescent to adult. David must decide if he should support the illegal activities of his friend Benno. Benno must choose between being an honest businessman and working for the Mafia. The only acting work Anna can find is in dubbing porno films. Their love lives are just as beset with moral dilemmas. David and Benno love the same woman. Anna loves both men, but also wants to realize her own ambitions and not simply become one or the other's girlfriend.

Finally the clash between adult world, youthful ambition, and general angst precipitates disaster in the youth film. Jopp, however, changes the dynamic of the tragic events. Whereas the adults in *Rebel without a Cause*, *The Wild One*, *The Hooligans*, *The Rowdies*, and *Berlin—Schönhauser Corner* learn as much or more from the death of their children, Jopp's adults are left out of the final tragedy. The problems may have been caused by the adults, but the solutions are solely those of eastern Germany's youth.

Forget America offers viewers an early example of protest to the progress and direction of unification, protest continued a few years later by Wolfgang Becker's comedy *Good Bye, Lenin!* (2003). Occasioned by economic conditions that have allowed unemployment to hover between 17% and 20 %, films such as *Forget America* and *Good Bye, Lenin!* suggest that answers to problems will not be found primarily in the West or through western style paradigms. Nor will they be found in the East and old socialist paradigms. Rather, the youth of eastern Germany will have to forge their own future. (RCR)

Questions

1. Jopp is clearly trying to show a bleak situation for youth in Aschleben, a name that translates as "life in ashes." Identify specific areas of the movie which comment on the economy in the eastern area of Germany.

2. Locate the scenes with English language songs in the background and describe how these songs comment on the visual narrative.

3. Describe the final scene of the movie. What do you think this ending signifies for David and Anna?

4. The movie never says that Benno committed suicide. What in the film
    leads to such an interpretation of the accident? What might lead to a
    different interpretation?

RELATED FILMS

The following films all focus on youth or coming of age.

Berlin—Ecke Schönhauser (*Berlin—Schönhauser Corner*, Gerhard Klein 1957).
Klein looks at rebellious youth in 1957 East Berlin, showing that adults
need to do more to win their children over to the socialist state.

Die Halbstarken (*The Hooligans*, Georg Tressler 1956). *The Hooligans* made Horst
Buchholz a star. After the film he received a Hollywood contract, and
among other films made *The Magnificent Seven* (John Sturges 1960), the
ultimate film about outcasts or rebels.

Die Frühreifen (*The Rowdies*, Josef von Báky 1957). One of the few youth films
to look at economic conditions as a cause of the problems of the younger
generation.

Rebel without a Cause (American, Nicholas Ray 1955) The film was a hit in
Germany under the title ...*denn sie wissen nicht, was sie tun* (for they know
not what they do).

Sonnenallee (*Sun Alley*, Leander Haußmann 1999). Haußmann looks at youth
in pre-unification Germany.

The following two films are classics that focus on the theme of love
triangles.

Unter den Brücken (*Under the Bridges*, Helmut Käutner 1945). Käutner began his
film under the Nazis but released it after the war. Two men share a boat
with a woman they both love.

Jules et Jim (*Jules and Jim*, French, François Truffaut 1962). The classic love
triangle film against which all others are measured. Jopp clearly had
Truffaut's threesome in mind when making her film.

INFORMATION

Vergiss Amerika (2000), VHS, in German w/subtitles, color, 90 minutes,
available from Goethe Institute, Germany.

Buck, Caroline. "*Vergiss Amerika*: Gespräch mit Debütfilmerin Vanessa Jopp."
http://focus.msn.de/D/DF/DFU/DFU08/DFU08166/dfu08166.htm.
(November 9, 2000).

CHAPTER 29

Bella Martha

(*Mostly Martha*, **Sandra Nettelbeck 2001**)

Martha (Martina Gedeck) and Frida (Sibylle Canonica) working side by side with Mario (Sergio Castellitto) in the Lido kitchen.

CREDITS

Director ....Sandra Nettelbeck
Screenplay ....Sandra Nettelbeck
Director of Photography ....Michael Bertl
Music...Manfred Eicher
Producers ....Karl Baumgartner, Christoph Friedel
Production Companies.........................A consortium of European companies from Germany, Italy, Austria, and Switzerland: including Bavaria Film and Rai Cinemafiction
Length...107 minutes; color

Principal Cast

Martine Gedeck (Martha), Maxime Foerste (Lina), Sergio Castellitto (Mario), Sibylle Canonica (Frida), Katja Studt (Lea), Idil Üner (Bernadette), Oliver Broumis (Jan), Antonio Wannek (Carlos), August Zirner (Therapist), Ulrich Thomsen (Sam).

THE STORY

Bella Martha (*Mostly Martha* 2001) begins with Martha (Martina Gedeck) on her therapist's sofa, describing the details of a recipe for truffles cooked with pigeon. From Martha's description, the therapist develops a craving for Martha's food, and even attempts to create some himself.

Martha creates culinary masterpieces as a chef in the Lido, a small gourmet restaurant in Hamburg. Her everyday existence is rather monotonous. She is introverted, has hardly any private life, and exists only for her work. When things get hectic, she withdraws to the walk-in freezer of the restaurant to cool off. Martha's only weak point comes when a customer criticizes her foie gras (see recipe below), for upon hearing the complaint, she begins to argue with her guests and her boss threatens to fire her.

All of that changes when her sister, a single mother, dies in an accident and Martha is left to care for Lina, her sister's eight-year-old daughter (Maxime Foerste). The little girl suffers greatly from the loss of her mother, but Martha understands very little of children and is not of much help to her. It is only the presence of Mario (Sergio Castellitto), Martha's merry Italian colleague, who brings light and pasta into the lives of the two. After an initial fight ending with Mario threatening to leave his new position as chef if Martha does not accept him, Mario becomes her friend and helps Lina overcome her eating disorder with his pasta dishes. He prepares a meal at Martha's home and changes from a rival into a friend. A sensitive romance starts between them.

Meanwhile, the little girl's Italian father appears and wants to take Lina back with him to Italy, where the movie ends on a light note. Martha and Mario decide to follow Lina to Italy. From the sketchy style of the ending we can only guess that Martha and Lina and Mario will finally leave the tough, damp German Hamburg for good and also settle in the sunny realm below the Alps to enjoy the delights of the Italian cuisine.

BACKGROUND

Mostly Martha provides a sense of watching a restaurant documentary with its impeccable kitchen equipment and the professionalism with which the actors move. This professionalism is the result of Nettelbeck's cuisine consultant, Rocco Dressel, a first rate chef, who trained and worked with the actors for several weeks before the film was shot. They all sat around a table in the restaurant, very much like they do later on in the film, and ate together in their work clothes.

During class, Dressel taught the actors – none of whom had any cooking skills whatsoever – how to move and look like professional chefs. They learned how to gut a fish, how to use a knife, and how to properly handle the pots and pans. The actors took these lessons very seriously. "They worked at this little restaurant that was closed during the day, and in their training sessions, they would prepare a three to four course meal every day, dessert and everything," explains Sandra Nettelbeck.

Martha (Martina Gedeck) and Mario (Sergio Castellitto) share an intimate moment over food, as one chef puts the other through a blindfolded taste test.

When it came time for the actors to shoot their scenes in the kitchen, Dressel's instruction was immediately apparent as each looked and moved with the skill and grace of true chefs. As the food designer, Dressel made up an entire menu for the restaurant and created every dish in the film. Dressel and his food stylist worked in a separate kitchen where they were constantly making new plates to replace those ruined from sitting out under hot lights.

The following recipes have been developed by Nettlebeck's cooking consultant Rocco Dressel.

> **Duck Foie Gras:** Open the lobes of a duck liver and remove the veins, nerves, fat and greenish parts. Add salt, pepper, nutmeg, quatre épices, Porto, and Armagnac. Let it marinate for 24 hours. Cook no less than 1000g of it in an 80°C waterbath in a 140°C oven, for 25 to 30 minutes. Don't overcook it. Let it rest in a cool place for at least two days before serving.

> **Lemon tart:** Fold the sweet short pastry into a buttered tart tin. Let it rest in the refrigerator overnight. Pre-heat the oven to 180°C. Line the pastry with aluminum foil, cover with baking beans. Bake for 15 minutes. Remove from oven, let it cool before removing the foil and beans. Grate the peel of two lemons, put in a blender with their juice, add 2 tablespoons of double cream, 50g of skinned almonds, 140g of sugar, 3 whole eggs and 60g of melted butter. Blend to smooth paste, spread onto the cool pastry and bake for about 15 minutes. Let it cool and decorate with a thick layer of confectioner's sugar.

EVALUATION

Bella Martha was first released in Germany with the title *Drei Sterne* and changed to its current title after it gained a lot of international attention, especially in the United States where the film was distributed under the name *Mostly Martha*. The Italian title is *Ricette D'Amore* (Recipe of Love).

Mostly Martha is not a serious movie needing a lot of analysis, but rather it is one of those rare German films that entertains and yet is still critically accepted.

With its casual elegance and leisurely pace, it represents a new quality in German film making. As critics pointed out, the movie was barely recognized as a German film since Germany has the reputation of producing only serious art movies.

Mostly Martha is a food movie, a "foodie," much like *Babettes gaestebud* (*Babette's Feast*, Gabriel Axel 1987) or *Chocolat* (Lasse Hallström 2000). It is a movie about our daily lives, with the ever-increasing fad of eating out in upscale restaurants, which look the same all over the world. Adding to this international feel is a definite European sense of community. Castellitto, the Italian male star and Gedeck, the German female lead, were cast, it seems, to appease the German and Italian production companies, which insisted on having an actor represent each country in order to insure a financial success in their respective countries. Castellitto's lines even had to be dubbed into German as the actor did not speak the language, but he is a major Italian star. Thus *Mostly Martha* continues a trend started in the 1980s of consortia of film studios from various European countries underwriting film production.

Food of course is a symbol for Martha's repressed character that she can only express with her fantastic culinary creations. As Nettelbeck observed, most first-rate chefs are obsessed with their work: they are artists in their own right. Nettelbeck's movie is neatly divided into two parts, work and pleasure. While Martha in her dour German ways is all work, Mario is all play, somewhat of a cliché between Germany and Italy, but a cliché most audiences would readily accept.

Martha lives in her own world, a world she constructed with her exclusive focus on work. Various scenes suggest that work has become her identity, for example when she blows up at a customer who dares criticize the quality of her duck foie gras. Martha is a perfectionist, representing yet another cliché that German culture will demand perfection, at the workplace or in everyday life. And since Martha's life is intensely work-oriented, she has no private life. When a new tenant, Sam the architect, moves into her building, she can only connect with him through her food. Since she cannot engage in small talk, she surprises Sam whom she barely knows with a dinner invitation. Martha is socially inept in her emotional isolation, which the movie shows in her repeated withdrawals to the chiller room. She also cannot relate to her niece Lina, who eventually runs away from home. The fact that Martha cannot eat in the presence of others seems to indicate a severe case of anorexia.

It is surprising that Martha chose cooking as her profession, since cooking and eating is a social activity. Martha is so dysfunctional that her boss requires her to visit a psychiatrist (August Zirner). The movie shows Martha's complex character in an ironic way when her descriptions of the recipes totally overwhelm her psychiatrist. Martha is a powerful figure in spite of her one-sided fixation on cooking.

Compared with the complex Martha, Mario presents another cliché, the southern European male who can offer northern Europeans a lesson in life. Mario has to save Martha from her misery with his Italian *joie de vivre*, the Italian cuisine, and his uncomplicated emotions, an attitude Martha's niece Lina relates to more easily than to Martha's heavy-handed approach. Mario represents *la dolce vita*: fun, love of food, play, music, and laughter. Most Germans love Italian culture and food: There is even a term for German lovers of Italian lifestyle, "Toscana Germans." At the end of the film, when he almost convinces Martha to join him in his Bella Italia, we recognize that Mario feels comfortable living in his sunny homeland, and that he loves his cooking and his music. Mario is an uncomplicated character and, as the movie suggests, Italy is an uncomplicated country without problems. Mario's only problem seems to be that he has to live in Germany.

The film's graceful flow originates in its soundtrack. Nettelbeck felt strongly that her film needed a good soundtrack and she found the right composer as a music consultant in Manfred Eicher. "I was very nervous when I showed him the rough cut. Thank God he liked the film," remembers Nettelbeck. "Collaborating with him was enlightening for me. He is a true master of his trade and he immediately understood what I was after with the film." Eicher was able to pull together a group of musicians and songs that ultimately created just the right background and atmosphere for the film. As Nettelbeck comments, "Keith Jarrett, Arvo Pärt and David Darling form the musical structure of the film and complement each other while at the same time allowing for the other songs to co-exist — the songs by Dean Martin, Paolo Conte, Louis Prima and others."

Mostly Martha takes full advantage of rock music, a trend since American rock music was first introduced to German films in the 1970s, with a series of almost nonstop tunes that give this film its even flow. Music enters into the story as it complements and underscores the competition between French and Italian food, the two culinary traditions and two different approaches to life favored by Martha and Mario respectively. The musical soundtrack reflects the polarity between French and Italian cooking, but in this case, the competition is between American and Italian music, with American rock standing in perhaps for the French. As the movie progresses, the Italian sound track becomes more dominant introducing such compelling songs as "Attenti Al Lupo," sung by Lucio Dalla, "Via Con Me," sung by Paolo Conte, or the mesmerizing "Angelina – Zooma Zooma," sung twice by Louis Prima in two key scenes when the tension between Martha and Mario rises. The music seems to indicate that as Martha constructs her life from various traditions, German, French and Anglo-American, Mario the character and Mario the chef remain and are the same person, who feels happiest when he sings. It is as if Martha's inability to sing represents the German proverb "Böse Menschen haben keine Lieder" ("Bad people have no songs"). Thus the film also is about Martha's musical education.

Like other food movies, such as *Babette's Feast*, *Tampopo* (Juzo Itami 1985), or *Chocolat*, *Mostly Martha* is a fun movie to watch in spite of its predictability: The film follows a love story formula, and we know from the beginning that Martha will fall in love not only with Mario but also with his lifestyle and follow him to Italy. (RZ)

QUESTIONS

1. What is Martha's approach to cooking? What does she feel makes a good cook? How does this compare to Mario's style? How do their different cooking styles reflect their approaches to their work and to life?

2. Sometimes we have expectations in life that are so ingrained that we are unaware of them until a situation does not meet them. What are some expectations people have with regard to dining/eating that are reflected in the various characters (major and minor) in this film? Can you imagine situations or cultures in which these expectations would not exist? Describe dining experiences in which you were surprised by the unexpected.

3. Construct a rough outline of the music titles in the film, determining how the changes from one culture to another play out on the sound track.

4. Imagine you are cooking for someone. How many people would you invite? What would you prepare? Why? How would you serve the meal?

5. Find a German recipe and compare it with one of the French recipes provided. What influences do climate and culture have on cuisine?

6. Martha uses food to connect with others. It is often a means through which she reaches out to others or a topic of discussion. Good food and good friends often make for a good evening. Families have long had "dinner table discussions" as a time for sharing the day and for announcing major life events. Describe a meal which you recently shared. With whom did you share it? What kinds of topics were discussed? To what extent did the food itself play a role in the discussion?

RELATED FILMS

The following German films like *Mostly Martha* contain more entertainment than message. Some even yield a warm glow in the viewer.

Männer (*Men*, Doris Dörrie 1985). Dörrie's Capraesque film explores the double standard that lets men stray but not women, in a light tone and with a happy ending.

Der bewegte Mann (*Maybe, Maybe Not*, Sönke Wortmann 1994). Wortmann's situational comedy tells the story of a straight man who, kicked out of the apartment by his girlfriend, moves in with a gay man and his buddies.

Keiner liebt mich (*Nobody Loves Me*, Doris Dörrie 1995). Dörrie's black comedy leaves viewers with a happy ending and humming Edith Piaf's "Je ne regrette rien." The movie is discussed elsewhere in the book.

Jenseits der Stille (*Beyond Silence*, Caroline Link 1996). This drama tells of a young hearing woman, raised by deaf parents, who grows up to win a place in a musical school as a clarinetist.

Lola rennt (*Run Lola Run*, Tom Tykwer 1998). Tykwer's film remains the feel-good champ in German films of the last decade.

INFORMATION

Mostly Martha (2001), DVD, in German w/English subtitles, color, 107 minutes, Paramount Home Video 2003.

http://www.paramountclassics.com/martha/index.html. Site of the press kit for *Mostly Martha*.

Cooper, Rand Richards. "Climate changes: mostly Martha." *Commonweal* 128 (11 October 2002), 22.

Liers, Sarah: *Bella Martha*: Roman. Berlin: Aufbau Taschenbuch Verlag GmbH, 2003.

CHAPTER 30

Nirgendwo in Afrika

(*Nowhere in Africa*, **Caroline Link 2001**)

Regina Redlich (Lea Kurka) stands in front of the first fire of the season, a portentous event in the African lore of the film. Fire again plays a part later in the film as Regina and her mother bond during an African ritual, and also when the plague of locusts is driven off.

CREDITS

Director	Caroline Link
Screenplay	Caroline Link (based on the novel by Stephanie Zweig)
Director of Photography	Gernot Roll
Music	Niki Reiser, Jochen Schmidt-Hambrock
Producers	Andreas Bareiß, Bernd Eichinger, Peter Herrmann, et al
Production Companies	Bavaria Film, Constantin Film Produktion GmbH
Length	141 minutes; color

Principal Cast

Juliane Köhler (Jettel Redlich), Merab Ninidze (Walter Redlich), Sidede Onyulo (Owuor) Lea Kurka (Regina as child), Karoline Eckertz (Regina as adolescent), Matthias Habich (Süßkind).

THE STORY

Having recognized the danger for Jews in his native Germany after Hitler and the Nazis come to power, Walther Redlich, a successful lawyer, has immigrated to Kenya, finding work managing the farm of a British landowner. Before Redlich can call for his family he contracts Malaria and is nursed back to health by Süßkind, a fellow émigré from Germany, who gives him quinine, the traditional cure, and Owuor, his African servant, who prefers homeopathic medicines. Süßkind's patronizing instructions to Owuor on how to administer the quinine and Owuar's rejection of the advice once Süßkind has gone introduce a major theme, the polarity between native and immigrant cultures that is not resolved until the final scene of the movie.

Once he is cured, Redlich sends for his family, his wife Jettel, a sophisticated but spoiled member of the Jewish professional class, and his young daughter. Jettel has difficulties acculturating into the life in Kenya: she rejects African culture from the beginning, denying to herself that the past is lost to her and she will have to make a new life in another culture. Reflecting her denial are an elegant party gown she bought with the last of the Redlich money and an insistence on bringing china rather than the refrigerator her husband had wanted. In contrast to her mother, young Regina Redlich, owing to her age, readily adapts to life in Africa, learning the language with ease and befriending the local children. Based on the novel *Nirgendwo in Afrika* (*Nowhere in Africa* 2000) by Stephanie Zweig, the film of the same name tells the story of a Jewish family faced with the physical and psychological realities of immigration. Each member of the family copes differently in a totally unfamiliar culture as the tragedy of the Holocaust unfolds off-screen.

BACKGROUND

Nowhere in Africa (2001) is one of the most recent films that try to come to terms to what happened to the Jews in Nazi Germany. Most of the countries engaged in the Second World War have produced films on the topic of Nazi persecution of the Jews. Most of the initial efforts to deal with the Second World War and Nazi Germany avoided referencing the Holocaust directly, as the years after the war were concerned with rebuilding Germany and creating bridges between Germany and the Allies. Notable exceptions were Wolfgang Staudte's 1946 movie *Die Mörder sind unter uns* (*The Murderers Are among Us*), which showed a brief headline proclaiming "2 Million Gassed," and *The Stranger* (Orson Welles, 1946), in which an ex-Nazi, who had practiced atrocities in a concentration camp, has assumed a new identity in the United States. But other postwar films until the sixties, if they dealt with the years 1933-1945, focused on issues outside the Holocaust. Although French director Alain Resnais devoted his documentary *Nuit et broulliard* (*Night and Fog*) to the horrific images of Auschwitz as early as 1955, concentration camps or death camps did not appear in a feature length fiction film until the East German director Frank Beyer took up the theme in 1963 with *Nackt unter Wölfen* (*Naked among Wolves*), a story of how inmates protected a young boy in Auschwitz from being discovered and killed. Italian director Roberto Benigni filmed a similar story in 1997, *La vita è bella* (*Life is Beautiful*).

Other notable examples of the Holocaust on film are Steven Spielberg's *Schindler's List* (1993), which takes place in the Auschwitz-Birkenau camp, and Roman Polanski's *The Pianist* (2002), which shows both the brutality of the Nazi Holocaust and one man's escape. West Germany's directors for the most part when dealing with the Holocaust have focused on escape from the Nazis rather than events in the camps. Among these are Peter Lilienthal's *David* (1979) and Polish director Agnieszka Holland's *Europa Europa* (1990), both of which show youthful protagonists as they hide from the Nazis among the Germans. Finally some directors have shown the lucky few who were able to get out of Germany before deportation to the camps. Austrian director Axel Corti's trilogy, *Wohin und Zurück* (*To Where and Back* 1982-1985) follows a young man from Vienna to France, where, just like the Redlichs in Kenya, he is arrested as a German sympathizer when war breaks out. Michael Hoffmann's and Harry Raymon's *Regentröpfen* (1981) likewise shows a German Jewish family finally able to escape the Nazis, only to be refused asylum by any of the Allied countries.

Link continues the change in perspective that has occurred in films that deal with the Holocaust. Whereas the early films focused on unnamed victims and later films told of individual tragedies, more recent films tell about the survivors, the witnesses to the tragedy. Link's characters cannot rightly even declare witness status, except to the early years of the regime, as they escaped before the tragedy began. Thus she takes the theme of Holocaust to another level, one that asks Germans and Jews to deal with the aftermath of the Holocaust; for Link's protagonists escaped but their friends and family did not. Moreover, they have lost a culture they once felt a part of, and which is responsible both for their leaving their homes and for the deaths of those not able to escape. Finally, now that the war is over and the Nazis defeated, they have to ask themselves how much they want to reintegrate into a society that spawned the tragedy. Süßkind, the family friend, cannot ever accept being German again. Walther's military superior, an Englishman, cannot understand why Walther would still consider himself German. And the narrator confesses to not "remembering Germany." Yet Jettel, Walther, and Regina repatriate themselves, an end that seems to offer viewers a sense of final resolution to one of the twentieth century's greatest tragedies.

EVALUATION

That *Nowhere in Africa* won the Oscar for best foreign film of 2002 is no surprise. Members of the Academy of Motion Pictures traditionally favor movies with a serious theme, and, without argument, few themes have dominated academic, intellectual, and public discourse as much as those related to the years of the Second World War in general and to the Holocaust in particular. But it would be unfair to attribute the film's success to the theme alone, for it is the manner in which Caroline Link addresses the past that has led to the film's success with critics and public. Unlike earlier films about the Holocaust (at least those since the American television miniseries, *Holocaust*), which foreground the atrocities committed by the Nazis, Link keeps Nazi Germany and the persecution of the Jews off screen. Indeed the scenes in Germany play in a German Jewish household, rather than in a public environment, and the only Nazi to appear is a helpful member of the Hitler Youth, who extends a hand when Jettel falls down while skating. And in the Africa sequences, which comprise most of the movie, Link's focus is on the problems of acculturation, marital and familial relationships, and coming of age. Yet the absence of the Holocaust in the film's story paradoxically heightens its presence in the minds of the viewers.

The seeming contradiction of presence through absence becomes a theme as soon as the film begins. Regina's (the narrator of the film) admission that she does not remember Germany places Germany and its past forward in our imagination, and yet Germany, other than for the opening scenes, will not be a visual subject for the remainder of the movie. In the same vein, in the opening scenes when Jettel, Regina's mother, stumbles while skating, she is offered assistance by a member of the Hitler Youth. As the boy extends his hand and Jettel sees his Hitler Youth armband, she refuses his help, a gesture that reminds viewers more strongly of the Jews' status within Nazi Germany than would have belligerent action on the part of the youth. Throughout the film, Link uses cinematography, music, characterization, and setting to create a story behind the one we are watching. Beneath or behind the family squabbles, the coming-of-age story, the African drums, and the learning of cultural tolerance lies a text of irreversible tragedy whose story continues.

The major and minor characters of *Nowhere in Africa* are beset with contradiction. Regina Redlich, played as a child by Lea Kurka and as an adolescent by Karoline Eckertz, narrates the film. It is through her eyes that we experience Kenya, hear about events in far-off Germany, and witness the troubles in her parent's marriage. She is thus our entry into the film. Her admission that she remembers little about the Germany of 1938 would be true for most viewers, and simultaneously distances that country from them, allowing them to experience the events there as vaguely as the narrator. As with another of her child/adolescent characters, Lara in *Jenseits der Stille* (*Beyond Silence* 1996), Link presents Regina as older than her age, possessing wisdom and selflessness not ordinarily found in children. Yet she embodies the cliché "from the mouths of babes," teaching the adults around them and helping them to grow. Regina is also the one character who, because of her age, acculturates completely. Indeed she assimilates into the local African culture even as she keeps and grows within her own. She visits the natives in their huts, climbs trees with her friends, and recognizes their culture as equal to her own. When she climbs a tree after returning from school as a sexually maturing teenager, she strips to the waist and climbs with her male friend in an act as natural as that of any of the local children. When her mother does this, at the behest of her husband, it is obviously a sign of how they only mimic the local culture and cannot be a part of it.

Jettel Redlich, played by Juliane Köhler, undergoes the most change in the film. Although told from Regina's persepctive, the film is more about the mother's coming to terms with Africa that it is about Regina's coming of age there. For while Link focuses the story on the daughter, she does so to contrast the genuineness of youthful naïveté with the deceit of sophistication. Although the mother learns the most in the film, and thus provides viewers with a focus for their own enlightenment, she is also the most difficult person to accept. On a personal level Jettel is unpleasant. She is a spoiled Jewish socialite, more interested in clothes and societal activity than making a life in Kenya with her husband and child. For the trip to Kenya she has ignored her husband's instructions to bring a refrigerator and leave the china at home. She has also used the last of her money for an expensive evening gown, suggesting her complete lack of awareness of what awaits. On a socio-political level she is insensitive and ethnocentric. She treats her

Jettel Redlich (Juliane Köhler) comforts an elderly African woman who has been put out to be killed by hyenas, a practice Jettel at first condemns and then understands. The scene represents another step on Jettel's acceptance and understanding of African culture.

cook as a servant for all things rather than a trained employee, and looks upon her life on the farm as a burden that she would rather not endure. She finds the African children dirty, the food monotonous, and the culture backward. On a moral level, she seems reprehensible. She has an affair with an officer of the country club-like prison she has been sent to, while her husband is in a genuine prison. Moreover, she is tempted to start yet another affair with a friend of the family rather than join her husband and daughter in returning to Germany. Yet in spite of all her hostility to the culture, to her "fish out of water" nature, and to her weakness in character, Jettel becomes one with the African culture. She learns and converses in Swahili, accepts African death rituals, and even teaches her daughter about the importance of keeping and yet accepting the differences among people.

Jettel carries the moral message of the movie, a lesson that is both obvious and complex. On the one hand she represents the person whose eyes are opened to cultural diversity. She is in Kenya because of persecution back home. And while she does not persecute her African neighbors, she does not respect them either. Only through intervention of her daughter and husband does she learn to live in another culture as an outsider. On the other hand she also represents the pre- and post-war Jew, who first ignored what was occurring in Germany and then, having survived, has to learn to accept her survival and return, either physically or psychologically, to the land of her persecutors.

Walther Redlich, played by Merab Ninidze, offers a counterweight to Jettel's seeming naïveté about the reasons they are in Kenya. He alone in his family recognized the danger the Nazis posed to the Jews. After the war he is again alone in his feeling of obligation to return to Germany, to face his persecutors and his family's killers, and to begin the process of healing still going on today. In a sense he is too good to believe. When letters are received, he has to interpret them for Jettel who still hopes to return to Germany and who still imagines her family as living in Breslau in the comfortable conditions of the middle class. He also holds together their marriage, which may have been in trouble already before emigrating from Germany. In a conversation between Jettel and Walther's father, her father-in-law tells her to love his son. He implies that he knows the marriage is in trouble and fears that Walther will be hurt. And indeed the relationship in Kenya revolves around Jettel's initial selfishness in her marriage to Walther. Against his nature he even tries hunting to satisfy her craving for something other than eggs and bread. And when the farm's harvest is threatened by a plague of locusts just before his departure for Germany, he returns to Jettel to help save the crop, giving up his desire to return home to once again practice law. Only Jettel's newly found wisdom overturns his selfless decision.

Owuor, played by Sidede Onyulo, represents both a strong African personality and a liberal cliché. When Jettel insists he learn German, he turns from her and continues to use Swahili to refer to items in the house. When she wants him to help in the garden, he is truly offended that she would ask him, a cook, to be an outdoor servant. He also refuses to get water for her, but then shows his strength by withstanding the taunts of village women when he carries Jettel's water jugs. Yet in spite of all his strengths, Owuor seems little more than a romantic's vision of the noble savage. He utters wisdom such as "Black women don't need help, white women are helpless." He introduces us to the customs of the Africans, generally presented as quaint: the need to watch the first fire, or the time when an African man must start his journey. Indeed, the fact that he finds the family after having been separated from them in time and distance says as much about his determination as it does about the native's devotion to *bwana*, familiar from countless movies about Africa.

Four minor British characters, a school headmaster, a lieutenant, a landowner, and the Jewish representative in Kenya, create an interesting subtext in the film. For together they represent the historical reality of how Non-German Europe ignored the plight of the Jews, either because of lack of concern or latent anti-Semitism. Anti-Semitism seems strongest in the headmaster, whose insensitivity to the Jewish children during assembly and whose patronizing questioning of Regina who has done well in school reveal the cultural gulf between British and Jewish culture. In contrast, the Jewish representative in Kenya reflects that non-German Jews could be insensitive to Jewish refugees from Hitler's Germany. Although willing to meet with Jettel to discuss the plight of incarcerated Jews, he does not see their problem as the responsibility of the non-German Jewish community. The British landowner is equally as unsympathetic to the German Jews, ignoring common sense, looking past the reasons the Jews have left Germany and firing Walther Redlich, believing him a German sympathizer. Finally the British lieutenant uses his position and Jettel's vulnerability to seduce her into an affair which will secure the release of her husband.

Underscoring the paradoxical behavior of the characters are lush cinematography, expressive camera movement, and evocative music, which say more than the simple images and melodies. Link's cinematographer captures the vastness of Africa's landscape, whether showing rivers, savannas or mountains. It is not a frightening landscape, indeed it is friendly. But in its vastness, it threatens to engulf the foreign inhabitants. Aided by crane shots that pull away from the scene, characters become part of the environment, are swallowed up by it. Their insignificance in the greater whole that is Kenya is further emphasized through contrast with the scenes that take place in Germany. Here, characters are not part of the environment, they are the environment. The surroundings hardly matter at all. Our attention is drawn to dialog, facial expressions, familial importance, and non-interaction with German neighbors. But the unseen world of Germans surrounding them poses more threat than the seemingly hostile Africa.

In the African scenes, the cinematographer also works with contrasting effects. As counterbalance to Kenya's vastness, emphasized through sun-drenched scenes that seem light and airy, he includes night scenes lit by candlelight and fire. The chiaroscuro play in these scenes forces attention on detail: a family Sabbath, a discussion of the concentration camps, Jettel's attendance at a native ceremony wearing her evening dress. Here also the cinematography is enhanced through camera work that moves over faces, circles rooms, and rests on poignant scenes. One of the most poignant of these is reminiscent of Jean Renoir's *La grande illusion* (*The Grand Illusion* 1937) also a film about war, about understanding the other. In Renoir's film, a German woman points out a table to some prisoners she is hiding. As the camera glides over the table, she recites battles from the war and ends by saying now the table is too big, a statement being reinforced by the camera work. In *Nowhere in Africa*, the family has just received a letter from Germany explaining the worsening situation. As the father reads the letter the camera pans the room, seemingly empty, moving closer to a table in the middle. The scene then cuts to Walther, panning to Jettel and then to Regina and pulls away, showing all three positioned at a distance from each other as the empty table sits in the middle of the room.

The musical score for *Nowhere in Africa* is reminiscent of the scores for classical films. It evokes place, time, and mood. It overarches scenes, allowing smooth transitions but also commenting on relationships. As the film begins, African drum rhythms sound behind the credits. In flashbacks to Germany, European style music plays. Yet European music bleeds into the scenes in Africa, carrying over the characters' European culture. This is especially true in early scenes as Jettel is still unable to shed her German culture. European music likewise plays as the Redlich china is unpacked or the parents discuss the need to send Regina to a British school. But in scenes with Regina, who has accepted African culture, the drums sound. Finally, once the mother has accepted the culture, even her scenes contain drum rhythms rather than violins. They beat as she takes over as manager of the farm, and they are joined by chanting voices while Jettel and the villagers fight invading locusts. They also sound as the Redlichs leave Kenya, the final shot freezing on an African peddler, perhaps as a reminder that alien cultures can coexist without obliterating each other.

Nowhere in Africa is both a simple and complex film, laying a straightforward personal tale of the difficulties of immigrants over a universal story of persecution and tragedy. Two things are immediately remarkable about the way Caroline Link handles these themes in her film. First, unlike many films set in Africa and unlike many films about immigration, the film does not for the most part patronize. In spite of the too good to be believed portrayal of Owuor, African culture, the dominant culture of the film, is depicted objectively, from the slaughtering of a goat to the abandonment of an old woman. Moreover, although the Redlichs balk at village customs, in the end, they accept local culture rather than teach the locals European ways. The mother's comment that "Tolerance does not mean that we all have to be the same" could well serve as a motto for multi-diversity. Within the world of the movie, the statement allows Africans and Europeans to allow the continued existence of the other without ultimately eliminating or leveling differences. Jettel accepts the custom of placing the sick out to die where the hyenas can get at them, yet stays to sit with the woman rather than abandoning her completely, comforting her as well as herself. Walther accepts Owuor's explanation of why he can take nothing of the father's on his safari, and Owuor, who had wanted to leave without seeing Regina, is able in the end to pick her up for a last hug.

Lying beneath this tale of acceptance, tolerance, and growth is the darker text of the Holocaust, which is always in the background threatening to disrupt the tale of immigration. The Holocaust comes to the foreground through letters, news reports, and newsreel footage. Letters from Breslau report how the members of the family who stayed behind in Germany are slowly being denied rights, reflected in their loss of spatial integrity. They are moved first to a ghetto, then to a concentration camp, and then are murdered. News reports and newsreel footage bring the reasons of the Redlichs' status as immigrants to the fore. These aren't immigrants looking for a better life, they are refugees hoping to continue living. (RCR)

QUESTIONS

1. Identify and discuss as many of the historical references in the film as possible. That is, when does the story include references to what is going on in Germany and elsewhere?

2. Link uses facial expression and glances to dramatic effect. Can you locate any specific scenes when just a glance or look gives meaning to what the camera shows?

3. What is the significance of the antelope's and the dog's names?

4. In what ways is Regina a device to tell the story rather than a child or adolescent?

5. European movies do not always end happily. When do we know that all will turn out fine for the Redlich family?

RELATED FILMS

The following German language films focus on Nazi persecution of the Jews. All are available with English subtitles.

David (Peter Lilienthal 1979). Lilienthal follows a teenage youth as he hides out in Nazi Germany awaiting a chance to escape.

Charlotte (Frans Weisz 1981). The film is based on the true story of a painter of water colors who died in a concentration camp. The film focuses on Charlotte Salomon's life before her deportation.

Europa Europa (Agnieszka Holland 1990). Known in Germany by the title *Hitlerjunge Salomon*, the film was rejected by the German film industry to be Germany's entry for the Best Foreign Film category of the Academy Awards on the ground that its director was not German.

Nackt unter Wölfen (*Naked among Wolves*, Frank Beyer 1963). This East German film is one of the earliest German language movies to focus on the Holocaust.

INFORMATION

Nowhere in Africa (2001), DVD, in German w/subtitles, color, 141 minutes, Columbia Tristar Home, released 2003.

Stefanie Zweig. *Nirgendwo in Afrika*. Munich: Heyne, 2000.

Zweig, Stephanie. *Irgendwo in Deutschland*. Munich: Heyne, 1998.

http://www.filmtracks.com/titles/nowhere_africa.html. Review of the soundtrack to the film offering insight into the mix of European and African sounds.

CHAPTER 31

Good Bye, Lenin!

(Wolfgang Becker 2003)

Denis (Florian Lukas) imitating a newsreader of the former East German "Aktuelle Kamera" news program, reads the evening news over closed circuit TV transmitting only to the room of Alex's mother.

CREDITS

Director	Wolfgang Becker
Screenplay	Wolfgang Becker, Bernd Lichtenberg
Director of Photography	Martin Kukula
Music by	Yann Tiersen
Producer	Stefan Arndt
Production Companies	Westdeutscher Rundfunk, X-Filme Creative Pool, Arte
Length	121 minutes; color

Principal Cast

Daniel Brühl (Alex), Katrin Saß (Mutter), Chulpan Khamatova (Lara), Maria Simon (Ariane), Florian Lukas (Denis), Alexander Beyer (Rainer), Burghart Klaußner (Robert Kerner, Vater), Christine Schorn (Frau Schäfer), Michael Gwisdek (Direktor Klapprath).

THE STORY

When Alexander's father (Burghart Klaußner) escapes to West Berlin during the last years of the German Democratic Republic (GDR), his mother (Kathrin Saß) has a nervous breakdown and refuses to speak for months, suggesting her difficulty in accepting what has occurred. When she starts talking again, she lets it be known that her husband has deserted the family and run off with a younger woman. She throws herself into political activity and becomes fanatical in her support of Communist ideals.

During a demonstration involving students and pro-democracy marchers, which she stumbles upon while walking home one evening, she suffers a heart attack and collapses in the street when she witnesses Alexander (Daniel Brühl) being arrested by riot police and bundled into a van. Alex is beaten when he attempts to run to her side and is subsequently taken away. For eight months, she lies in a coma, during which time the Berlin Wall is demolished, the government collapses, capitalism takes root and freedom of expression is restored.

When the mother regains consciousness and is brought back to her apartment, Alexander creates a false world for her in which nothing has changed since her heart attack, for fear that knowing the truth about the demise of the GDR might cause a second heart attack and kill her. To accomplish his ruse, he embarks on an exhilarating project to get hold of East German groceries which are becoming increasingly rare and for which Hanna so yearns: *Mokkafix* instant coffee, *Globus* peas and *Spreewald* gherkins have all disappeared. These GDR brands have been replaced by an onslaught of western products, and although much hated by Alexander and his sister Ariane (Maria Simon), the old GDR products gain tremendously in emotional value for them as symbols of the old life to which Hanna clings.

Alexander's loving project to keep the German Democratic Republic alive for his mother has a playful political element. Hanna asks for a television set to watch the news, and Alexander makes use of his new job with a western satellite-dish retailer and gets his workmate Denis (Florian Lukas) to produce GDR-style prime-time news videos, which are then transmitted into Hanna's living room. In a reversal of reality, they feature westerners flocking to the GDR because they have realized its socialist potential. They also show Sigmund Jähn, the only East German to have flown in outer space, as Erich Honecker's successor.

Alexander's quest to save his mother's little socialist world provides the film with many opportunities for humor, particularly slapstick situations. For example, Alexander organizes a birthday celebration for his mother with Young Pioneers in prim uniforms singing kitschy socialist tunes. At another time Ariane's new western boyfriend confuses Young Pioneers with Hitler Youth.

Alex's mother looks up and just misses seeing a plane under which hangs a statue of Lenin. The western-like advertising slogan behind her that "all wishes are fulfilled" seems to escape her notice also.

BACKGROUND

Wolfgang Becker, the director of *Good Bye, Lenin!* was born in 1954 in Hemer/Westphalia and studied German, History and American Studies at the Free University in Berlin. He followed this with a job at a sound studio in 1980 and then began studies at the German Film & Television Academy (dffb). He started working as a freelance cameraman in 1983 and graduated from the dffb in 1986 with his student project film *Schmetterlinge* (*Butterflies*), which won the Student Academy Award in 1988, the Golden Leopard at Locarno and the Saarland Prime-Minister's Award at the 1988 Ophüls Festival Saarbrücken. He directed the *Tatort*-episode, "Blutwurstwalzer," before making his second feature *Kinderspiele* (*Children's Games* 1992), the documentary *Celibidache* (1992), and the Berlinale competition features *Das Leben ist eine Baustelle* (*Life is All You Get* 1997), and *Good Bye, Lenin!* (2003).

EVALUATION

Good Bye, Lenin! was one of the most successful German post-unification movies. Indeed it has been one of the most successful German movies ever. Although a comedy, indeed one of the funniest German films in years, *Good Bye, Lenin!* also has a serious text. In the film's humorous look at nostalgia for the East or what Germans refer to as *ostalgie*, we see a requiem for a dream of a better world under socialism, a dream that was held by people in the West as well as the East. This better world is at first represented by the mother, who represents the type of GDR citizen engaged in socialism's creation of a new human being, but already seems dated at the time of unification. Her enthusiasm is compensation for her failed marriage. As Alexander comments ironically she is "married to the socialist system," a reaction of her husband's defection to the West, after which Mrs. Kerner redirects herself completely to the socialist cause, becoming the ombudsman for all those who complain of injustices in the system of the GDR and writing infamous *Eingaben* (petitions) with wit and humor. She becomes a literal and figurative mother figure, representing the maternal nature of the GDR as reflected in the novels of Thomas Brussig and Alexa Hennig. Brussig and Hennig portray the GDR as a *Muttirepublik* (nanny state), showing that even those who had been victimized, considered the state to be on their side.

The film begins with a longer series of introductory shots connected by Alex's voice-over narration. Such voice-over introductions have recently become a popular method to introduce movies in German cinema. It lends the film a semi-documentary style, especially in combination with the real documentary footage these films incorporate. This blend of fictional and appropriate documentary footage in the beginning of the film prepares viewers to accept the movie's later artistic subterfuge as possible, when Alex and his friend use documentary footage to recreate a false reality for the mother. The documentary effect of the movie's introduction is enhanced by the use of 8mm film images that were popular for family and vacation movies at that time. The introduction, taking about ten minutes, leads to the start of the main story, which begins with the events of 1989.

The film then introduces a number of important key scenes, the first being the demonstration against the celebration of the fortieth anniversary of the GDR when Alex's mother collapses while he is beaten up and taken away by riot police. This sequence offers the film's only criticism of the GDR regime. The second key scene, the removal of Lenin's statue from its traditional location at East Berlin's Lenin Square, elicits an emotional response and laughter from viewers familiar with the event. For the statue's removal entered into public discourse and memory as a moment when Communism ended. Becker models the removal of Lenin on a memorable scene in *La dolce vita* (Federico Fellini 1960) when a statue of Christ is flown above the streets in Rome, an event many understood as sacrilege, just as Lenin's removal was considered sacrilege at the time by some East Berliners. In the film, as Mrs. Kerner steps outside her apartment for the first time since her heart attack, she just misses seeing the statue in the air but knows something is amiss and asks for an explanation. It is at this point that Alex is challenged to use the old clips from the news show *Aktuelle Kamera* to reinvent history. His explanation of what the mother has seen, in particular for the huge Coca Cola sign going up on a building outside her window, is that the GDR granted tens of thousands of Westerners political asylum in East Berlin, since they had gotten tired of living in the stressful competitive West, an explanation Mrs. Kerner accepts without a doubt. She even immediately offers a room at their *dacha* to one of those needy refugees.

Alex, the film's protagonist, represents another facet of the dream. As the film's ever-present narrator, he looks back with critical distance, recognizing the old system's failures but also its successes. In the scenes before the mother's attack, despite her shining example of good Communism, Alex has become a rather passive GDR citizen who is not very exited about his career as a TV repairman. Indeed he even gets involved in political demonstrations against the GDR's fortieth anniversary, where he is beaten up by the police, the incident that causes his mother's near fatal heart attack.

Alex at first enjoys the changes the political *Wende* (turn of events) brought, when Berlin has become the center of the universe: "Everything was possible, everything was imaginable." When his mother wakes up from her coma he too seems to have become more engaged in life. He takes over the situation and is able to recreate a new version of the old world in order to insure his mother's survival.

What adds to the comic element is an exploration of the meaning of change. In a touching and comic manner, *Good Bye, Lenin!* shows how a loving son creates miracles to restore his mother to health by getting her to believe that Lenin really did win after all! In his fantasy news items Alexander and his friend Denis create the humane German Democratic Republic of their own dreams.

As carrier of the film's dream, Alex constructs the image of a GDR which he himself would have liked to see. With his creation of Siegmund Jähn, the GDR's only space hero, to replace Erich Honecker as head of state, he puts words into Jähn's mouth that resemble his own nostalgic dreams of a nicer GDR:

"Socialism means moving towards the other person and trying to get along with him, not dreaming of a better world, but creating it. Many have looked for an alternative to the hard struggle of survival in the capitalist system, not everyone wants to participate in careerism and consumerism. Not everyone is made for the *Ellenbogen* (pushy) society. These people want a different life in our midst."

These ideas resemble those of the citizen groups that brought about the change during the revolutionary events of 1989/90, ideas of a new fear-free society that would soon be pushed aside by the harsher realities of Western power players. Alex however feels he has to voice them and in voicing them discovers how much he and GDR citizens really lost by abandoning socialism. His words also reflect the views of many in the West who had hoped an eventually united Germany could someday be a bridge between Eastern and Western Europe. They had hoped this united country could show the world socialism with a human face.

The movie deals with reality and the perception of reality, communicated through TV images. It challenges viewers who got used to seeing the conventional perception of the events following the fall of the Berlin Wall as liberating, and applauding the West as victorious. Alex's task is to use the traditional images and turn them around by using the language of the *Aktuelle Kamera*, East Germany's former news program. TV again becomes a propaganda instrument in the socialist language that Alex and his friend learn to apply with increasing skill. The charm of the movie consists in Alex's ability to insert attractive utopian ideas into his version of GDR TV when he constructs a pleasant and utopian GDR that eventually deviates from the real GDR. Atrocities, such as the Berlin Wall, border guards instructed to kill, and the *Stasi* (secret police) are never mentioned, only Alex's and Jähn's idealism. At the same time, the charm also provides the film's pathos, as the idealism represented in the dreams was never realized, and now with the victory of the West and market capitalism never will be.

The constructed reality is reflected in the movie through the mother's family situation. Both the GDR and the mother have created their own lies. And thus Alex follows this model with yet another lie, the construction of a GDR that could have been, but never was, full of humanism and idealism. During the visit to the *dacha*, when Alex is ready to tell the truth, the mother preempts him with her own tragic story, the story of the father wanting the entire family to escape, and the sad story of a mother too scared to follow the plan. Therefore she decided to stay behind. Her story resembles very closely that of the protagonist Konrad in Margarethe von Trotta's *Das Versprechen* (*The Promise* 1995) treated elsewhere in this book. The unstated assumption is that nobody really wanted to live in the GDR, some people just missed their chance of a better life style in the West.

Once the mother reveals her secret, the movie takes on a different and more creative or more bizarre direction (depending on how one sees it). It is also when

Alex's picture of the socialist GDR gets ever rosier. At this point he has won over his viewers, and also his mother. Despite the mother's death at the end of the film, where the facial expression and head movement of the actress playing the mother (Katrin Saß) reveals she knows her son has tricked her, the ending is happy. She dies knowing how much her children love her and what they did to keep her alive, and Alex goes on believing his ruse worked.

The movie achieves a final accomplishment in the scenes from the *Sandmännchen* (a children's TV series popular in both the East and West) which Alex watches at his father's house. As he and his half-siblings watch the East German sandman take off to the moon in a spaceship there is bonding of familes, East and West. More importantly, this scene is followed by Alex's encounter with the real East German space man, Siegmund Jähn, whom he subsequently employs to make his dream come true. *Good Bye, Lenin!* then turns into a real fairy tale with Jähn as the benevolent dictator. *Sandmännchen*, documentaries and Alex's fantasies are merged into a utopian fairy tale. (RZ)

QUESTIONS

1. Look at the central scene, the removal of the Lenin monument. What is its significance for the character of Alex's mother?

2. Find examples of how the West is portrayed in the movie.

3. Try to determine what the original text might have been for some of the *Aktuelle Kamera* news stories.

RELATED FILMS

Go Trabi Go (Peter Timm 1991). The first of the post-Wall comedies to laugh at residents and life in eastern Germany, *Go Trabi Go* was highly successful with the public, if not with the critics.

Das Leben ist eine Baustelle (*Life Is All You Get* 1997). This is another of Becker's successful movies taking place in Berlin.

Sonnenallee (*Sun Alley*, Leander Haußmann 1999). Haußmann's comedy cashed in on and contributed to *ostalgie*, the post-Wall phenomenon that looked back with longing on the "good old days" under Communism.

INFORMATION

Good Bye, Lenin! (2003), DVD, in German w/English subtitles, color, 121 minutes, Columbia Tristar 2004.

Good Bye, Lenin! Berlin: Schwarzkopf & Schwarzkopf, 2003.

PHOTO CREDITS

The authors wish to thank the following for permission to reprint photographs from the films.

Das Cabinet des Dr. Caligari (pp. 7, 11), *Nosferatu* (pp. 15, 21), *Berlin: die Sinfonie der Grosstadt* (p. 25), *Der blaue Engel* (pp. 33, 37), *M* (pp. 43, 47), *Kuhle Wampe* (p. 51), *Triumph des Willens* (p. 59), *Die Mörder sind unter uns* (pp. 75, 81), *Die Brücke* (p.107), *Aguirre, Der Zorn Gottes* (pp. 111, 115), *Angst essen Sele auf* (pp. 125, 129), *Die Ehe der Maria Braun* (p. 143), *Die Blecktrommel* (pp. 149, 153), *Die bleierne Zeit* (pp. 159, 163), *Der Himmel über Berlin* (pp. 175, 177), *Keiner liebt Mich* (pp. 187, 191), *Lola rennt* (cover and p. 217), *Bella Martha* (pp. 233, 235), *Nirgendwo in Afrika* (pp. 239, 243), *Good Bye, Lenin!* (p. 251), © Photofest

Jud Süss (p. 67) © Christian Unucka, Verlag für Filmschrift

Die Brücke (pp. 105) © Beta Cinema

Die Legende von Paul und Paula (pp. 119, 121) © Waltraut Zech

Die verlorene Ehre der Katharina Blum (pp. 133, 137), *Das Versprechen* (pp. 195, 199) © Bioskop-Film

Die Ehe der Maria Braun (p. 141) © Rainer Werner Fassbinder Foundation

Das Boot (pp. 167, 171) © Bavaria Film International

Das scheckliche Mädchen (pp.181, 183) © Sentena Filmproduktion München

Rossini (pp. 203, 205) © Diana Film GmbH

Sonnenallee (pp. 209, 213) © Delphi Filmverleih GmbH

Lola rennt (p. 221), *Good Bye, Lenin!* (p. 249) © X-Filme

Vergiss Amerika (pp. 225, 229) © AVISTA Film- und Fernsehproduktion